THE EUROPEAN SPORTS HISTORY REVIEW

Volume 1

D1604367

Editors and Advisers

THE EUROPEAN SPORTS HISTORY REVIEW

Volume 1

SPORT IN EUROPE
Politics, Class, Gender

Edited by

J.A. Mangan

International Research Centre for Sport,
Socialisation and Society, University of Strathclyde

FRANK CASS
LONDON • PORTLAND, OR

First published in 1999 in Great Britain by
FRANK CASS PUBLISHERS
Newbury House, 900 Eastern Avenue
London, IG2 7HH

and in the United States of America by
FRANK CASS PUBLISHERS
c/o ISBS, 5804 N.E. Hassalo Street
Portland, Oregon 97213-3644

Website: http://www.frankcass.com

British Library Cataloguing in Publication Data

Sport in Europe : politics, class, gender. – (European
sports history review ; v. 1)
1. Sports – Europe – Sociological aspects – History
2. Sports – Europe – Philosophy – History
I. Mangan, J. A. (James Anthony), 1939–
306.4'83

ISBN 0-7146-4946-5 (cloth)
ISBN 0-7146-8005-2 (paper)
ISSN 1462-1495

Library of Congress Cataloging-in-Publication Data

Applied for.

Printed in Great Britain by
Antony Rowe Ltd, Chippenham, Wilts

Contents

Prologue

J.A. MANGAN

Sport is now a mirror in which nations, men and women and social classes see themselves. The image is sometime bright, sometimes dark, sometimes distorted, sometimes magnified. This metaphorical mirror is a source of exhilaration and depression, security and insecurity, pride and humiliation, association and disassociation.

As sport has grown to a gargantuan size, progressively replacing religion in its power to excite passion, provide emotional escape, offer fraternal (and increasingly sororital) bonding, it has come to loom larger and larger in the lives of Europeans and others. The force of its appeal surprises only the ignorant, yet its appeal is astounding.

Athletes of all persuasions now have the capacity to win the affection of not millions but scores of millions within their own nations. Super athletes transcend national boundaries and become international icons – glamorous, wealthy, 'healthy' and deified. Nations are sustained through economic recessions, political disasters and identity crises by triumphant athletes who 'symbolise' national virtues. Moreover, men regain some confidence when male athletes win, while women grow in greater confidence when female athletes succeed. And middle-class social certainties diminish when middle-class performers in essentially middle-class activities do badly and vice versa.

Such is its contemporary power that sport beckons the historian more persuasively and compellingly than ever, to borrow an expression from the innovatory historian Peter Gay, 'to explore its familiar terrain and to wrest new interpretations from its inexhaustible materials'.[1] Its subject matter is replete with 'questions unanswered and for that matter, questions unasked'.[2]

It encompasses so many dimensions of experience involving politics, gender and class, that this is a 'resonant moment', as the Millennium approaches and sport seduces the modern world, for cultural historians as they consider the evolution of one of the most significant human experiences of the late twentieth century.

'An experience,' Peter Gay has reminded us, 'is an encounter of mind with world, neither of these ever simple or wholly perspicuous.'[3] He continued, 'Far more than simply providing occasions for the stereotyped exercise of thought and action, experience participates in creating objects of interest and passion; it gives form to inchoate wishes and defends against besetting anxieties ... an experience is thus more than a naked wish or a casual perception; it is an organization of passionate demands, persistent ways of seeing, and objective realities that will not be denied.'[4]

In one form or another, sport is now among the earliest, and most continuous, experiences of modern men and women – as spectators or performers or both. It infiltrates their emotions, it determines their enthusiasms, it serves their fantasies, it shapes their adulthood – because it 'blends memory and desire, none of them unalterable or ready made'.[5] To quote Gay once again, 'Experiences ... testify to the uninterrupted traffic between what the world imposes and the mind receives, and reshapes,'[6] and the materials received for this reshaping 'are by and large, public property'.[7] Nothing is more public, for better or worse, than modern sport. For some time, sport has been an inescapable reality linking public environment with intimate experience. It offers, therefore, a stimulating opportunity to historians to inspect and attempt to grasp *all* the dimensions of the recent past and their relative share in individual and collective experience.[8] 'To write the history of the bourgeois experience in the nineteenth century,' wrote Gay, 'is to hazard risky generalisations. Only the individual loves and hates, develops tastes in painting and furniture, feels content in moments of consummation, anxious in times of peril, and furious at agents of deprivation; only the individual glories in mastery or revenges himself upon the world. The rest is metaphor, but,' he adds wisely, 'it is a necessary metaphor. For all humans share at least their humanity – their passions, their paths to maturation, their irrepressible needs. And each develops social ties, belongs to part-cultures that expose him to predictable clusters of experiences ... By the time a child is ready for school, he is a little living anthology for his particular culture – partial, indeed unique, a true individual, but still a highly instructive witness to his several worlds.'[9]

All this is true of the cultural history, not simply of the bourgeoisie, but of modern sport – an opium of nations, classes and the sexes. In the following pages, in a more modest manner than Gay, we have attempted 'to recover, reconstruct and recount' merely some aspects of the recent history of sport in Europe as it relates to politics, gender and class, and to recapture sport as a recent human experience.

NOTES

1. See Peter Gay, *The Bourgeois Experience: Victoria to Freud* [volume 1, Education of the Senses], (Oxford, 1984), p.9. Peter Gay has much to offer the cultural historian with an interest in sport and society by way of inspiring and innovatory approaches to, and arguments about, cultural history. In particular, he advocates a psychoanalytic approach to history. He writes: 'What psychoanalysis can contribute to the interpretation of experience is a set of methods and propositions designed to wrest from the past its recondite meanings and to read its full orchestrated score. My aim is to integrate psychoanalysis with history. These volumes [his studies of the bourgeois experience], then, are not psycho-history; they are history informed by psychoanalysis, [*The Bourgeois Experience*, p.8]. The utilisation of Gay's approach – a systematic and detailed concentration on middle class culture – in the history of sport, incidentally, would ensure an invaluable contribution to the cultural history of Europe and European sport. By definition it would be a multi-faceted analysis of sport in Europe covering arguably its most influential segment of nineteenth- and twentieth-century society, which has had such a powerful part to play in the creation, adoption and diffusion of what Eric Hobsbawm has rightly and perspicuously called one of the most significant practices of the nineteenth century.
2. Ibid.
3. Ibid., p.11.
4. Ibid.
5. Ibid., p.12.
6. Ibid.
7. Ibid., p.12.
8. Ibid., p.15.
9. Ibid, pp.15–16.

Women and Football – A Contradiction? The Beginnings of Women's Football in Four European Countries

GERTRUD PFISTER, KARI FASTING,
SHEILA SCRATON and BENILDE VÁZQUEZ

Our interest in the history of women's football developed from our involvement in the project 'The experiences and meanings of physical activities in women's lives: an intercultural comparison in four European countries.' As part of this research project we carried out 240 in-depth, qualitative interviews with women tennis players, gymnasts and footballers in England, Germany, Norway and Spain (highly competitive and recreational). In our analysis of the data from the footballers it became obvious that in order to understand their experiences as sportswomen, it was important to locate women's football in its specific historical and cultural context. This essay first examines how football spread as a male domain to various countries in Europe in the period up to 1945 and to the end of the Second World War. This is followed by a reconstruction of the first attempts by women to participate in physical activities in general, as well as football in particular. Here, we focus specifically on the following questions: under which conditions and circumstances did women succeed in penetrating this male terrain? Which reasons and arguments were put forward either to support or hinder the participation of women in this 'unfeminine' sport? Are there noticeable differences in the development of women's football in the different countries? And, finally, what explanations can be given for differences as well as similarities in this development?

We take as our starting point that body and movement are both 'biologically grounded'[1] and are, to a large extent, shaped by culture. This means that on the one hand the sexual hierarchy 'embodies' itself in men and women and that, on the other, body and movement cultures play a role in constructing the gender order. As a result of body and movement being 'engendered' in this fashion, sports have developed either a masculine or feminine image and thus appeal to men and women in different ways.[2] Further, the myths of masculinity and femininity which are associated with different body or sport practices are dependent on the prevailing social and gender orders. This can be demonstrated with many examples taken from the history of physical activities in Europe. From the very beginning, the participation of men and women in certain forms of physical exercise or certain types of sport was tied to numerous rules and norms pertaining to gender. It was above all women who – in compliance with existing gender roles – were barred from sporting activities. One of the sports which in many countries was regarded as a male preserve was the game of football.

The cross-cultural comparison will, it is hoped, throw light on the factors which gave rise both to opportunities and to problems not only in women's football but also in women's sports more generally. One of the major aims of the article, furthermore, is to identify common features and differences of culture and thus to uncover structural links between women's sport and the special circumstances of women's lives.

THE DEVELOPMENT OF MEN'S FOOTBALL

The game of football as it is played today developed in England in the nineteenth century.[3] In the wake of the social and economic changes taking place at that time and in connection with the development of modern sport, old games resembling football (which were played in many places on public holidays without any strict rules and often with large numbers of people taking part) lost their appeal.[4] However, the idea of the game of football had been taken up by the public schools where this originally wild and uncontrolled game was 'tamed', and used as a way of teaching schoolboys discipline and manliness.[5]

Public schools were private boarding-schools of the British upper class and in the first half of the nineteenth century were 'godless, cold, harsh and brutal places'. The law of the survival of the fittest governed relations between pupils, whose values and code of behaviour were oriented towards those of the upper class. Fellow-pupils were bullied, teachers were 'ragged' (i.e. made fun of, played tricks on and generally harrassed), and fights and mutinies were not infrequent. The last rebellion, in 1850, 'brought about an educational revolution in the schools – the advent of compulsory team games – as an antidote to uprisings, the creation of extensive and expensive playing fields and the establishment of cups and cup-ties, leagues and league tables – and the construction of the attendant myth of the gentleman sportsman endowed with a national instinct for "fair play"'.[6] The code of behaviour encapsulated in 'fair play' developed into an ideology whose purpose was clearly to keep disputes and conflicts under control by transposing them to the playing fields. J.A. Mangan pointed out in this connection that 'it was eventually a system rather than any single man, or indeed any group of men' that produced the new ideal of masculinity characterised by athleticism, and that 'the system fitted functionally into the times'.[7]

The year 1863 saw the founding of the Football Association, which established standardised rules, thus making a clear distinction between Association football and rugby football.[8] After the introduction of the Football League (association) in 1888, the popularity of the game increased and aroused the enthusiasm of great sections of the population. As the working class became more involved so the game became more professionalised. By the end of the nineteenth century thousands of football clubs had been formed with a total membership of approximately 60,000.

In England, football had been a 'typical man's' game from the very beginning and it played an important role in boys' socialisation and education towards manhood: 'Boys learnt how to drink and tell jokes as well as the language of physical aggression … Football clubs were only a part of the wider process of male socialisation …'[9] Rugby, too, offered young Englishmen the opportunity to build up and participate in a male subculture. Mangan demonstrated how, at the end of the nineteenth century, with growing imperialism, the increasing glorification of militarism and the idealisation of heroism on the battlefield, a new ideal of masculinity developed. Sport and war became central elements in the character training of future British and imperial officers.[10] The close link between games field and battlefield produced the ideal of 'martial masculinity' and men who embodied this ideal.

Even today rugby is, for E. Dunning (1994), one of the few remaining 'male preserves', where myths of masculinity can be passed on, masculinity demonstrated and male identity developed.[11]

In Germany, too, games were played (such as football in the round) in which the ball was kicked. These games were part of the physical exercising of German *Turnen* and were recommended at the end of the nineteenth century by the 'games movement', which supported the

Sport in Europe

propagation of popular games. The characteristics of these, often traditional games, were co-operation amongst the players, lack of competition and a moderate degree of technical and tactical competence demanded of the participants.[12]

At first, English football was played in a number of German towns by resident Englishmen who infected German young men with the enthusiasm for the game. In the 1880s the first clubs were founded in Berlin and other German towns. Although football was gaining support, it also met opposition from various quarters. Many physical education teachers claimed that the game was ugly, crude and dangerous.[13]

In spite of this opposition, by 1914 the German Football Federation (DFB) controlled approximately 2,200 clubs with roughly 190,000 members. After the First World War the popularity of the game still increased not only among players but also among spectators, and football developed into Germany's national sport,[14] which was played more by members of the middle classes than by workers in industry as was the case in England.[15]

Norway, too, came into contact with football in the mid-1880s, when the first games were played by English army and navy officers while staying in Norwegian towns. Nevertheless, the game did not, at first, find any wide acceptance among the Norwegian population. In spite of its apparent 'cultural neutrality', football was difficult to integrate into Norway's sport tradition, partly because it differed quite considerably from typical Norwegian physical culture. During these early years, football only just survived as a school sport – 'as an activity for boys in secondary and higher school, both as a compulsory part of physical education and as a voluntary game after school'.[16] It is important to note that during this period girls did not receive any formal physical education in schools. In 1902 the Norwegian Football Association was founded, although it was made up of only three clubs which mainly consisted of academics and sons of the bourgeoisie. In the years that followed, however, football gained, also an increasing number of supporters, among the working classes, and, after the First World War, it became just as popular as skiing or athletics. In contrast to the early professionalisation of football in England, the best Norwegian football players remained amateurs until 1970-80. Although by the 1930s the Norwegian Football Association had more members than any other of the country's sports organisations, football never gained first place as a national sport: 'Norwegians were not born with bats in their hands or footballs by their feet, but with skis.'[17]

In Spain neither the government nor the great majority of the population showed any great interest in physical education and sport. Political circumstances – conflicts raging between conservative and liberals, as well as between the church and nobility on one hand and the bourgeoisie on the other – certainly played an important role in the omission of physical education from schools until 1887, when the first law about physical education was launched. However this law did not guarantee the realisation of physical education in schools, primarily because of the lack of resources.[18] However, by the end of the nineteenth century, due to the influence of French culture, physical education became more popular and was incorporated into the schooling system.

At the end of the nineteenth century, Englishmen who were living in Spain for professional reasons founded the first sports clubs, one of them being reportedly the country's oldest football club, the 'Club Recreativo' in Huelva.[19] English teachers at international schools in Spain brought their lifestyles including their sport participation to the country. According to Polo del Barrio (1986), we can distinguish three periods in the development of football in Spain before the Civil War (1936–39). The first period is characterised by the centralism of Madrid when football was promoted by the aristocracy and their ideas of 'regenerationism', where football was used to develop 'strong and virile' men. The second period involved the popularisation of football. More facilities were created, the association was founded in 1909, and the National League in 1928, connected with the 'internalisation' of the Spanish football team that played in the Olympic Games in 1920 in Antwerp. The third period is characterised by the professionalisation of football players, a development which was stopped by the Civil War. The Franco régime subsequently gave systematic support to football for political reasons. It was hoped on the one hand that football would distract the population from the troubled political situation and, on the other, that successful clubs might favourably reflect the régime abroad.[20]

It is not possible to discuss here in detail why in all four countries the game of men's football developed into one of the most popular types of sport in terms of club membership. Among the decisive factors leading to the rise of football were not only processes of modernisation, above all the development of road and rail networks and the growth of telecommunications, but also changes in working conditions and the increasing significance of leisure.

If the state of industrialisation is taken as a parameter for the development of sport, the four countries under study exhibit clear differences as well as parallels. The belated success of football especially in Spain might be attributable, for example, to the country's lack of industrialisation. In other countries, it was perhaps the globalisation tendency of football – together with the opportunities which this opened up for national presentation and identification – which contributed to the popularisation of the game. It may also be assumed, moreover, that processes of sportification, i.e. emphasis on performance and tendencies towards professionalisation, as well as the growing interest of the spectators, provided increasing impetus in the development of the game in all four countries.

There are great differences, however, in the development of football in the countries studied. Only in England, for example, did the game become professional; and only in England, too, did the different forms of association football and rugby football, develop. In Norway and Germany football had to assert itself against 'national' traditions of physical culture. In Germany success came quicker than in Norway, where football, according to M. Goksøyr (1996), never acquired the status of a national sport. This was in spite of the fact that from the 1930s football was the most popular sport in terms of membership. In Spain, football's breakthrough was hindered above all by economic conditions, and the fact that the prime national sport was bull-fighting.

THE EARLY PHASE OF WOMEN'S SPORT

In each of the countries under study the development of women's football was very closely connected to the general situation of women's sport. It can be assumed that women had more difficulties in participating in soccer in the countries in which women's sport, especially competitive sport, was confronted with prejudice and resistance.

Germany

At the beginning of the nineteenth century it was quite unthinkable that girls and women should take part in German *Turnen*, not only because of its emphasis on bringing forth able-bodied men capable of fighting for their country, but also because of the political goals which it pursued. Although, even at the end of the century, male *Turnen* were still adamantly pursuing the cause of education and the demonstration of masculinity, the number of female *Turnen* had begun to rise steadily from the 1880s onwards. At the turn of the century, it was the new types of sport from England which were labelled 'unfeminine' in Germany, especially the ones related to performance and competition.[21] Despite all the opposition, girls and women became increasingly interested in sports, including the so-called traditional exercises involving running, throwing and jumping. In 1913 these were incorporated in the first guidelines to be drawn up for girls' physical education. Physical education which had been introduced in girls' schools since the 1850s had been an obligatory subject for girls in higher education since 1894 (in Prussia).[22]

In the wake of the processes of modernisation which followed the First World War, great changes took place both in the situation of women and in the situation of women's sport. These changes can be observed especially in the attitude towards the engagement of women in athletics, which, for a long time, had been looked upon as a typically male domain.[23] In 1919, for example, the German Athletic Federation (Deutsche Sportbehörde für Athletik) urged all track and field clubs to set up women's sections.[24] In the 1920s and 1930s Germany developed into one of the leading nations in the area of women's sport. German athletes, for example, were the most successful team in the Women's World Games in 1930.[25] In the 1920s, too, there was general consensus, among not only sports officials, doctors, sports journalists and the general public, but also many physical education teachers and women athletes that the femininity of girls and women should on no account suffer from exaggerated sporting activities. Numerous precautionary measures were introduced in order to prevent any imagined masculinisation of women athletes.[26] It was the renowned athlete and later functionary Karl Ritter von Halt who, in the 1920s, declared that 'men were born to compete; competition is alien to a woman's nature'.[27] Women should be excluded not only from all contests but also from those types of sport 'not suited to women's natures, which have an alienating and distorting effect and therefore should be better left to the male sex'.[28]

England

Until the middle of the nineteenth century English girls were excluded from physical education with the exception of those attending private schools, who were allowed to practise moderate, 'feminine' forms of physical exercise such as callisthenics. However, towards the end of the century, in view of the changing role of women and the discussion which was taking place on eugenics, it was generally considered necessary to introduce and regulate girls' physical education.[29] The London School Board decided to adopt Swedish gymnastics, which was provided at girls' secondary schools and colleges together with games such as hockey, netball and tennis. These activities gained approval because of their benefits to both the girls' health and education. Nevertheless, these team games were harshly criticised by a great many doctors since, besides allegedly offending standards of decency, they were thought to have harmful effects on the girls, both physically and mentally – and, what was even worse, it was believed they would cause the girls to lose their femininity and become more masculine. Adult women had even more obstacles to face than girls with regard to dress, ideals of femininity and standards of decency and it was not until the end of the nineteenth century that well-to-do Victorian women began to practise 'feminine' sports such as cycling, tennis or croquet.[30]

In the twentieth century, English women began to become increasingly active in a number of sports ranging from golf and hockey to netball and lacrosse and even athletics. J. Hargreaves (1994) attributes the 'proliferation of twentieth century women's sport' to the fact that it 'occurred in separate spheres from the sports of men'.[31] It is not until after the First World War, however, that traces can be found of organised women's athletics. In 1921 the Kensington Athletic Club opened a women's section and in 1922 an independent Women's Athletic Association was established.[32]

In spite of this development, even in the 1920s women's sport in England had to put up with all manner of prejudice and ambivalence and met with strong opposition, as Hargreaves has been able to demonstrate: 'The discourse on female sports during the interwar years accommodated to reactionary accounts of female biology as well as challenging them: the new athletic image of womanhood both embodied power and was vulnerable.'[33]

Norway

In nineteenth-century Norway, women participated in many kinds of informal sporting activities such as ice skating, skiing, hiking and swimming.[34] A women's group existed as early as the 1850s in Christiana Turnforening (gymnastics).[35] In 1895 women participated, for the first time, in public gymnastics demonstrations, but there was strong resistance to competition. According to F. Olstad and S. Tønnesson

(1987), there were only a few sports: tennis, swimming, figure skating and equestrian events, where from the beginning women were allowed to compete to almost the same degree as men.[36]

From 1924 sport in Norway was organised under two umbrella bodies. One of them, Arbeiderenes Idrettsforbund (AIF – the workers' sports federation), was more positive towards the introduction and development of women's sport than the other one (Landsforbundet for Idrett). Women in AIF were permitted to compete in track and field, swimming and gymnastics, which became the major women's sports. However, shooting, cross-country skiing and bicycle roadracing were also permitted in the late 1920s. On special occasions even 'tug of war' and football were put into the programme.[37] The 'blooming' of women's sport in the AIF plus the international development forced the 'bourgeois' federation (Landsforbundet) to accept and increase the number of competitive sports disciplines for women.

By the end of the 1930s, Norwegian women participated in badminton, fencing, track and field, handball, orienteering, equestrian events, rowing, skiing, skating, swimming, tennis and gymnastics. The last one was by far the most popular sport among women.[38] By 1940 competitive sport for women, however, was not accepted in the same way as competitive sport for men. Women's role in society was first of all that of wife and mother. The resistance to women taking part in competitions was connected, to a large degree, with the widespread myth of femininity which focused on motherhood and judged all activities according to their alleged effect on the health and beauty of mothers and children. Women and men were deemed to be different and this had to be taken into account in planning and organising women's sport. Health, beauty and the norms of femininity should not be threatened. The legitimising of the dichotomous roles of the two sexes was strongly supported by the medical discourse. As in Germany and England, Norwegian doctors took a sceptical stance in the discussion of women's competitive sports. Frequently, doctors and journalists combined medical and aesthetic arguments, particularly when it came to questions of women's performance and competition: 'When they desire and aim to compete with others, however, they overstretch their capacities and talents. What follows is not only unhealthy but also ungraceful.'[39]

Spain

Women and sport were scarcely reconcilable entities in Spain before the

Second Republic (1931). Here, besides the prejudices familiar in other countries – especially the scepticism shown by the medical profession, there was a further significant obstacle to women's sport. Spanish women were far more strongly bound to the single goal of motherhood than women in Germany, for example.[40] In Spain, 'there were also sharp gender divisions. In all but the most advanced industrial areas (and, to a considerable degree, even there), men and women lived almost entirely separate lives. Most women were economically dependent on men, their lives circumscribed within the larger domestic arena – though it should be noted that their identification with the domestic arena did not mean that they did not engage in labor'.[41] This meant that they were confronted with rigid rules about lady-like behaviour: 'Deportistas no, madres si' (female athletes no, mothers yes) was thus the catchphrase of opponents of women's sport. Only women from the higher social classes were able, from the end of the nineteenth century onwards, to participate in upper-class sports such as golf, tennis, horse-riding or skiing. Here, the emphasis was on meeting people rather than on sporting performance, and sport was a means of social distinction and demonstrative consumption.[42]

The Instituto Cultura i Bibliotheca Popular de la Dona, founded in Barcelona in 1909, provided women of the middle classes with an opportunity to take part in sporting activities. Besides offering vocational training and a cultural programme, the institute organised sports activities such as hiking. As far as sport was concerned, the same strict rules applied as elsewhere in the country. The first concern was health, and the greatest danger to health was considered to be the masculinisation of women who practised sport. In 1928, the Club Femeni i d'Esports was founded in Barcelona, a women's sports club whose programme – including hockey, basketball, swimming as well as cultural activities – sounded almost revolutionary. As far as women's issues were concerned, however, the club (which had a membership of several thousands) was rather conservative: family and motherhood were propagated as the highest goals of women's lives.[43]

It was not until the Second Republic that the myths of femininity started, also, to lose their force in sports.[44] In 1931 the first women's athletic championships were held, followed in 1933 by the first women's swimming championships. Nevertheless, the most popular sports among Spanish girls and women continued to be swimming and tennis. A measure of the diffusion and significance of women's sports is the participation of women in the Olympic Games. Before 1960, Spanish women competed only once in the Games, which was in 1924 when two tennis players took part.[45]

SUMMARY AND COMPARISON

Although women's sports met with opposition in all the countries studied, women who wanted to practise sports were faced with specific opportunities as well as obstacles. In Spain during the monarchy, few girls or women were active in any form of physical exercise; women's sport was élitist and limited to women of the upper class. In 1931, during the political and social changes in the Second Republic, attitudes towards women's sport changed as girls and women were encouraged to participate in some physical activities and sport.

In Norway, gymnastics was very popular among women while sports, especially competitive sports, were rejected as being 'unfeminine' up to the Second World War. In Germany, in spite of the many warning voices, a relatively strong women's sports movement was able to develop during the 1920s. As an alternative to sport, however, German women had German gymnastics (*Turnen*). In England, sporting activities developed from the end of the nineteenth century, primarily among the middle and upper classes with the provision of sports for young women being largely confined to middle-class education establishments. In England and Spain the segregation of the sexes in sport was the rule whereas in the other countries it was more the exception.

WOMEN AND FOOTBALL – FROM ITS BEGINNINGS TO THE SECOND WORLD WAR

Germany

The German 'games movement', which from the beginning of the 1880s had propagated physical exercise, especially with games practised in the open air derived from *Turnen*, also sought to attract girls and women because of the belief that 'strong offspring can only be born of strong mothers'. Among the activities that were recommended for girls were ball games in which the ball was only allowed to be moved by kicking it with the feet, for example 'football in the round'. Like all *Turnen* games, this type of football game completely lacked both a competitive impulse and any orientation towards performance. Although P. Heineken claimed in 1898 that 'for many years football has been played by girls, too, and they enjoy playing it',[46] he gives neither details nor the slightest evidence for his assertion.

While proponents of sport, as well as of the games movement, wished to restrict 'proper' football to boys and men, there were advocates of women's football to be found among the first women doctors, who were in favour of physical fitness for women. These included A. Fischer-Dückelmann and H.B. Adams-Lehmann, both of whom encouraged the women readers of their popular guidebooks to practise sports as they pleased, and keep active, building up strength and stamina through exercise.[47] Fischer-Dückelmann even went as far as recommending football for women, provided that they wore the right clothing. As far as we know, this unconventional proposal was never put into practice; throughout the 1920s there was absolutely no question about the fact that the football field was no place for women. 'All types of sport which exceed women's natural strength, such as wrestling, boxing and football, are unsuitable sports for women and are, moreover, unaesthetical and unnatural in appearance' is Vierath's lapidary comment in his book *Moderner Sport*, published in 1930.[48] Reasons why women should be prohibited from playing football were seldom given. In 1927 an article appeared in *Sport und Sonne* under the heading 'Should the female sex play football?' The author had been prompted to put this question (understood merely rhetorically here) because of the 'great women's football associations which exist' in England. According to the author, German women disapprove of football, firstly, because the 'rough way' in which the game is played is contrary to women's sensibilities and, secondly, because the game is not suited to the 'build of the female body'.[49] A rare reference to women football players – and one, moreover, which did not contain a fundamental rejection of the game played by women – can be found in the 1930 edition of the journal *Leibesübungen*. A report on the founding of a women's football club in Frankfurt included the following comment: 'The lady footballers ... intend to play a cheerful, combative kind of football. Whether it will be worse than hockey, we will have to wait and see. ... It will be interesting to see what will come of this venture.'[50] Today we know that nothing came of this venture. At first, the 35 young women who had founded a women's football club in 1930 trained regularly on Sundays. Reports of this 'scandal' in the press led soon to a 'storm of indignation', and many of the players yielded to pressure from both their families and the general public and left the club, which was subsequently disbanded in 1931.[51] On the whole, reports of women's football in Germany are rare, most of them being critical opinions voiced about football-playing women in England or France.[52] One women's magazine, the *Damenillustrierte*, commented in 1927, 'Women may be playing football in England and America, but it is to be hoped that this bad example is not followed in German sport'.[53] This hope came true and it took until 1970 before the German Football Federation officially allowed German women to play football.

England

The development of women's football in England, the motherland of this game, was much more comprehensive. As early as in 1894, a 'British Ladies' Football Club' was founded and in the following year football matches were played between various women's teams.[54] A match took place in 1895, for example, between a team from the north and a team from the south of England. A detailed report of the match appeared in the *Manchester Guardian*, although the reporter restricted himself almost exclusively to a discussion of the women's outfits.[55] The general public gradually became aware of this new sensation and a women's football match played in Newcastle in 1895 was attended by 8,000 spectators. In Scotland, too, a number of women began to take interest in this new game in the 1890s, and Lady Florence Dixie, a well-known writer and suffragette (who also supported women sitting astride a horse instead of riding side-saddle) managed a 'travelling ladies' football team'.

Football matches did take place, apparently, between women's and men's teams, although in 1902 the English Football Association forbade the clubs which belonged to the association from playing against women's teams. Whereas the first women football players were looked upon as a curiosity and the games they played were treated as some kind of fairground spectacle, women's football developed during the First World War into a popular sporting event. The women, who had to take the men's places in the factories, sought distraction and recreation in the game of football, and were even supported in this by their employers, who were interested in maintaining and improving the health and fitness of their workers – and possibly in promoting their firm's name, too. Furthermore, the boom in women's football was due to the national enthusiasm for the war effort since the matches were played to raise money for charity. On Christmas Day, 1917, for example, a game took place between Dick, Kerr's Ladies and another team from Preston with 10,000 spectators looking on. The money taken at the gate, all of £600, was donated to a fund for wounded soldiers. The character of the events – occasionally against men's teams or games played in fancy costumes – indicated that more importance was attached to the charitable purpose rather than to sporting performance. In this context playing football was not seen as a sign of moral decadence but as evidence of the patriotism of the women playing football. And when games were played to raise money for charity, the women had a great advantage over the men since they were, after all, an attraction for the masses hungry for sensation. The number of spectators grew to such an extent that the Football Association allowed its clubs to put their grounds at the disposal of the women: 'By early 1920 it was no idle kick about on a ploughed field with a few curious onlookers on the touchlines; it was Stamford Bridge, White Hart Lane and Goodison Park, all bastions of the male preserve with packed terraces enjoying an entertaining match for a good cause.'[56]

During the First World War women's teams were set up in a number of companies, among them the five Lyons Ladies teams whose players worked in Lyons cafés in and around London. Women's football matches were organised, also, by sports clubs and in 1921 there were about 150 women's teams in England, the main centres of women's football being the Midlands and the North.

The most successful women's team was Dick, Kerr's Ladies FC. This team was founded in 1917 by workers at Dick, Kerr's, a munitions and engineering factory, and its first game, played in the same year, was organised by a woman named Grace Sibbert. She was replaced as the team's manager by Alfred Frankland and under his management Dick, Kerr's Ladies went from success to success. In 1920, for example, they played almost every Sunday – a total of 30 games over the whole year, of which they won 25 and, of the rest, three were draws. In their most famous match they beat St. Helens 4–0 at Goodison Park before a crowd of 53,000 spectators.[57]

Women's football even became international, with English teams first of all playing teams of Scottish and Irish women. In Spring 1920, for example, Dick, Kerr's Ladies defeated a Scottish team with a score of 20–0.[58] In the same year a match between Dick, Kerr's Ladies and a French team caused much excitement in the English press. The French team (accompanied by Alice Milliat, who later became president of the International Federation of Women's Sports) was given a tremendous reception on its arrival in Preston and was followed through the streets of the town by an enthusiastic crowd. In the week that followed, they played four games in four different English towns. In October of the same year, the players from Preston travelled to France on an exchange tour, which turned out to be another highlight of women's football. In 1921 a match was played between a French team and the Plymouth Ladies and in 1922 Dick, Kerr's Ladies even travelled to the United States and Canada, where they earned great respect from the spectators for their performance against men's teams.

The standard of women's football had risen considerably since its early years and players now trained regularly and systematically not only in order to improve their condition but also to refine their ball skills and practise tactical moves.

However, the rise of women's football did not meet with approval from every quarter, and in the phase of 'normalisation' after the war, there were calls also, for a return to normality in the gender order. In the press and elsewhere in public life, heated debates flared up on the question of women's football: 'It was the most ludicrous exhibition of the noble sport I have ever witnessed,' commented a reader of the *Western Morning News* in 1921.[59] On the one hand, women football players were criticised for their lack of skill; on the other hand, if they did demonstrate ball-playing qualities, they were attacked because of their lack of femininity. Moreover, the arguments which were put forward against women's football were not only of an aesthetic or moral nature, but also to a great extent medically motivated.

The women players were anxious to rebut such accusations and made every effort to try and convince the public that playing football was neither dangerous nor harmful: 'If football was dangerous, some ill-effects would have been seen by now,' observed the team captain of Huddersfield Atalanta FC in 1921. She said that she felt much better than she had the previous year and even the housework was no longer a problem since she was 'refreshed' after playing football.[60] One problem was certainly the fact that after the war the argument of raising money for charity as a legitimisation of women's football matches began to lose its validity. In addition, since the standard of football the women played was relatively high, it could no longer be declared to be a harmless pastime; on the contrary, it was hard 'unfeminine' sport. Further, the matches between women's teams seemed to divert public attention from boys' and men's football. In the reactionary political climate of the post-war years, in which women 'by a national campaign in the press and in Parliament should be persuaded, even forced back into the home',[61] women's football seemed to upset the long awaited reshaping of the gender order. The real threat appeared to come from the joint activities of the women: 'The success of single women in public life threatened the status quo. Independent women were accused of sex hatred and pilloried for preferring their own sex to men. Amid a wholesale effort to revive marriage and delicate womanhood, single women and their communities were covertly and overtly attacked.'[62]

The 'official' explanation for taking measures against women's football matches was based on the alleged lack of clarity about how revenues from the games were used. In 1921 the Football Association decided that women's teams would have to seek the permission of the FA before matches could take place at the grounds of clubs belonging to the FA. At the end of 1921, a resolution was passed by the FA's advisory committee in which it was observed: 'The game of football is quite unsuitable for women and should not be encouraged.'[63] Football clubs were now urged to stop the practice of putting their grounds at the disposal of women's teams.

The women, of course, objected strongly to this; the captain of the Plymouth Ladies accused the FA of living 'a hundred years behind the times', adding that behind the measure lay 'purely sexual prejudice'. Looking back, Gail Newsham came to a similar evaluation of the events: 'The chauvinists, the medical "experts" and the anti-women's football lobby had won – their threatened male bastion was now safe.'[64]

The FA's decisions were the first steps in the decline of women's football in England, especially since it meant the end of, at least some, appearance of official recognition. The end of support from established football clubs made it necessary for the women to organise their own matches and, in 1921, 25 women's clubs came together to form the English Ladies' Football Association (ELFA). By the time the Association held its second meeting, the number of affiliated clubs had already risen to 60. Nevertheless, the ELFA was faced with enormous difficulties, since it lacked not only support, but also, an organisational basis. A great part of the credit for the success of women's teams was due to their managers and trainers, who had had long years of experience and formed the necessary contacts.[65] After the FA's decision it was difficult 'to find grounds that were not used by FA affiliated clubs, referees who were not associated with affiliated football, and even the professional players who had helped train the women and refereed matches had to be careful of associating with the ladies' teams'.[66]

Little is known to date about the activities of women footballers in the period which followed: 'Undoubtedly, the women's game continued in a more or less "underground" fashion, staging matches at local festivities and for fund-raising and charity events.'[67] Dick, Kerr's Ladies, at any rate, continued to play football until 1965; through the years the team played a total of more than 800 games, winning the great majority of them.

Spain

During the Second Republic, Spanish women began to take a more active part in sports. Photographs, moreover, provide conclusive evidence that some women even dared to take part in football games. However, little is known up to present about the development of women's football in Spain. Pointing to the tendencies towards modernisation and the new freedoms gained by women during that period, García Bonafé noted: 'El futbol femenino cuenta con representacion en diversos clubs y el esqui incluye categoria oficial para mujeres.'[68] Nevertheless, Spanish women's football was short-lived. In the Franco régime women were made aware, once again, of their roles as mothers, which could or should not be, combined with sporting activities.

Norway

Similarly in Norway we found few traces of women's soccer before the Second World War. In a German magazine, *Damen-Sport Damen-Turnen*, of 1919, a very short note was published about a soccer match between a women's and a men's team in Kristiania. 'It seems this game was not to be taken too seriously. Newspaper reports talk about 'standing ovations' and 'enthusiastic applause'.[69] No further information about this game is available.

Another sign of women playing football is a game which took place in Brumundal in mid-summer 1931.[70] When there was a soccer match between a team of women and a team of older men. It was common at that time, the author writes, to arrange amusing soccer matches between different groups. An announcement in *Hamar Arbeiderblad* (a newspaper) states: 'Humorous soccer match. Women's team against old men.' The result of this match is not known, but according to the author it inspired some sportswomen in the district to start a women's team. The women in Hamar took the initative to develop their own team as an alternative to their 'sweethearts' team. They arranged and played matches between themselves and were supported by the men in the club (Hamar idrettslags soccer group). The women's 'baptism of fire' was a match against Bolton Wanderers that consisted mainly of English tourists. This historic match took place in connection with a tournament called 'the olympic games' held in Hamar on 19 July 1931. The result is unknown, but according to the newspaper *Hamar Arbeiderblad* it was a victory for the Norwegian women's team. Following this success, they started to look for other female opposition and managed, finally, to find some women from Kapp sports club who had played some soccer on playgrounds, with the support of their fiancés. This sports club put together a women's team and played against Hamar in August 1931. Hamar won 3–0. This is probably the first recorded soccer match between two Norwegian women's teams.[71]

FOOTBALL AND MASCULINITY

In each of the countries studied, these initiatives did not seem to lead to an upswing of women's football. Indeed, many female players quickly gave up playing. Although there is no evidence for why these women gave up football, we can assume that they were constrained by dominant ideals of acceptable female behaviour. In all the countries, femininity and soccer was looked upon as a contradiction which could only be tolerated in a 'humorous' situation. Women entering male domains were regarded as ridiculous. In Norway, the strong resistance to women's sporting competitions seems to have rendered female football unthinkable.

In this concluding section we focus on two key questions. First, why did women who wished to play football not succeed in building up a women's soccer movement? Second, why did attitudes towards women's football differ in the countries studied?

It can be assumed that in all four countries opposition to women's football was closely connected to the characterisation of the game as a competitive sport.[72] In contrast to the games of the German *Turnen*, or to games such as hockey, football was considered to be competitive, strenuous, aggressive and potentially dangerous. On these grounds, football was disapproved of even for boys and men by German *Turnen* and physical education teachers. In 1928, for example, Fischer attested in his popular book on 'body culture' to the 'markedly combative character' of football[73] and advised women to play team handball, an 'altogether more subdued and civil game'.[74] In none of the countries under study did football, based as it was on performance and competition, appear to be reconcilable with the prevailing ideals of femininity. It did not matter, of course, for such images to be effective, that the qualities attributed to football were based on imagination and association and did not necessarily have much to do with the reality of this game.

The body, physical activity and forms of presenting oneself (including sport) play a major role in the reproduction of the gender order. Ideologies and myths, concerning the body and the limits of physical achievement with regard to both sexes, are key factors in reinforcing and reproducing structures. From the beginning, people were afraid that women's sport would have adverse and undesirable effects on both gender identity and gender hierarchy. Sport, or certain sports at least, have continuously provided a means, right up to the present day, of constructing and demonstrating masculinity.[75] As mentioned above, the development of football in England was closely connected with the construction of 'martial masculinity'. The ideology of militarism was an inherent part of the ideology along with the practice of team games. Mangan has demonstrated that 'it was team games like rugby and cricket that were supposed to give Englishmen an inherent superiority when it came to the supreme sacrifice in battle'.[76]

Dunning (1994) was able to reveal, using the example of rugby, that sport is especially vital as a resource in shaping male identity in times in which the balance of power between the sexes is undergoing change. Football teams (and this can be seen in the rituals that they enact) may be regarded as male preserves and male allegiances.[77] Male allegiances are formed precisely through the exclusion of women and the rejection of femininity and all the qualities attached to it such as softness and tenderness. Efforts to keep women away from football fields can, therefore, be interpreted as attempts to preserve and protect the domains and the privileges which men have secured for themselves.

Further, it must be taken into consideration that in the countries studied, football is – more or less – a national sport – the sport with which the (male) population or, at least groups of the population, identify. National sport and myths of masculinity are intricately interwoven: 'Each country's national sport contributes towards producing and securing the male identity specific to that particular country. This explains not only why in all societies the national sport is a male preserve ... but also why it is linked to sexual demands, needs and anxieties.'[78]

On the whole, in all the countries the aim was to preserve the gender order both inside and outside sport. That the differences between the sexes should disappear, that women should become more masculine, that 'certain limits' should be exceeded – this was more or less strictly rejected.[79]

WOMEN'S FOOTBALL – SIMILARITIES AND DIFFERENCES

The development of women's sport, and of women's football in all countries involved, shows clearly that universal ideologies of femininity and masculinity cut across culture and nation.[80] Sport was associated with hegemonic masculinity and, therefore, women faced barriers to their entering and participating in physical activities. Competition was a contested terrain for women in all four countries researched. However, women's competitive sport increased after the First World War in Germany and, to a lesser degree, in England. There was considerable resistance to competitive sport for women in Norway, and, during the monarchy, in Spain. The general judgement of football as a male combative sport and attitudes towards women football players were in many respects very similar in all the countries studied. Everywhere football was viewed as a challenge to hegemonic beliefs around appropriate femininity relating to women's role as mothers, their physicality and sexuality. The power and influence of the myths of femininity were, however, different in the countries involved. The ideology of motherhood was especially strong and powerful in Spain.

Why, then, was women's football tolerated in England, at least for some time, but spurned in Germany and Norway? Why were women prevented from playing football under the monarchy in Spain, but started to participate in football in the Second Republic? Were women's sports in England more developed and 'progressive' than in Germany or Norway? This latter hypothesis is not supported by the relatively broad-minded attitude to women's sports generally in Germany, which is reflected in the way women's athletics was encouraged.

Explanations for the differences in the development of women's football need to be situated in their specific social, political and economic contexts. If we use the percentage of women in the labour force as an indicator for women's 'emancipation', there are large differences between the countries involved. However, we have to take into consideration that working outside the home does not necessarily equate with 'liberation' or 'empowerment'. In Germany in 1933, 36% of the economically active population were women. In Great Britain the percentage was 30% (1931), in Norway 27% (1930) and in Spain 14% (1920) and 12% (1940).[81] At least for Spain it is clear that women's role was to be housewives and mothers.[82] This conclusion can be drawn, also, in relation to the introduction of political and civil rights for women. Moreover, the development of women's political rights seemed to be linked to their ability to access sport. In Norway, women gained civil rights in 1888 and the right to vote in 1913, in Germany in 1896 and 1919 respectively, in Great Britain 1888 and 1928 and in Spain 1875 and 1931.[83] However, political influence was denied women (and men) in Spain during the dictatorship of Franco. The presented data may help to explain the exclusion of women from football in Spain during monarchy. That Spanish women started to play soccer at the same time as their role changed during the Second Republic is clear evidence that women's sport was closely connected with the political situation.

It is probable that the short success of women's football in England, as well as in Spain during the Second Republic, was made possible by the particular historical constellations and specific contexts. For women's football in England, the First World War undoubtedly played a considerable role. If women had to take the place of men in numerous fields of life, then why not in sport, too? Lopez (1997) explains the popularity of women's football in England in the following terms: 'Women were able to take the opportunity to play because millions of men went off to fight the invading Germans at the war front in France, many never to return. Therefore, not only did women have to fill the void in the factories left by the absent men and take on their traditional work role, but they also took on traditional male pastimes such as football.'[84] In England, where football already had a long tradition, the First World War and the necessity of raising funds for charity provided women with a suitable opportunity of taking up a sport which had hitherto been a male preserve. As many of the players came from the working class, it was easy to look upon the games as entertainment for the masses, instead of earnest sport; the respectability of middle-class girls was in no way compromised. Last but not least, football was not the only sport in England which was regarded as a 'male preserve'. Rugby constituted an alternative path to the demonstration and the preservation of manhood.

That it did not occur to German women to play football during this period may have been connected to the widespread misgivings which people had about this competitive game. After all, football had not found universal acceptance in Germany at that time. Moreover, German women were provided with an alternative to sports, which emphasised performance and competition, in the form of *Turnen*. In handball, they had a substitute for the combative team game of football.

In Norway, by contrast, women were largely confined to gymnastics, which was considered to be the feminine form of physical exercise. In Norway, as has been described above, until the Second World War even athletics was held to be incompatible with femininity and, as in England, the few women's football games that were played were perceived as 'humorous' or a spectacle.

In neither Germany, Norway nor Spain was there a women's sports association that could have organised and supervised women's football. In England, the tradition of gender segregation in physical education and sport and the existence of the English Ladies' Football Association may have contributed to the continuity of a women's football movement, however marginal. From the early 1930s, due to factors including an economic recession, social upheavals and political developments, traditional ideals of womanhood and the family gained new significance in all the countries under study. In a period in which criticism of emancipation and new culture was rife, there was no room for women's football.

Soon after the Second World War initiatives were taken by women in Germany and England to become officially licensed to play football. However, it was not until the 1970s that a new women's football movement began to develop world-wide – a movement which in the meantime has succeeded even in having women's football recognised as an Olympic discipline.

NOTES

1. Ute Frevert, *'Mann und Weib, und Weib und Mann.' Geschlechterdifferenzen in der Moderne* (Munich, 1995).
2. The term sport is used in many European countries in a broad sense; it is often synonymous with physical activities.
3. See, for example, Ph. Heineken, *Das Fußballspiel* (Hannover, 1898. Nachdruck 1993) (hereafter *Das Fußballspiel*); E. Dunning and K. Sheard, *Barbarians, Gentlemen and Players* (Oxford, 1979).
4. In the following account of the history of football and the development of women's football, the working-class sports movement has been neglected since, to date, virtually nothing is known in sport history on the subject of women's football in the working-class sports movement. The proletarian sport movement played quite an important role in Germany and in Norway; however, the vast majority of men and women engaged in sport were members of 'bourgeois' sport organisations.
5. See J.A. Mangan, '"Muscular, Militaristic and Manly": The British Middle-class Hero as Moral Messenger', in R. Holt and J.A. Mangan (eds.), *European Heroes: Myth, Identity, Sport* (London, 1996), pp.28–47 (hereafter *Heroes*); J.A. Mangan, 'Sport in Society: The Nordic World and Other Worlds', in H. Meinander and J.A. Mangan (eds.), *The Nordic World: Sport in Society* (London, 1996), p.i.
6. Mangan, *Heroes*, p.30.
7. Ibid., p.32.
8. On the history of football in England, see, for example, Ph. Heineken, *Das Fußballspiel*; J. Walvin, *The People's Game – The Social History of British Football* (London, 1975); S. Wagg, *The Football World – A Contemporary Social History* (Harvester Press, 1984); J. Williams and S. Wagg (eds.), *British Football and Social Change* (Leicester, University Press, 1991).The FA Cup was awarded for the first time in 1871; and in 1888, 32 clubs came together to form the football league.
9. Holt, quoted in J. Williams and J. Woodhouse, 'Can play, will play? Women and football in Britain' in Williams and Wagg, *British Football and Social Change*, p.89.
10. J.A. Mangan, 'Games field and Battlefield: A Romantic Alliance in Verse and the Creation of Militaristic Masculinity', in J. Nauright and T.J.L. Chandler (eds.), *Making Men: Rugby and Masculine Identity* (London, 1996), pp.140–57 (hereafter 'Games field'); J.A. Mangan, 'Duty unto Death: English Masculinity and Militarism in the Age ot the New Imperialism', in J.A. Mangan, *Tribal Identities: Nationalism, Europe, Sport* (London, 1996), pp.10–38.
11. E. Dunning, 'Sport as male preserve: Notes on the Social Sources of Masculine Identity and its Transformations', in S. Birell and Ch. Cole (eds.), *Women, Sport, and Culture* (Champaign, Human Kinetics, 1994), pp.163–9.
12. See G. Steins (ed.), *Spielbewegung - Bewegungsspiel. 100 Jahre Goßler'scher Spielerlaß* (Berlin, 1982).
13. See, for example, Ph. Heineken, *Das Fußballspiel*, p.222. See also G. Pfister, 'Sport auf dem grünen Rasen. Fußball und Leichtathletik' in G. Pfister and G. Steins (eds.), *Vom Ritterturnier zum Stadtmarathon. Sport in Berlin* (Berlin, 1987), pp.68–96.
14. K. Koppehel, *Geschichte des deutschen Fußballsports* (Frankfurt, 1954).
15. C. Eisenberg, 'Fußball in Deutschland 1890–1914', *Geschichte und Gesellschaft*, 20 (1994), 181–210; O. Nerz, 'Fußball' in E. Neuendorff (ed.), *Die deutschen Leibesübungen* (Berlin/Leipzig, 1927), p.339.
16. Matti Goksøyr,'"We are the best in the world! We have beaten England!" Norwegian football's function as carrier of nationalism', in G. Pfister and T. Niewerth and G. Steins, *Spiele der Welt im Spannnungsfeld von Tradition und Moderne* (St. Augustin, 1996), p.368 (hereafter '"We are the best in the world!"'). A survey of physical exercises practised in Norway which was published in 1891 noted: 'Possibly the future will show that these amusing English ball games may prosper also in our country. For the time being, however, these games have such a weak popular basis that I dare not call them Norwegian', quoted in M. Goksøyr, '"We are the best in the world!"', p.369.
17. M. Goksøyr,'"We are the best in the world!"', p.370. See also M. Goksøyr, 'Winter sports and

the creation of a Norwegian national identity at the turn of the nineteenth century', in M. Goksøyr and G. v.d. Lippe and K. Mo (eds.), *Winter Games Warm Traditions* (St. Augustin, Academia, s.a.), pp.26–35.

18. See A. Martinez Navarro, 'Anotaciones a la historia de la educacion fisica Española en el siglo XIX', *Historia de la' Educacion. Revista interuniversitaria* , II (1983), 153–64; M. Piernavieja del Pozo, 'Spanien' in H. Ueberhorst (ed.), *Geschichte der Leibesübungen*, Bd. 5 (Berlin/München/Frankfurt, 1976), pp.188–224 (hereafter 'Spanien'). An important role was played by the desolate economic state of a country where 'in 1900 tens of thousands of Spaniards suffered hunger and more than half of the population could neither read nor write', W. Herzog, *Spanien* (München, 1989), p.53. See also M.A. Ackelsberg, *Free Women of Spain. Anarchism and the Struggle for the Emancipation of Women* (Bloomington, 1991) (hereafter *Free Women*).

19. M. Piernavieja del Pozo, 'Spanien', p.221. Especially in the south of Spain there were a great many English (and also French and Belgian) firms involved in mining, W. Herzog, *Spanien*, p.51. See also X. Pujadas and C. Santacana, 'Reflexions per a un estudi sobre els valors de l'sportman' en els inicis de l'esport a Catalunya (1870–1910)'. *Acàcia* (1995), 47–61.

20. See J. Polo del Barrio, 'El futbol espanol hasta la guerra civil', *Revista de Occidente* No.62–63 'Deporte y Modernidad'. Julio-Agosto 1986; also L. Crolley, 'Real Madrid y Barcelona. The State against a Nation. The Changing Role of Football in Spain', in A. Krüger and A. Teja (eds.), *La Commune Eredità dello Sport in Europa* (Rome, 1997), pp.450–7.

21. See, for example, G. Pfister and H. Langenfeld, 'Die Leibesübungen für das weibliche Geschlecht – ein Mittel zur Emanzipation der Frau?' in H. Ueberhorst (ed), *Geschichte der Leibesübungen*, vol. 3/1 (Berlin, 1980), pp.485–521. Exceptions here are upper-class games such as tennis, golf and hockey. It is only possible to go into the development of the bourgeois *Turnen* and sports movements. Taking the worker's sports movement into consideration is problematic on account of the lack of research; it would also exceed the scope of this essay.

22. Ibid.

23. G. Pfister and G.von der Lippe, 'Women's Participation in Sports and the Olympic Games in Germany and Norway – A Sociohistorical Analysis' *Journal of Comparative Physical Education and Sport*, XVI, 2 (1994), 30–41.

24. For a brief account of this, see H. Bernett, *Leichtathletik im geschichtlichen Wandel* (Schorndorf, 1987).

25. G. Pfister and G.von der Lippe, 'Women's Participation in Sports and the Olympic Games', 30–41.

26. See G. Pfister, 'The Medical Discourse on Female Physical Culture in Germany in the nineteenth and Early 20th Centuries', *Journal of Sport History*, XVII (1990), 183–99. See, for example, Deppe in *Die Leibesübungen* (1930), p.225.

27. Quoted in G. Pfister, '"Der Kampf gebührt dem Mann ..." Argumente und Gegenargumente im Diskurs über den Frauensport', in R. Renson (eds.), *Sport and Contest* (Madrid, 1993), pp.349–65.

28. *Sport und Gesundheit* (1932), 1, 16.

29. See S. Fletcher, *Women First: the Female Tradition on English Physical Education, 1880–1980* (London, 1984); S. Scraton, *Shaping Up to Womanhood. Gender and Girls' Physical Education* (Buckingham, 1992); J. Hargreaves, *Sporting Females* (London/New York, 1994), p.141 (hereafter *Sporting Females*).

30. M. Müller-Windisch, *Aufgeschnürt und außer Atem. Die Anfänge des Frauensports im viktorianischen Zeitalter* (Frankfurt, 1995).

31. J. Hargreaves, *Sporting Females*.

32. S.A.M. Webster, *Athletics of To-Day for Women* (London/New York, 1930), p.33; G. Pallett, *Women's Athletics* (Dulwich, Normal Press, 1955), p.248.

33. Hargreaves, *Sporting Females*, p.134.

34. G. von der Lippe, 'Women's Sports in Norway in the 1930's. Conflict between Two Different body cultures', *Stadion*, 19/20 (1993/1994), 178–87.

35. M. Goksøyr, *Idrettslive I borgersleanets by* (PhD Thesis, Norwegian University of Sport and Physical Education, Oslo, 1991), 202.

36. F. Olstad and S. Tønnesson, *Norsk Idretts Historie 1861–1939* (Oslo, 1987).

37. Ibid. p.270.
38. Ibid. p.271.
39. *SportsManden* (1928), 88.
40. S. Behn and M. Mommertz, 'Wir kämpfen für Spanien. Frauen im antifaschistischen Widerstand und in der sozialen Revolution während des Bürgerkriegs 1936–1939', in *Wiener Historikerinnen* (eds.), *Die ungeschriebene Geschichte. Dokumentation des V. Historikerinnentreffens in Wien 1984* (Wien, o.J.), pp.102–13; M. Nash, 'Two Decades of Women's History in Spain: Reappraisal', in K. Offen and R. Pierson and J. Rendall (eds.), *Writing Women's History: International Perspectives* (London, 1991), pp.1–32.
41. Ackelsberg, *Free Women*, p.43.
42. M. García Bonafé, 'Los Inicios del Deporte Femenino' in Ajuntament de Barcelona (ed.), *Mujer y Deporte* (Barcelona, 1989), pp.23–39.
43. M. García Bonafé and M. Nash, 'Women and the World of Sport in Catalonia' (Unpublished paper, Barcelona, 1993).
44. See, for the struggle for emancipation Ackelsberg, *Free Women*.
45. E. Kamper, *Enzyklopädie der Olympischen Spiele* (Stuttgart, 1972).
46. Ph. Heineken, *Das Fußballspiel*, p.228.
47. A. Fischer–Dückelmann, *Die Frau als Hausärztin* (Dresden, 2. ed. 1905); H.B. Adams–Lehmann, *Das Frauenbuch* (Stuttgart, sine anno).
48. W. Vierath, *Moderner Sport* (Berlin, 1930), p.61.
49. *Sport and Sonne* (1927), p.24. Unfavourable comments on football in other countries are to be found, for example, in an article in *Sport und Gesundheit* (1938), 9, 18.
50. Quoted in G. Pfister, *Frau und Sport. Frühe Texte* (Frankfurt, Fischer, 1980), p.179.
51. B. Schreiber-Rietig, 'Die Suffragetten spielten Fußball', *Olympisches Feuer* (1993), 2, 36–41. See also *Das Illustrierte Blatt*, dated 27 March 1930.
52. *Sport und Gesundheit* (1932), 1, 16; *Sport im Bild*, dated 22 Nov. 1895, 334. See also *Sport im Bild*, dated 5. 2. 1987, p.87; *Berliner Illustrierte Zeitung* (1933), 11, 401.
53. *Die Damenillustrierte* (1927), Special Issue 'Frauensport', 7.
54. The following text is based on information in D.J. Williamson, *Belles of the Ball* (Devon, 1991) (hereafter *Belles*); Williams and Woodhouse, 'Can play, will play? Women and Football in Britain', pp.85–111 (hereafter 'Can play') and S. Lopez, *Women on the Ball – A Guide to Women's Football* (London, 1997) (hereafter *Women*).
55. D.J. Williamson, *Belles*, p.4.
56. Ibid., p. 12.
57. S. Lopez, *Women*.
58. Williams and Woodhouse, 'Can play', p.91.
59. D.J. Williamson, *Belles*, p.47.
60. Quoted in Williams and Woodhouse, 'Can play', p.85.
61. E. Roberts, *Women's Work 1840–1940* (London, 1988).
62. M. Vicinus, *Independent Women, Work and Community for Single Women, 1850–1920* (London, 1985), p.285.
63. D.J. Williamson, *Belles*, p.69.
64. Quoted in S. Lopez, *Women*.
65. D.J. Williamson, *Belles*, p.10.
66. S. Lopez, *Women*, p.4.
67. Williams and Woodhouse, 'Can play', p.94.
68. M. García Bonafé, 'Los Inicios del Deporte Femenino' in Ajuntament de Barcelona (ed.), *Mujer y Deporte* (Barcelona, 1989), p.32.
69. *Damen-Sport Damen-Turnen* (1919), p.156.
70. R.-K. Torkildsen, *Norsk Kvinnefotball. En historisk undersckelse om norsk kvinnefotballs utvikling. Master thesis* (Hogskolen i Levanger, 1993).
71. Kretsstyrets moteprotokoll. Bergen og Fylkenes Arbeideridrettskrets 1932–1934.
72. See especially E. Dunning, 'Sport as Male Preserve: Notes on the Social Sources of Masculine Identity and its Transformations', in S. Birell and Ch. Cole (eds.), *Women, Sport, and Culture* (Champaign: Human Kinetics, 1994), pp.163–9.
73. H. W. Fischer, *Körperschönheit und Körperkultur* (Berlin, 1928), p.73.

74. Ibid. p. 78.
75. See also M. Messner, 'Sports and Male Domination: The Female Athlete and Contested Ideological Terrain', in Birell and Cole, *Women, Sport, and Culture*, pp.65–81.
76. Mangan, 'Games Field', 140.
77. For the *Turner* movement as male allegiance which combined a glorification of masculinity and nationalism, see G. Pfister, 'Physical Activity in the Name of the Fatherland: Turnen and the National Movement (1810–1820)', *Sporting Heritage*, 1 (1996), 14–36.
78. M. Klein (ed.), *Sport und Geschlecht* (Reinbek, 1983), p.18; see also G. Pfister, 'Physical Activity in the Name of the Fatherland'.
79. H.W. Fischer, *Körperschönheit und Körperkultur* (Berlin, 1928), p.10.
80. Because of the restricted space we could not discuss the connections between gender, sport and class which showed specific patterns in the different countries.
81. B.R. Mitchell, *European Historical Statistics* (London, 1976); these numbers have to be interpreted very carefully because it is difficult to compare the available statistics which are based in each country on different material. See for a more detailed discussion about similarities and differences of womens roles in Europe the article in volume 5 of the *History of Women* edited by Thebaud (1995). In the contributions of this series edited by Georges Duby and Michel Perrot special emphasis is laid on the role of women in France and England.
82. See especially Ackelsberg, *Free Women*.
83. M. Sineau, 'Recht und Demokratie', in G. Duby and M. Perrot (eds.), *Geschichte der Frauen*, Vol. 5 (Frankfurt, 1995), pp.529–59; S. Lopez, *Women*, p.2.

Cultural Differentiation, Shared Aspiration: The Entente Cordiale of International Ladies' Football, 1920–45

ALETHEA MELLING

On Thursday 29 April 1920 an important international football match took place at Preston North End ground, Deepdale in Lancashire, between Dick, Kerr's Ladies representing England and a team comprising the best eleven out of the nine major women's football teams in the Paris region of France.[1] The tour, consisting of four matches and lasting twelve days, was organised by the manager of Dick, Kerr's, Alfred Frankland and Madame Alice Milliat, of the Fédération des Sociétés Féminines Sportives de France, which controlled French women's athletics.[2] All expenses for the tour were to be met by Dick, Kerr and Company Engineering, who were acting as the sponsors.[3] The objective of the tour was to promote international peace and goodwill between the allies and raise money for those affected by the First World War. Alice Kell, a Dick, Kerr's player and spokeswoman, stated: 'If the matches with the French serve no other purpose, I feel they will have done more to cement the good feelings between the two nations than anything which occurred during the last fifty years, except of course, the Great War.'[4]

The First World War acted as a vehicle for many changes in both England and France, both culturally and politically. Firstly, hostilities in Europe threw the two nations, who usually regarded themselves as natural enemies into alliance. Each nation held damaging stereotypes about the other. In 1906 Bardoux explained to the French that the English were lacking in aesthetic sensibility, weak in critical intelligence, yet strong in will power and in general the people of England reflected the weather in personality; rather damp and miserable with a tendency to occasional storms. The English disliked all foreigners, of whom the French were the nearest.[5] After the war, the alliance disintegrated into

bitterness and regret over the weight of the burden each country had to
bear in terms of casualty and mortality.[6] Secondly, the war had serious
implications for the women of both nations, throwing them into roles at
home and in the work place from which they had previously been
excluded.[7] The women rose to the challenge of the war with enthusiasm,
proving they were physically and mentally capable of accommodating
traditional male roles. A whole new modernist culture for women
developed from the war experience, manifesting itself in the 'Femme
Moderne' in France and the 'It' girl or 'Flapper' in England. The
modern woman cut her hair into a 'Bob', shortened the hem of her skirts
to the knee, wore trousers, smoked cigarettes, suppressed her breasts in
favour of the new androgynous figure and sought to emancipate herself
from the constraints of the pre-war era.[8]

In addition to throwing herself enthusiastically into male spheres in
the work place, the modern woman involved herself in 'men's' sports. In
England, a craze developed for women's football, which was endorsed as
part of the war effort as a means of lifting moral and raising money for
ex-servicemen.[9] In France, women began to get involved in athletics, an
area from which they had previously been excluded, and the playing of
football was regarded as an extension of this.[10] After the war, in the 1920s
spirit of promoting internationalism and global peace through sport, the
two groups of women met in an effort to raise money for ex-servicemen.
However, the endorsement of women's football was to be short lived and
in an effort to return to pre-war social forms women's involvement in the
sport was to be undermined by the establishment on both sides of the
channel.[11] The women's football internationals between the Paris region
and Lancashire teams grew out of unique circumstances resulting from
the war. Their significance is in the way they transcended both cultural
and ideological barriers to form a long-term tradition in women's
football.

Despite measures to dismiss women's role in football, their involvement
has a long and significant history in England, with the first official match
being recorded at Crouch End Athletic in North London on 23 March
1895, organised by Nettie Honeyball, the Secretary of The British
Ladies' Football Club. Nettie Honeyball promoted ladies' football as a
'Manly game that could be womanly as well'.[12] The club president was
Lady Florence Dixie, the youngest daughter of the Marquess of

Queensbury. Florence Dixie was fundamental in organising the sport in Scotland, playing mainly exhibition matches for charity.[13] Women's sport of any description was the preserve of the educated middle class. However, this was to change with the onset of the First World War.[14]

In 1917, Grace Sibbert, the founder of Dick, Kerr's Ladies' football team, challenged her male colleagues to a match. The men's team had not been performing very well of late, resulting in some lunch-time teasing from the women. The result of this was a friendly contest between the sexes on a field near Penwortham, Preston, Lancashire. The result of this first match was never recorded, but it led to the formation of Dick, Kerr's women's team, whose official objective was to raise money for ex-servicemen and other war-time charities. Sibbert's interest in those affected by the war was also personal, as her husband Jimmy had suffered appalling treatment in a German POW camp.[15] The nature of 'modern' warfare was to cause the condition of ex-servicemen to become a national concern on a scale unknown before[16] and this was fundamental to the future direction of women's football during the early post-war years.

Women's football in England became phenomenally successful during the early post-war period up to 1921. J. Williams and J. Woodhouse note that by 1920 crowds of spectators had become 'unmanageably large', filling FA stadiums rather than factory yards and farmers fields.[17] Teams spread over the north, midlands and the south east of England, with estimates in the region of 150 teams.[18] D. Williamson notes that the first Ladies' Football Association was formed at Blackburn on 10 December 1921, comprised 25 teams and grew to 60 by the second meeting.[19] Women's football developed rapidly in Lancashire during and shortly after the war due to a combination of environmental and ideological factors. Firstly, football was already established in Lancashire as the most popular sport of the working classes and conscription had seriously affected the game, with 4,765 players from the Lancashire League teams conscripted into the forces, there left a huge gap in popular culture which could be filled by women.[20] Secondly, the ideology of the 'plucky heroine' taking on men's roles in the factory and on the farm, whilst the men were fighting in France, created an environment which endorsed women playing football as part of the war effort to boost morale and raise money for war related charities.[21] However, this endorsement was short lived and by 1921 steps were in motion to return women to pre-war social forms, shifting them from the factory back to the home to create employment for demobbed troops.[22] This agenda was also applied to football, starting with a FA ban on women using their grounds, which was effective from December 1921. This resulted in the sudden collapse of the game as only FA stadiums could accommodate the crowds of up to 53,000 which the women's game attracted.[23]

Women's football in France followed a similar pattern of growth in the Paris regions and other provinces such as Marseille, Reims, Toulouse and Roubaix.[24] The first game was a private affair in 1917, followed by a public match preceding the men's international between Belgium and France in 1918.[25] This was between two of the new French women's sports clubs, which included En Avant, Femina, and the Fauvettes, which had developed during the years before the outbreak of the First World War.[26] Association football had established itself in France at the beginning of the twentieth century and along with other 'English' sports such as rugby, took over from traditional gymnastics.[27] The public preferred them as an escape from the regimentation of formal gymnastic exercises, as Association football and rugby were far more spontaneous, combining a 'sense of the importance and freedom of the individual player, with a belief in the value of team work'.[28] It was evident that football was developing into a dominant sport in France as early as 1906, when 1,500 out of 3,000 youngsters voted football as their favourite sport in a poll organised by a popular boys' magazine.[29] The *Revue Olympique* noted that 'the most important feature of European sport at the present time is the steady growth of association football'.[30] Football was spread in France through ports and towns by travelling businessmen and artisans. The sport spread during the Great War when it was played by soldiers in the trenches. After the war, football took off as a major sport. In 1920 the Fédération Française de Football (FFF) had 1,000 clubs. Over the next five years this quadrupled, reaching 6,000 by the late 1930s.[31]

During the decade leading up to the First World War football infiltrated gymnastic and athletic clubs, therefore it is of little surprise that women's football developed from such a background. During the war women's football was nurtured in the Paris district under the blanket of the Fédération des Sociétés Féminines Sportives de France, which organised women's athletics.[32] In his study of French sport Richard Holt fails to mention this federation, yet it was unique in France. Women made very little impact on French sport before the First World War.

Holt suggests that even as late as the 1930s there were few French sportswomen but, as Gertrud Pfister points out, there has been only limited research on the subject.[33] The situation, therefore, is neither fully explored nor absolutely clear. Certainly the predominantly patriarchal nature of French sport actively excluded women. Vigorous sport was considered an exclusive 'man-to-man' activity where men could meet and socialise away from their families and households. Women were denied even the most gentle of pastimes such as cycling which, if not initially, was eventually considered quite acceptable in England.[34]

Women's football in France was managed by Alice Milliat of the Femina Sports Club, the first women's football club in Paris.[35] Milliat originally made a name for herself in 1917 when she challenged the IOC's ruling that prevented women from competing in the Olympic Games, resulting in a breakdown of the IOC's previously unanimous stand against women athletes.[36] Milliat emphasised that women's football was simply another way of demonstrating the athletic ability of French women and girls.[37] French women's football was fundamentally different to that played by working-class women in Lancashire in the sense that it originated in an intellectually motivated phenomenon, based on modernist ideas, rather than a spontaneous reaction to the war effort. The Lancashire women were primarily interested in football, which occasionally led them to other sports. The French, however, were primarily interested in athletics, which in turn led them to football. The Lancashire team was working class, whereas the French came from a variety of backgrounds, but predominantly white collar occupations; Duray, shop assistant and interpreter; Laloz sisters, machine workers; Pomies, dental student; Rinbaux, shorthand typist; Brule, shorthand typist; Bracquemonde, shorthand typist; Delpierre, student of philosophy; Billac, bookkeeper; Patuneau, dressmaker; Trottmann sisters, English mother from Leeds; Janiaud, no details; Viani, no details; Ourry, no details; Lévèque, married.[38] Regarding social composition, they appeared to have more in common with the Atalanta Sports Club from Huddersfield, which recruited women from a wide section of the community.[39] However, intellectually Milliat's ideas were comparable to those disseminated by Bergman-Osterburg and the nineteenth-century advocates of women's football who looked towards fit women improving the quality of the race.[40] What the Lancashire and the French sides did have in common was that they both developed out of the infrastructures put in place during the First World War. Both were sanctioned by the dominant patriarchal hegemony as part of the war effort, acting as a temporary service to raise money and the morale of those affected by the war, and both faced clearly focused pressure to return to pre-war gender roles in the early 1920s.

The relationship between the two teams was founded on a shared vocation; the promotion of international peace through sport and the assistance of those disaffected by the war. In order to appreciate why these women were drawn into internationalist roles, it is important to understand the development of the internationalist 'peace through sport movement' in both countries and also how profoundly the ex-servicemen's condition affected all spheres of society on both sides of the Channel. The spirit of sporting internationalism had already begun to flourish in the decade before the First World War. The first sports internationals developed in Europe during the latter end of the nineteenth century and spread to Germany, Switzerland, and the Czech lands of the Austro-Hungarian Empire by 1900. Shortly after, similar organisations were developed in Belgium, France and England. David Steinberg states that a Belgian, Gaston Bridoux, attempted to develop cross-boundary sports events between the French and Belgians to an international level, resulting in a congress organised at Ghent in 1913 by representatives of workers' sports associations from England, Belgium, France and Germany belonging to the Socialist International, and resulting in an official international workers' sport association.[41]

The outbreak of war put an abrupt end to the proceedings. However, the concept transcended the war and promoted a new message of peace and reconciliation during the early post-war years. Bridoux, assisted by another Belgian, Jules Devlieger, arranged a conference in Seraing, Belgium 1919, followed by another in Paris at Easter 1920, leading to the convocation of a congress on 13 and 14 September 1920 at Lucerne. The new organisation was anti-military and due to pressure from the French dropped socialist from the title in order to embrace non-socialist workers. It became known as the International Association for Sport and Physical Culture: 'the tasks facing the international in 1920 were to recreate among worker sportsmen the unity which had been shattered by the war, to develop the national workers' sports movements and to generate among workers, sport activity that was truly international'.[42] This ideology flourished in both France and England during the early post-war years.

A sense of sporting internationalism began in France in 1908 with the formation of the Fédération Sportive et Athlétique Socialiste (FSAS). By 1913 the FSAS had about 1,000 members and produced its own newspaper, *Sport et Socialisme*, with columns on athletics, cycling and sport. In 1913 the FSAS joined the Belgians, Germans, English and Swiss to form the first sports international at Ghent. The French organisation was destroyed during the First World War. However, it was re-established in 1919 as the Fédération Sportive du Travail (FST), by means of which the spirit of sporting internationalism was resurrected in France after the War.[43]

A parallel experience was taking place in England in part due to work on the British Workers' Sports Federation. According to Stephen Jones, the main drive behind the formation of the Federation in 1923 was the desire 'to further the cause of peace between nations'.[44] The main protagonist was Tom Groom, a confirmed internationalist, who as chairman of the Labour-orientated Clarion Cycling Club, attended the conference at Ghent in 1913 and at Lucerne in 1921. Groom promoted internationalism and sport, using slogans such as 'footballs instead of cannonballs' and 'peace through sport'. The objective of the BWSF in pursuing internationalism was to ensure that 'the future peace of the world may be secured in the democratic arenas of international sporting Olympiads'.[45] These pacifist and internationalist ideas shaped the directions of women's football in the early post-war era. During the war the role of the women's football was directly associated with the war effort and the subsequent development of sporting internationalism in the context of peace provided a new direction which would extend popular endorsement into the early post-war years. In England, women's football had won considerable acclaim for the work it did raising money for war-related causes, therefore it was logical to give their efforts an international perspective, particularly given the widespread revulsion at the condition of ex-servicemen.

The condition of ex-servicemen was an international concern. Nearly 8,000,000 Frenchmen were mobilised during the First World War. Out of these 1,322,1000 (16.6%) died. To bring the scale of this mortality home, in an article in *French History* in 1987 David Englander quoted a demographer, stating 'if laid head to foot, the dead would have formed an unbroken line from Berlin to Paris three times over', or 'they would have filled to capacity some 2,500 average sized living rooms'.[46] Once the war began, the sufferings of the French people were far greater than those of the English, as the war was carried out largely on French ground and it was the French army that bore the brunt of the fighting for the first two years. The English army lost approximately 750,000 men compared to the 1,322,100 suffered by the French and this loss was compounded by the sharp fall in birth-rate during the war.[47] The English never really understood the full effects of the war on the French: they were too busy grieving the loss of what they regarded as the 'élite' of society, as a disproportionate number of recruits came from the professional classes; whereas French recruits came from a cross-section of society. Neither side appreciated the loss of the other.[48]

The long-term condition of ex-servicemen was a growing concern as an enormous number suffered severe mental and physical scars. The outcomes of the First World War were instrumental in challenging traditional cultural and social concepts regarding the effects of war on soldiers. Ted Bogacz notes that in England, two years after the Armistice, 65,000 ex-servicemen were drawing disability pensions for neurasthenia; of these, 9,000 were still undergoing hospital treatment.[49] Press articles disseminated the issues relating to the terrible effects of the war to the general public. In addition to neuroses, the extent of mutilation was unprecedented due to the new war technology employed such as grenades. Over 41,000 Englishmen had their limbs amputated in the First World War: 69% lost one leg, 28% lost an arm, 3% lost both arms and legs, another 270,000 suffered disabling injuries to limbs. Head or eye wounds afflicted 60,500, 89,000 had other serious injuries. In 1920, 31,500 men were still receiving compensation for loss of limbs. In the years leading up to the Second World War 222,000 English officers and over 419,000 servicemen were still on disability pensions. Dr Doyan of the French army medical services reported in 1915 that military surgeons were removing limbs in 'a haphazard kind of way ... In some places amputations multiplied to a rather dangerous extent'. Joanna Bourke's comment that in every street in every town someone was affected is fully substantiated. 'Mass mutilation,' stated Bourke, 'was there for all to see.'[50]

In March 1920 Alfred Frankland, the manager of Dick, Kerr's Ladies, issued an invitation to the organisers of the nine Paris clubs, inviting a representative eleven to organise a tour in order to raise money for the ex-servicemen, whose condition was a concern to all nations involved in the war. The English men's amateur side were already due to play an international match at Rouen in France and it was originally hoped the Lancashire women would follow them and also play an international there in May.[51] However, this was postponed until the autumn of 1920. The invitation to play the Lancashire side was accepted by the French, who contacted Frankland by telegram one week before they were due to arrive on 20 April 1920.[52] The *Lancashire Daily Post* gave details of the imminent arrival of the French team the following Wednesday, with plans to play the opening game at the Preston North End ground on the Thursday.[53] What is striking about the arrangements for this tour is the apparent lack of organisation. The tour was only confirmed one week before their arrival and the venue for the opening match had not yet been finalised, although Preston North End had been 'approached'. Secondly, although Dick, Kerr's representatives had been approached by London, Leicester, Manchester, Stockport, Burnley and Blackburn for matches to be held at their respective facilities, the complete itinerary for the tour had not yet been decided.[54]

By 22 April an itinerary for the tour was nearly complete. The French would be met at Preston Station by the officials of Dick, Kerr and Co. and the works band. Then they would be driven to the Bull and Royal Hotel, which would be their headquarters during their stay in the town. The first match with Dick, Kerr's would take place at Deepdale on Friday evening and the second at Stockport on the following afternoon. On Wednesday 5 May the team would appear at Manchester City Ground, Hyde Road, with the final match at Chelsea's ground, Stamford Bridge, in London.[55]

John Bell, the special correspondent of the *Daily News* in Paris, provided the following commentary on the French team:

> Wearing horizon blue jerseys, navy blue breeches and black stockings, black caps and a tri colour badge on their breast, the team will show English crowds the progress made in French athletics in France. Tomorrow night, the team which will play the association game against the girls' team in England, will be chosen at the Elisabeth Stadium. The players belong to the clubs affiliated to the Fédération des Sociétés Féminines Sportives de France and are drawn from all ranks of society. Social position counts for nothing among the girl football players in France and the team visiting England will consist of students of medicine and dentistry, school teachers, typists and work girls. The Federation which is

run entirely by women athletes, has formed four football clubs in Paris, and so great has been the desire of the players to perfect themselves in the game and so be chosen to visit England that numerous matches have been played against men's teams.[56]

The French players were beaten 2–0 in the opening match of their tour at Deepdale by Dick, Kerr's. The sports column in the *Lancashire Daily Post* stated that although the French girls lacked the skill of the English girls, they played with 'pluck and zest' and were often 'saved by their superior stride'. The paper added that although Dick, Kerr's had not played their best, the crowd of 25,000, which paid a total of £1,295 for admission, 'enjoyed itself hugely'. The money went towards building an ex-servicemen's club. The match was refereed by Percy Smith, a first division referee, and Frank Jeffers and Joe McCall of Preston North End acted as linesmen.[57]

The tour provided an interesting insight into English working-class attitudes towards the French and the insular nature of society in Lancashire. The press represented this in several articles. However, the most interesting popular commentary comes in the form of a cartoon from the *Lancashire Daily Post*, illustrating the opening match between Dick, Kerr's and the French (Figure 1).[58] The cartoon is not only significant in the way it draws attention to popular cultural stereotypes of the French, but also as a starting point in looking at the differences between the methods of the French and Lancashire teams. The first striking feature is the regimentation of the French women compared to the Lancashire team. Although the spectacle of the French marching onto the field to the strains of the 'Marseillaise' may have amused and fascinated a relatively insular society, who found the visit of the French novel, it is an interesting reflection of French physical education and its preoccupation with the aesthetic aspect of athletics.[59] Regimentation in sporting activities was a reflection of the French interest in improving the race by military-style physical exercise. This developed into a tradition in the mid-nineteenth century as a reaction to the Prussian defeat of Austria. The French middle class had always resisted anything regimental, but a group of theorists pushed forward the idea of military-style drill on the English model as the most efficient method of physical training for the youth of France.[60] Unlike England, ball games on the continent 'followed in the wake of more systematic methods of physical training'.[61]

FIGURE 1

FRENCH LADIES v. DICK, KERR'S LADIES AT DEEPDALE

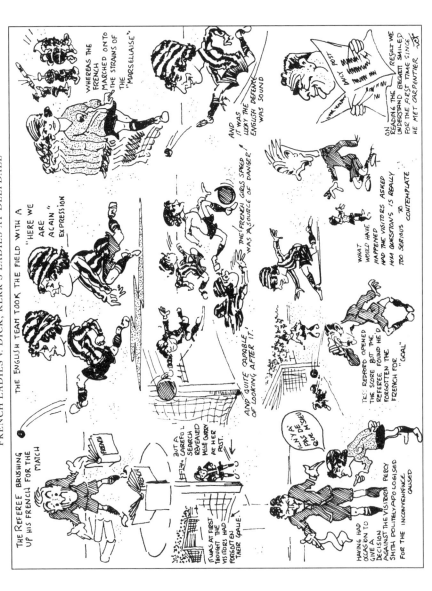

Rather than being a free-standing sport, football was regarded as an element of French women's athletics. This may explain why they were trained in a far more regimented manner than the Lancashire women. As members of a sporting federation, they took part in other more systematic sports such as tennis, rowing, swimming, basketball, cross-country running, putting the weight and javelin throwing.[63] The Fédération des Sociétés Féminines Sportives de France controlled women's and girls' athletics and the tour was not simply a demonstration of the girls' soccer skills, but more significantly, a representation of the development of women's athletics in France.[64] It reflects Milliat's defiance of continued resistance to women partaking in athletics previously monopolised by men and the determination of a section of French women to have women's sporting achievements recognised by the IOC. It is also significant to note that the French women played men as part of their training before the tour to emphasise further their physical capabilities, although Milliat rejected this for political reasons as Frankland, among many others, declared it immoral.[65] The French instigated Fédération Sportive Féminine Internationale (FSFI), became, according to Jennifer Hargreaves, an important mover for women's international athletics, organising its own Olympics in Paris, 1922, which became the Women's World Games, as the IOC claimed exclusive rights to the term 'Olympic'.[66] By comparison, the Lancashire team of 1920 was not firmly associated with more systematic sports. Also the cult status of football in working-class Lancashire would have eclipsed other sports and there is little to suggest that the 'munitions girls' of 1920 were genuinely preoccupied with anything else.

However, although Milliat and the French women's sporting federations made significant moves in the cause of women's athletics, they have to be viewed in the context of the era and in that context their apparent polish and organisation is an illusion. Women's sport was, and remained so for several decades, virtually non-existent in France. French sport was monopolised by men and the level of chauvinistic hostility towards women was intense. Secondly, the majority of French women consented to the dominant ideology that they were physically and mentally unfit for sport. The French workers' sport organisation, which was against chauvinism, tried unsuccessfully to interest French working-class women in sport by arranging activities and giving them positive coverage in their press. Rosette Guérard, a workers' sports correspondent, urged women to spend less time at the cinema and more time involved in sport.[67] The weekly journal of the FST, *Sport*, was forced to conclude that the organisation of women's sport in France via the Fédération Française des Sports Féminines (FFSF) was in fact a 'farce'. Sports journals such as *L'Auto* were only interested in women's sport to sell beauty cream.[68] The 'Deepdale' cartoon, mentioned above, presents the French as a strong, united team in contrast to its depiction of the Lancashire women, who take to the field in an undisciplined manner with the 'here we are again' expression. The 'Deepdale' cartoon says more about English working-class perceptions of the French than of the real organisation and structure of French women's football.

The modern woman's body and body image were a point of debate in post-war culture, and the deconstruction of the cartoon depiction of French and Lancashire women's bodies provides an important insight into popular perceptions of the Femme Moderne, the working-class girl and what their respective body shapes represented. Firstly, the French were characterised by their slightness of build compared to the robust and sturdy Lancashire lasses. The French goalkeeper, Ourry, is depicted as being so tiny the crowd cannot see her from the stands: 'It was at first thought that the visitors had lost their goalie, but a careful search revealed Mlle Ourry at her post' (Figure 1). The *Lancashire Daily Post* observed that the French team were 'mostly of slim build, and thus gave a lot of weight away'. On their arrival the media noted that only one or two French girls looked strongly built and the general question appeared to be, despite their so-called speed, would these predominantly white collar workers be physically capable of competing with 'munitions' girls?[70]

From her statements regarding sport and body image, Milliat appears to be influenced by the modernist aesthetic. She refers to her players as 'beautiful, Grecian dancers', who play 'fast but not vigorous football'.[71] After their defeat by the Lancashire team, Milliat praised her team by saying they played 'beautifully'. Alice Milliat's preoccupation with the modernist aesthetic pre-empts Mary Bagot-Stack's League of Health and Beauty founded in England in the 1930s.[72] The League, states Hargreaves, made 'bodily form pre-eminent, revealed in thin loose flowing clothes. Greek style costumes were designed to allow complete freedom of movement, producing a sense of the fluid, mobile, female body'.[73] Anne Hollander remarks that the ideal of female slenderness, presented by the French football team, began in the 1920s and that 'the look of a possible movement became a necessary element in female beauty and an important feature of modernisation'.[74]

Hollander further states that sport became an expression of eroticism and this, according to Hollander, was best offered in 'a self contained, sleekly composed format: a thin body, with a few layers of covering'.[75] Eroticism is subtly alluded to in the 'Deepdale' cartoon where the Lancashire women appear asexual in comparison to the French with their slightly coquettish march to the 'Marseillaise', the significantly greater expanse of exposed thigh, the coy posturing of the girl who is being 'politely' ruled against by Percy Smith: 'Il n' y a pas de que m'sieu' (Figure 1). This treatment was not exclusive to Lancashire. Williamson uses a photograph from an unnamed national newspaper showing the French versus English match at Stamford Bridge, London, entitled, '"Shorts". Very Short'. '... Many wore knickers so scanty as would be frowned upon by the FA if worn by men.' The photograph depicted French and Dick, Kerr's players, the French players' shorts being marginally the shorter of the two.[76] The French were being subtly sexualised for the male gaze. Once a woman's sport is sexualised, it is simultaneously trivialised. Turning sports women into the objects of titillation is a chauvinistic ploy which automatically undermines the women's achievements.

D. Mrozek, in his study of sporting women in America, touches on a universal theme in Western society. Men and women occupied separate cultures, each not understanding the world of the other. Women were still regarded as morally weak and without patriarchal controls to keep them in their place, promiscuity and associated evils would follow. This belief was also applied to sport and although the benefits of sport were being discussed in terms of improving the race, vigorous athletics and exuberant displays of physical behaviour were still associated with promiscuity and poor morals. Respectable women were expected to behave with 'restraint' in all things including exercise, 'any departure from the most restrained and proper behavioural code could be interpreted as a start down the road to depravity'.[77] The patriarchal dominant culture which still placed clear distinctions in gender roles and modes of behaviour, found it difficult to accept a concept of modernism and the modern woman which filtered into popular culture in the early post-war era. After the war Mrozek's observation, 'it was bad enough if a man could not manage to behave like a man; but his dilemma worsened if women refused to behave like women', was to resonate around Europe.[78] Athletics and sports had traditionally been a male sphere establishing and reinforcing their masculinity.[79] The way that patriarchal hegemony dealt with women intruders was to dismiss them as eccentric, lesbian or sexually promiscuous. These traditionally held beliefs are evident in the 'Deepdale' cartoon and expressed with a racist bias against the French rather than the English girls, who in 1920 had just over a year's grace before the full force of chauvinism would be directed against them. The French girls were being deliberately associated with a cultural stereotype, the Parisian Femme Moderne, liberated, exuberant and sophisticated. Images of Gay Paris, the Cancan and the Belle Époque era were never far from the surface. Alternatively, the Lancashire women, 'our lasses', were depicted as sturdy, robust, square-jawed Tomboys – immature and unsophisticated 'munitions' girls, doing their bit for Britain. The promiscuous versus the eccentric, 'the flighty capricious Marianne versus the solid John Bull'.[80] However, regardless of the ethnic bias, how both teams are depicted supports Mrozek's overriding hypothesis that athleticism for women in the 1920s was a major social challenge.[81]

According to Eugene Weber, 'acquaintance across ethnic lines does not generate favourable judgements or friendly feelings. Stereotypes are negative.'[82] The racial stereotypes in the 'Deepdale' cartoon are clichés and contrary to the spirit of internationalism. Percy Smith puzzling over French textbooks may be designed to provoke a popular nationalist sense of humour, but it is also representative of the English insular attitude. Despite the internationalist rhetoric of the likes of Tom Groom, there was an ideological dislike of the French deeply entrenched in popular opinion, cultivated by years of traditional hostility. The 'adoration of French culture' was confined to an educated élite and according to P. Bell had limited impact on the English working class, who still regarded the French as natural enemies.[83] The final caption on the 'Deepdale' cartoon reinforces these nationalistic tendencies. It shows the boxer Beckett taking vicarious revenge on the French: 'Beckett smiled for the first time since meeting Carpentier'. This refers to his defeat by the suave French boxer Georges Carpentier. The English were contemptuous of the French adopting their sports. Holt provides a quote from Lewis Hemon's novel, *The Battling Malone*, 1909, to illustrate the point:

> One fine day, they [the French] had suddenly grown tired of kicking each other in the face and had determined to learn the art of using their fists like men – of boxing, in short. All England had roared. 'A boxing Frenchman!' It was the absurdest of paradoxes, a challenge to common sense![84]

If a boxing Frenchman was the 'absurdest of paradoxes', the sight of a French woman playing that most masculine of English sports, football, must have been anathema. It was a sad irony on the part of the English working-class male that their self-respect was restored somewhat by 'munition' girls beating 'Marianne' at football.

Despite inherent racism and chauvinism, the tour was successful, raising over £3,000. Alice Milliat was presented with something suitably French, a manicure kit, by the Discharged Soldiers' Association in recognition of the fact that the proceeds of all the matches were in aid of ex-servicemen.[85] The media noted at the end of the final match, Mlle Bracquemonde of En Avant, flung her arms around the stoic Alice Kell of Dick, Kerr's and gave her a kiss.[86] This was the first recorded example of the spontaneity and demonstrative behaviour of the French that was to fascinate the Lancashire girls in the decades to come.

The French tour was followed by a visit to France by the Lancashire team on 28 October 1920. This tour was also given popular endorsement as an extension of the girls' role in the war effort as one of the main objectives was to place wreaths on the graves of Lancashire football players who had been killed in France during the First World War.[87] Some of the girls had relatives who had been killed in the war and they wanted to visit their graves and the public memorials to the English soldiers in the four towns where the matches would be held. One of the objectives was to place a wreath in Blackburn colours on the grave of Eddie Latherton, the Blackburn Rovers international inside right, who was killed in active service with the Royal Artillery at Passchendaele. They also intended to visit the battlefields of the Ypres Salient.[88] It was an important symbolic gesture for the women to visit the memorials as part of the national mourning process. This was an extension of their response to the war and as Jay Winter points out, the role of a woman was important to national sentiment: 'a grieving woman, a wife, mother, sweetheart, who suffered in silent agony, and without complaint. She stands in the attitude of sad but stoic sorrow, holding in her hand a wreath of remembrance.'[89]

The act of remembrance and the erection of memorials to the dead was common to both nations. Bell states that 'other wars have had their memorials, but none to match those in number, in significance or in solemnity with which they were inaugurated'.[90] The memorials stretched all over north-eastern France, The Somme and Vimy Ridge, to Arras and Bapaume. The mourners on both sides of the channel shared one desire and that was for peace, so that future generations would not have to make the same sacrifices. This desire for peace manifested itself in two responses, which according to Bell would divide the people of the two nations. The first was a national patriotic response which was essentially insular. The second was a pacifistic nationalist response, which led to the League of Nations and a rejection of all alliances. After the war, each nation felt bitter about the share of the burden they had borne and this led to deep-rooted resentment towards each other. Although they had stood together closely during the war, the remembrance of it drove them apart.[91]

The gesture of the women football players setting out on what was to be endorsed as a tour of remembrance is very significant in light of what Bell has written. Despite a growth in popular antagonism between the two peoples in the post-war years, the English and French women football players were able to transcend this and develop their own entente cordiale which would extend beyond the Second World War. Although at the time it is unlikely that the Lancashire team realised the implications of the tour. In fact laying wreaths at the tombs of dead soldiers, whose football boots they had metaphorically worn during the war, was the last act of service to the war effort before they were decommissioned by public opinion and establishment pressure in an effort to return to pre-war gender practices. Both the English and the French women's football had developed directly as a result of the war and was only endorsed as part of the war effort. After 1921, in England, and more so in France, pressure was put on women by the establishment to avoid 'masculine' spheres of sport. Following the 1921 ban on women playing on FA grounds, the local Lancashire media ran many articles on the subject such as 'women and athletics' by the 'Captain', who wrote the 'Athletic Field' column in the *Bolton Evening News BUFF*:

Both East and West Lancashire are keenly affected by the FA edit against football for women. I have urged for a long time that there are certain competitions quite unsuitable and I fail to see what good certain strenuous athletics on the track or across the field for women could do for them or for the sport.

I place women's races on the same category as children's events – they might be all right as variety turns in a programme (and only when carefully designed) but from the athletic or competitive stand points they do not serve any useful purpose ...[92]

Despite opposition and pressure to undermine the sport on both sides of the channel, the English and French were still able to continue successful international tours and exchange visits throughout the inter-war period. This is significant as the teams demonstrated they could function effectively independent of the pre-war patriarchal structures, as they developed and formed international relationships which transcended those of their respective domiciles.

After 1921 women's football in both England and France became in effect, a subculture. The Lancashire teams carried on playing in the name of charitable causes at public events. Many of the teams that had been associated with munitions work lost the support of their sponsors, as public attitudes and popular ideology demanded a return to pre-war gender forms. In their study of football in Europe in this volume,[93] Gertrud Pfister and her colleagues note that many women gave up playing in the early post-war years: 'Although there is no evidence why these women gave up football, we can assume that they were constrained by dominant ideals of acceptable behaviour.'[94] Bolton Ladies quickly disbanded and so did Manchester Ladies, Liverpool Ladies and many others; although the former two were reformed with a completely new side on the eve of the Second World War.[95] Dick, Kerr and Co. disassociated themselves from the women's team in 1926 and they subsequently became known as Preston Ladies.[96]

The continuation of this subculture in England, according to Pfister *et al.*, was due to the existence of the English Ladies' Football Association.[97] However, the influence of the English Ladies' FA is debatable. The main reason why the sport continued at a low level was demand. Despite the dominant post-war ideology, people wanted to see women play football. They added an extra spectacle to any event, and the English love a spectacle.[98] The women continued to raise money for charity and regularly attended after-match gala dinners, hosted by a variety of VIPs. Ironically the presence of the girls at charitable functions added both a touch of traditional glamour and a frisson of daring modernity. The girls would leave the football pitch covered in mud, bathe, change and arrive at a charity dinner in full length satin ball gowns. The *Lancashire Daily Post* stated in 1937 that 'the football girls are going to make whoopee, casting aside shorts and jerseys, they are preparing to wear their daintiest frocks for a celebration dinner on

November the 24th'.[99] The French tours continued for the same reason, there was a demand. They presented a different culture that appeared sophisticated, glamorous and liberated, and people wanted to see them. However, by banning women's football from FA stadiums, the establishment had placed the sport, in the words of the 'Captain', 'as variety turns in a programme...'. Pfister *et al.* quote Klein stating, 'each country's national sport contributes towards producing and securing the male identity specific to that particular country'[100] and they go on to remark that 'on the whole, in all countries, the aim was to preserve the gender order both inside and outside sport'. Gender order was an important issue for all European countries especially from the beginning of the 1930s: 'Due to economic recession, social upheavals and political development, traditional ideals of womanhood and the family gained new significance ... In a period in which criticism of emancipation was rife, there was no room for women's football.'[101]

From the 1930s to the Second World War, the 'Femme Moderne', as the woman of modernist culture was referred to in France, came under increasing attack. In 1933 the Alliance Nationale began to develop the ideas of pro-nationalist and familial organisations into government policy on the roles of men and women in a social, cultural and political context, looking at sexuality in relation to national identity.[102] Using the rhetoric of the Fascist dictators, Hitler and Mussolini, the Femme Moderne was attacked as a 'central threat to society', with 'denatality' as a fundamental issue. During the First World War the French had a deficit in births of 1,770,000 compared to 670,000 in England. This 'demonisation of the modern woman' in France was instigated by Fernand Boverat, Secretary General of the Alliance Nationale and Paul Haury, a history professor and president of the group's Lyon section. Between them they denounced young independent women as 'threatening to set self interest as the standard for young girls, thus corrupting the future life givers of France'.[103] Shortly after the Second World War, Nan Thomson, a Preston Ladies' veteran, recalls an interesting incident related directly to the French ideology:

Most of the [French] girls were employed in schools as P.T. teachers, and would have immediately lost their jobs had the French authorities found out about their football activities. They never played in France. In fact, the team was entirely unofficial and formed amongst themselves.

I remember one occasion when a reporter interviewed them in Hull and they all gave him fictitious names, in case a French paper got hold of it.[105]

It is clear from the description of the mood of the time described above why female physical training teachers would have faced disciplinary action for playing football, as they would have allegedly 'corrupted' pupils, particularly as it was fashionable to associate vigorous sports with lesbianism and female infertility, neither of which is conducive to pro-natalism.

Despite pressures in France to conform to the dominant patriarchal ideal of womanhood, embracing 'her biological destiny and social responsibilities by raising a large family',[106] the French women football players, however, remained the 'Femme Moderne', particularly in the eyes of their Lancashire working-class counterparts, who were fascinated by what they regarded as the sophisticated and liberated nature of the French. From their arrival in 1920, the French 'aesthetic body' was a great source of interest in comparison to the Lancashire 'athletic body'. Joan Whalley, who played for Preston and Manchester Ladies' describes the French: 'They were more like models, lovely figures, boobs and their shorts were short! Some had white football boots, lovely white football boots.'[107] The Second World War effectively put a stop to international football matches between women's teams. The last match against the French was at Fleetwood on 29 June 1938, in aid of Fleetwood Social Welfare Committee and the unemployed, with the last international against Belgium in 1939, just before the outbreak of war.[108] Whalley remembers the Belgian players being afraid to return on 24 August 1939. War was declared on 3 September.[109] Women's football matches continued in Lancashire up to 1941, mainly due to Frankland and the manager of the newly reformed Bolton Ladies, Ernest Hunt. However, due to rationing Frankland did not arrange any more after a match at Horwich, Lancashire on Saturday 25 October 1941.[110]

Joan Whalley remembered that during the war 'there were blackouts and all sorts happening when we were playing and we had to take our gas masks with us where ever we went'.[111] The experience of the women in France, however, was far more profound. Carmen Pomies, who was one of the original 1920 team and who played for Dick, Kerr's for a while, gave an interesting account of her experience in France to the *Daily*

Mail. She allegedly belonged to a Paris region partisan unit of the FFI. 'Oh, of course I was FFI and I did it with all my heart and strength ... I went on the barricades and fought my part.'[112] If this information is accurate, incidentally, Carmen Pomies was indeed a unique case. Contrary to popular myth, women among the Partisans were rare and extremely difficult to identify. French resistance women who were involved in active combat have been hard to study; because of the nature of their role, they are reluctant to discuss it. These women were trained in secrecy. Paula Schwartz states that it was a 'rare partisane, poised on the barricades, with machine gun in tow [that] inspired the popular cliché of the woman resister, immortalised in legend and even in song'.[113] Nevertheless, regardless of her role, what Pomies goes on to say is interesting.

After the Liberation in 1944, Pomies wrote to Frankland of the 'delirious joy of deliverance' and of the freedom to play and discuss women's football as the Germans had banned it. Pomies stated in the *Daily Mail* that the sport had suffered 'dreadfully' during occupation and the girls had only managed to keep it alive by risking jail. Pomies and her team played on a field, which the men of a tennis club 'fearfully' allowed them to use.[114] Pomies' comments regarding the German attitude towards women playing football are not unrealistic. Firstly, according to Pfister, although there was an active 'games movement' in Germany from the 1880s, advocating physical exercise in the open air for women, with the understanding that 'strong offspring can only be born of strong mothers', football was not encouraged. In 1930 the journal *Leibesubungen* announced the formation of a women's football club in Frankfurt. The 35 women who founded the club trained on a Sunday, thus causing a national scandal, leading to a 'storm of indignation' in the press. The result was a disbanding of the team. In fact, it was 1970 before the German Football Federation acknowledged the women's game.[115]

Pomies was involved in maintaining sporting activities during the Occupation via her membership of the Cercle Athlétique de Montrouge Club in Paris. She stated that the French Ministry of Sport and Education would support her effort to reorganise internationals after the war.[116] However, in light of French Government policy towards women and sport and Nan Thomson's oral evidence, this seems improbable. Nevertheless, post-liberation euphoria created an enthusiasm on both sides of the channel to recommence women's football internationals.

Frankland was keen to associate them with the war effort as in 1920. He told a *Lancashire Daily Post* reporter that as soon as he obtained the services of experienced players, he would be able to present a good side; 'Those who have been in the Services should be in good trim especially,' said Frankland. He went on to point out that the matches would be a 'good attraction for the troops'. A massive relaunch of women's football was planned on a First World War scale. A national newspaper ran the following article in 1944:

> The women of Britain are all set for a football revival after the war and are planning how to launch in this country many all female football clubs, with an estimate of between 50 and 60 teams.
>
> And to this growing movement in Britain has been added recently a new impetus from abroad. With the liberation of Europe, Ladies' football teams in France and Belgium, who once played British Clubs at home and away, have been sounding our women again...[118]

Women's football and international matches did resume after the war, but never on the scale of the First World War. In 1947 there were only 17 clubs in England compared to 150 in 1921.[119] Society and ideology had gone through many different transitions, and the role of women had been questioned by pro-natalists on both sides of the channel. Feminism during the inter-war period tended to follow the Havelock Ellis form, emphasising women's roles as mothers and pushing for better maternity care and so on, rather than protecting women's rights at work and striving for equality in other spheres, including the sports field.[120] This ideology was augmented by a deep economic recession during the 1930s, which affected all of Europe. Women were pressurised into maintaining traditional gender roles in order to maintain an equilibrium in the workplace. The Second World War yet again turned this around and women were once more expected to become the guardians of male spheres. However, women's football never regained the significance it had in the first war and this was due to a combination of reasons. Firstly, according to Colin Veitch, football itself had a great symbolic significance during the First World War to both soldiers and exservicemen and this was not repeated to the same extent.[122] Secondly, popular culture provided women with alternative leisure such as the cinema and dancing, which was extremely popular during the Second World War.[123] Also, current fashion trends favoured a glamorous womanly image, epitomised by Dior's 'New Look', in contrast to the 1920s Flapper, who was androgynous in appearance. Nevertheless, a hardcore of players and supporters remained in England and France, maintaining strong links across the Channel which extended into the 1950s and paved the way for a gradual growth of internationalism within the sport.

Football is now the fastest growing international sport for women, with teams in such 'far away places' as China, Brazil, New Zealand and Japan.[124] Although France is no longer as eminent in international women's football, what the French and English teams achieved during the inter-war period had significance for the development of international women's football today. Firstly, both teams developed out of the patriarchal infrastructures of the First World War, yet proved they could operate independent of them. This is important as women's football has had to function without the support of male football organisations. It was not until the 1970s that 'a new women's football movement began to develop world wide – a movement which in the mean time had succeeded even in having women's football recognised as an Olympic sport'.[125] The struggle with the IOC, of course, was incidentally something Milliat had initiated in the early 1920s. Secondly, teams from both countries had to develop strategies to overcome the opposition of a dominant ideology, which advocated pro-natalism and denounced vigorous sports as damaging to women. Thirdly, in contrast to male football, these teams overcame damaging racial stereotyping and cultural differences to form strong links of friendship which transcended the sport.[126] Therefore, through their achievements, they set a precedent from which international women's football could develop, starting with the Belgians in the 1930s and progressing to the first official women's football World Cup in 1991.

NOTES

The author wishes to thank Professor John Walton of the University of Central Lancashire, Gail Newsham, Professor J.A. Mangan of the University of Strathclyde and Professor Gertrud Pfister of the Freie Universitat, Berlin for advice and support, and Gaynor Campbell for translations.

1. *Lancashire Daily Post*, 31 March 1920 (hereafter *LDP*).
2. Ibid., 29 April 1920.
3. Ibid., 31 March 1920.
4. G. Newsham, *In a League of their Own!* (London, 1997), p.32.
5. P. Bell, *Britain and France 1900–1940* (London, 1996), pp.3, 18, 20.
6. Ibid., pp. 99–112.
7. C. Koos, 'Gender, Anti Individualism and Nationalism: The Alliance Nationale and the

Pronatalist Back Lash Against the Femme Moderne, 1933–1940', *French Historical Studies* (hereafter *FHS*), 19,3 (1996), 669–724. See also P. Summerfield and G. Braybon, *Out of the Cage: Women's Experience in Two World Wars* (London, 1987), p.31.

8. A. Holdsworth, *Out of the Dolls House*, series for BBC Television (1987).
9. Newsham.
10. G. Pfister, 'Die Konstruktion von Weiblichkeit un Mannlichkeit im Sport–Ein Vergleich der Entwicklung des Frauen–Furbballs in Deutschland, England und Frankreich', from K. Hardman (ed.), *Proceedings, ISCPES Congress 1998* (hereafter *ISCPES 1998*).
11. Ibid.
12. J. Williams and J. Woodhouse, 'Can Play, Will Play?' in J. Williams and S. Wagg (eds.), *Women and Football in Britain: British Football and Social Change* (Leicester, 1991), p.87.
13. Newsham.
14. Williams and Woodhouse, p.87.
15. Newsham.
16. J. Bourke, *Dismembering the British Male: Men's Bodies, Britain and the Great War* (London, 1996), pp.33–4.
17. Williams and Woodhouse, p.92.
18. D. Williamson, *Belles of the Ball* (Devon, 1991), p.83.
19. Ibid.
20. C. Sutcliffe and F. Hargreaves, *The History of the Lancashire Football Association 1878–1928* (Yore, 1992), pp.144–5.
21. S. Ouditt, *Fighting Forces, Writing Women: Identity and Ideology in the First World War* (London, 1993), p.73.
22. Summerfield and Braybon, p.119.
23. Newsham, pp.1–23.
24. Pfister, *ISCPES 1998*.
25. Ibid.
26. Ibid.
27. R. Holt, *Sport and Society in Modern France* (London, 1981), p.62.
28. Ibid.
29. Ibid., pp.70–1.
30. Ibid.
31. Ibid.
32. *LDP*, 29 April 1920.
33. Holt, p.164 and Pfister, *ISCPES 1998*.
34. Holt, pp.163–4. Of course, while cycling may have been more acceptable in England than in France by the 1930s, it does not mean it was immediately and wholly acceptable on its earlier introduction. To imply this is to simplify a complex issue. For an interesting and succinct discussion of cycling and female physical emancipation, see John Lowerson, *Sport and the Middle Classes* (Manchester, 1993). For equally succinct discussions of various aspects of the struggle for female physical emancipation in Britain, its Dominions and the United States to juxtapose with events and attitudes in France, see all 12 chapters in J.A. Mangan and Roberta J. Park (eds.), *From Fair Sex to Feminism: Sport and the Socialisation of Women in the Industrial and Post-Industrial Eras* (London, 1987). This volume was published by Frank Cass who will shortly re-issue it with a new Introduction to take account of research in the last decade.
35. *LDP*, 29 April 1920.
36. J. Hargreaves, *Sporting Females* (London 1994), p.211.
37. *LDP*, 29 April 1920.
38. Newsham, p.25.
39. Williamson.
40. Williams and Woodhouse, p.89.
41. D. Steinberg, 'The Worker's Sports Internationals 1920–28', *Journal of Contemporary History* (hereafter *JCH*), 13 (1978), 233–51.
42. Ibid.
43. W.J. Murray, 'The French Workers' Sports Movement and the Victory of the Popular Front in 1936', *International Journal of the History of Sport* (hereafter *IJHS*), 4,2 (1987), 203–30.

44. Stephen J. Jones, 'Sport, Politics and the Labour Movement: The British Workers' Sports Federation 1923–1935', *British Journal of Sports History*, 2,2 (1985), 154–78.
45. Ibid.
46. D. Englander, 'The French Soldier', *French History*, 1,1 (1987), 49–69.
47. F. Field, *British and French Writers of the First World War* (Cambridge, 1991), pp.2–3.
48. Bell, pp.93–4.
49. Ted Bogacz, 'War Neurosis and Cultural Change in England 1914–1922', *JCH*, 24 (1989), 227–256.
50. Bourke, pp.33–4.
51. *LDP*, 29 April 1920.
52. Ibid.
53. Ibid.
54. Ibid.
55. Ibid., 22 April 1920.
56. Ibid.
57. Ibid., 1,5 (1920). See also, *Bolton Evening News BUFF* (hereafter *BUFF*), 1 May 1920.
58. 'French Ladies' versus Dick, Kerr's at Deepdale', *LDP*, 3 May 1920, adapted from the original by Stuart Grey for the purposes of this article.
59. Ibid.
60. M. Spivak, 'Un Concept Mythlogique de la Troisième République: Le Renforcement du Capital Humain de la France', *IJHS*, 4,2 (1987), 155. This point is of current interest since Richard Holt dismisses drill in British elementary education as insignificant, see Holt, 'Contrasting Nationalisms: Sport Militarism and the unitary state in Britain and France before 1914,' in Mangan (ed.), *Tribal Identities*, pp.38–54. It was far more significant than he appreciates. See Alan Penn, *Targeting the Schools: Militarism, Elementary School and Drill, 1870–1914* (London, 1998) passim and see also the consideration of this issue in J.A. Mangan, 'Sport in Society: The Nordic World and Other Worlds', in H. Meinander and J.A. Mangan, *The Nordic World: Sport in Society* (London, 1998), pp.189–91. There is also the point raised in this volume by J. A Mangan and Colm Hickey in their article on 'Athleticism, Drill and the Elementary School', namely that on occasion military drill masqueraded as non-military drill to comply with liberal and progressive Education Boards' regulations, and in this form alone was more widespread and significant than Holt realises. Finally, the fact that France borrowed ideas on military drill from Britain is surely of some significance!
61. Holt, p.62.
62. *LDP*, 29,4 (1920).
63. Ibid.
64. Ibid.
65. Pfister, *ISCPES 1998*; *LDP*, 29 April 1920; oral evidence: J. Burke and N. Thomson.
66. Hargreaves, p.211.
67. Murray, *IJHS* (1987), 216.
68. Ibid.
69. *LDP*, 1 May 1920.
70. Ibid., 28 April 1920.
71. Ibid., 29 April 1920.
72. J.J. Matthews, 'They Had Such a Lot of Fun: The Women's League of Health and Beauty', *History Workshop*, 30 (1990), pp.22–54.
73. Hargreaves, pp.134–6.
74. Ibid.
75. Ibid.
76. Williamson, p.51.
77. D. Mrozek, 'The Amazon and the American "Lady": Sexual Fears of Women as Athletes, in Mangan and Park (eds.), *From 'Fair Sex' to Feminism*, pp.282–98.
78. Ibid.
79. G. Pfister, K. Fasting, S. Scraton and B. Vázquez, 'Women and Football – A Contradiction?: The Beginnings of Women's Football in Four European Countries', *European Sports History Review* (hereafter *ESHR* 1998).

80. Bell, p.20.
81. Mrozek, pp.282–98.
82. E. Weber, 'Of Stereotypes and of the French', *JCH*, 25 (1990), 169–208.
83. Bell, pp.19–22.
84. Holt, p.43.
85. Newsham, p.37.
86. Ibid.
87. Ibid., pp.32–9.
88. Ibid.
89. J. Winter, *Sites of Memory, Sites of Mourning: The Great War in European History* (Cambridge, 1995), p.96.
90. Bell, pp.109–11.
91. Ibid.
92. *BUFF*, 10 Dec. 1921.
93. For a full discussion of this point see the first essay in this volume, passim.
94. Pfister *et al.*, *ESHR* (1998).
95. S. Lopez, *Women on the Ball* (London, 1997).
96. Ibid.
97. Pfister *et al.*, *ESHR* (1998).
98. Ibid.
99. Press cutting from Joan Whalley's scrap book, courtesy of G. Newsham.
100. Pfister *et al.*, *ESHR* (1998). Pfister and her colleagues draw, for example in particular on the extensive research of J.A. Mangan on British middle-class socialisation into masculinity and militarism through sport, in support of this assertion. See Pfister *et al.*, above. For detailed and specific reference to the making of British middle-class militaristic masculinity by means of the playing field (and football), see especially J.A. Mangan, 'Duty unto Death: English Masculinity and Militarism in the Age of the New Imperialism', in J.A. Mangan, *Tribal Identities* (London, 1996), pp.10–38, also J.A. Mangan, 'Gamesfield and Battlefield: a Romantic Alliance in Verse and the Creation of Militaristic Masculinity', in John Nauright and T. Chandler (eds.), *Making Men: Rugby and Masculine Identity* (London, 1996), pp.146–52. For the social context in which this male identity was developed by way of sport, see J.A. Mangan, *Athleticism in the Victorian and Edwardian Public School* (Cambridge, 1981).
101. Koos, *FHS* (1996), 669–724.
102. Bell, pp.93–4.
103. Koos, *FHS* (1996), 669–724.
104. Oral evidence: N. Thomson.
105. Koos, *FHS* (1996), 669–724.
106. Oral evidence: Joan Whalley.
107. Press cuttings: J. Whalley.
108. Newsham, p.95.
109. Press cuttings: J. Whalley.
110. Newsham, p.98.
111. *Daily Mail*, 24 Oct. 1944.
112. Ibid.
113. *Daily Mail*, 24 Oct. 1944, courtesy of G. Newsham.
114. Pfister *et al.*, *ESHR* (1998).
115. *Daily Mail*, 24 Oct. 1944.
116. *LDP* (1944), undated clipping: J. Whalley.
117. Ibid.
118. Lopez.
119. S. Rowbotham, *Hidden from History* (London, 1974), pp.71, 141.
120. Summerfield and Braybon, p.119.
121. C. Veitch, 'Play Up! Play Up! and Win the War!: Football the Nation and the First World War 1914–1915', *JCH*, 20 (1985), 363–78.
122. Notes from A. Melling, 'Leisure, Community and control in the Districts of St Helens, Wigan and Leigh: An Assessment of the Nature of Working Class Women's Leisure

Activities 1914–1945' (Unpublished MA dissertation, Edge Hill College of H.E, 1994).
123. Lopez, p.111.
124. Pfister *et al.*, *ESHR* (1998).
125. R. Holt, *Sport and the British* (Oxford, 1989), pp.221, 330, 339–40.

A Contribution to the History of Jewish Sport and Physical Education in Poland: The City of Poznań, 1904–39

TERESA ZIÓLKOWSKA

THE GERMAN TIMES (1904–18)

The Grand Duchy of Poznań and its capital, Poznań, were established under provisions of the Congress of Vienna in 1814–15. The Duchy was composed mainly of areas in the West of Poland known as Wielkopolska (Greater Poland) and it was to be a temporal part of the Prussian monarchy under the sovereign rule of the Prussian kings and their successors, i.e. the emperors of united Germany.

After the unification of Germany and the establishment of the German Empire in 1871, the name Grand Duchy of Poznań was changed to the Province of Poznań (*Provinz Posen*). Poznań, however, did not lose its status and remained the capital of the new Prussian province, populated by three main nationalities: Poles, Germans and Jews. The Poles, still sensitive about their lost independence, kept their distance from the Germans and did not consider themselves citizens of the Reich; the Jews were soon assimilated into German culture and actively participated in the economy and municipal government.

At first the Jews joined various German organisations of physical culture. Later, however, some of these German organisations showed clear signs of anti-Semitic bias, for example, the Deutschvölkisher Turnverein, 'Bismarck' added the so called Aryan ruling to its statutes directed against any *Turner* of non-Aryan and non-Teutonic origin. The organisation was clearly involved in anti-Semitic activities and recruited only Germans. All this contributed to the foundation of Jewish organisations of physical culture.

In 1902 Weltverband aller National – Jüdischen Turn – und Sportorganisationen (The Makkabi World Union of Jewish Gymnastic and Sports Organisations) was established. From the outset the union was a satellite body of the World Zionist Organisation (The Jewish Agency) which was founded in Basel, Switzerland in 1897 and had its Central Committee Office in Berlin.

All newly founded independent Jewish, gymnastic, sports and tourist societies were regarded by the Agency as an important contribution to the maintenance of Jewish identity and the biological strengthening of the Jewish diaspora.[1] Promotional activities featured in papers such as the *Jüdische Turnzeitung*,[2] the official organ of the Jüdischer Turnverein 'Bar Kochba' based in Berlin. At the 4th Zionist Congress in London the issue of Jewish organisations of physical culture was given considerable attention.[3]

In 1904, two years after the foundation of The Makkabi World Union of Jewish Gymnastic and Sports Organisations, the Jews of Poznań founded the Posener Turnerbund gymnastic society. Its main objective was the improvement of Jewish physical fitness by organizing fitness training, sports and hiking trips. In addition, the connection between physical culture and spiritual culture was given considerable emphasis. The Posener Turnerbund hoped that regular physical exercise would raise awareness of Jewish identity. To this end it organised activities to promote a knowledge of the origins, history and solidarity of all Jews. However, the society excluded political goals. For the Jewish community physical exercise 'served the purpose of fostering physical development, hygienic upbringing and the cultivation of Jewish national consciousness. It was a means in the struggle against antisemitism, against the influences of a big city; together with the school and the home, it exerted educational influence on young people.'[4]

Anyone over 18 years old with a good reputation could become an ordinary member of the Posener Turnerbund. Honorary members were elected at the members' assembly by a three-quarters majority. The monthly fee was 50 pfennig. The management consisted of the chairman, deputy chairman, instructor, treasurer and secretary. For many years the chairman was Dr Jeremias (first name unknown) who not only did sterling work for the society but also for the whole Jewish gymnastic movement. He was well known as the patron of the Jewish '*turnerism*'. His successors were Leo Calvary and, from 1913, Dr Leo Cohn.

In 1911 it was suggested that the Posener Turnerbund should merge with the Jüdischen Turnverein Berlin 1905 to form an association called 'Kartell deutscher Turnen jüdischen Glauben', which was a sign of the

growing popularity of the gymnastic movement among the followers of
the Jewish religion.

In Poznań, physical exercise took place in age groups. There was one
female group and one male group (*Männerriege*). Classes were held once
a week in the gym of the Frederich Wilhelm Grammar School under the
supervision of the country secretary (*Landessekretär*) Fuhrman (first
name unknown) assisted by two foremen (*Vorturnen*), Alex Jüffner and
Max Schwartz. The exercises used were for general fitness. They were
usually free exercises using equipment such as poles and dumbbells.
Sometimes there was wrestling as well. Each session ended with a
contest of some sort. The active participants could demonstrate that the
ancient Jewish tribe (*alte Stamm*) was composed of agile and well-trained
gymnasts. In 1910 the exercises were practised by 64 people with an
average attendance of 21 people per session. In 1911 the number of
active members dropped to 56 and the average attendance was 18 people
per session.

Another group consisted of senior male citizens (*Alten Herren –
Riege*). In 1913 it had eight to ten members. Mainly merchants and men
from an academic background. They took part in regular weekly sessions
in the gym under Adler's supervision (first name unknown) and did
exercises appropriate to their age – free and easy gymnastics.

Yet another group were 16–18-year-old school students
(*Zöglingsriege*). It was led by Max Krombach, Georg Baer and Brull (first
name unknown), members of the Posener Turnerbund. Classes took
place once a week. In 1913 the average attendance was 11 youths. The
society also tried to attract boys from more advanced classes to common
exercises in order to familiarise other people with Jewish gymnastic
ideals and spread them more widely in the Jewish community. On
average the classes were attended by 25 schoolboys of higher and lower
grades.

From the end of June to the beginning of October physical exercises
were also conducted within the gymnastic group of military recruits
(*Rekrutenriege*) once a week in the gym of Berger Grammar School. The
classes were attended by five or six members. At first the participants
became proficient in military gymnastics under supervision of the
gymnastics instructor, Itzig (first name unknown). From 1913 the
exercises were done under supervision of the non-commissioned officer
Konczak (first name unknown) of the Twelfth Infantry Company of the
Forty Seventh Regiment. Apart from military gymnastics he conducted

bayonet combat training sessions. The management of Posener Turnerbund hoped that well-trained conscripts would prove to be excellent soldiers and bring honour to the organisation and the whole Jewish community. Training sessions for foremen were also organised by Adler (first name unknown), and usually attended by eight gymnasts.

The participants in gymnastic evenings were well-trained Jewish gymnasts who were either resident in Poznań or students on vacation. They came from all parts of the Jewish community.

In addition to the male groups there was one female group (*Damenriege*), led by a special committee headed by Emma Cohn, Gertruda Nehab and Clara Engländer. Exercises were conducted by a grammar school teacher, Schober (first name unknown), assisted by the aforementioned inspector Itzig and others. The exercises were free with use of props. They took place once a week in the gym of the secondary school on Naumann Street (currently Działyńskich Street) and were attended by 14–20 women. A training course for prospective gymnastic forewomen (*Vorturnerinnen*) was set up in 1913 and was attended by about 12 gymnasts. The exercises were conducted in the gym of the Berger Grammar School by the school coach, Moritz Sachs. Exercise groups for senior female citizens and children were planned as well.

At a special general assembly on 29 July 1913, women were admitted as the society as full members. This led to an increase in activities and to an even more active participation in the exercises. The women practiced gymnastics, swimming and fencing. Foil fencing lessons were given by Dr Schultz (first name unknown), a member of a German Fechtklub, were attended by six women. Dr Schultz taught also épée and sabre fencing to the male gymnastic group. On the sports field in the north-east of the city, the Brama Wildecka, members of the Posener Turnerbund practised various kinds of games including slingshot throwing, soccer, boxing, bear run, chain tussle and 'thief beating'. Soon a tennis section was started, attended by 30 people. Games of tennis took place on Sundays at the courts in Kunkel's Garden (first name unknown). From 1913, the main venue was a sports field on Bukowska Street, where there were also ball games. A rowing section was planned.

Hiking trips outside Poznań to various recreational places such as Luboń, Puszczykowo, Osowa Góra, Jarosławiec, Murowana Goślina, Złotniki and some other ones were extremely popular. In 1913, 439 people went on these trips, virtually 100% of the membership since there were 488 members in the organisation on 1 January 1911. When anti-Semitic trends were observed in the Poznań 'Wandervogel', the German youth tourist society, the Posener Turnerbund started hiking trips for Jewish school students.

In 1913 the Posener Turnerbund owned about 140 items of moveable equipment including long and high jump facilities, a springboard, 75 pound iron dumbbells, a 15 kg iron putting shot, a clock, a gymnastic box, a wrestling mat, 2 épées, 2 sabres, 4 foils, a first aid kit. The society's library had over 32 publications on gymnastic exercises such as *Geschichte der Leibesüngen* by Fr. Iselin, *Der Turner und sein Einfluss auf die Entwicklung der Menschenheit* by M. Zettler, *Die gesundheitliche Bedeutung der Leibesübvngen für die Grosstädte* by Dencke (first name unknown) and a work by the Chief Mayor of Poznań, Dr Ernst Wilms, on F.L. Jahn's activities.

The society also delivered lectures on the role of physical education in social life. The first lecture, 'Unsere Ideale' (Our Ideals), was given in December 1910 by a lawyer, Dr Kaempfer (first name unknown). Some lectures also touched on Jewish roots, for instance, the slide-aided public lecture 'On Palestine' by a school teacher, Aurback (first name unknown). Other lectures were: 'Warum sind wir jüdische Turner in der Zöglingsriege?' (Why Are We Jewish Gymnasts in Pupil Groups?) by Georg Baer, 'Die Ziele der jüdischen Turnerschaft' (The Objectives of Jewish Gymnastic Societes) given by the lawyer, Greifenhagen (first name unknown), and 'Die jüdische Turnbewegung in der Zöglingsriege' (The Jewish Gymnastic Movement in a Pupil Group) presented by Fritz Bernstein. It was emphasised that the Posener Turnerbund ought to become a worthy representative of Jewish youth. Appeals were made for participation in all events and for new members. The activities of the Association and daily work intended to demonstrate the greatness and dignity of the Jewish nation.

The Posener Turnerbund held annual celebrations of the anniversary of its foundation. These took place in the hall of the Zoological Garden or in the hall of the Apollo Theatre and included gymnastic demonstrations by members.

The Association competed with German gymnastic associations in sporting events in Poznań. One such competition was organized on 4 September 1910 on the initiative of Poznań's mayor, Dr E. Wilms. It took place in the square behind the barracks of the 6th Infantry Regiment. Three German *Turner* associations were represented, Männer-Turnverein Posen, Deutscher Männer-Turnverein 'Jahn',

Männer Turnverein 'Posen-Wilda', as well as Posener Turnerbund. A total of 70 gymnasts took part (in free exercises) including 27 from the Posener Turnerbund of whom seven achieved good places in the competition and Georg Ilüttner won a prize. The Association was pleased with their performance.

Representatives of the Posener Turnerbund also took part in celebrations held by Jewish gymnastic associations in other cities. In September 1910 in Leszno another significant town in Western Poland, the Turner Association of Jewish Students celebrated the anniversary of its foundation and the Poznań Association sent several representatives of its board and two students to take part.

Members of the Posener Turnerbund also participated in Der erste Turntag des deutschen Kreises der Jüdischen Turnerschaft (The First Gymnastics Day of the German Circle of Jewish Gymnastics Associations) organised in Berlin, 22–24 March 1913. The group of the delegates was composed of women: Flora Brand and Laufer (first name not known), and men: Bernstein (first name not known), the chairman. Dr Leo Cohn, the treasurer, Leo Kollenscher and the instructor, Moritz Sachs. In addition, a group of six men participated in the free exercises and exercises on the high horse with a springboard and Messrs Wohl and Brüll (first names not known) took part in the free exercises on the bar and were admired by all.

Eight gymnasts from Posener Turnerbund took part in gymnastic shows (*Schauturnen*) organised on the occasion of the Ninth Zionists' Congress in Vienna, 7–8 September 1913. They performed free exercises and group exercises on the bar and were praised for the jump with a rifle (*Gewehrsprung*) that they had prepared under the direction of the gymnastics instructor, Moritz Sachs.[5]

The evidence extant reveals that the Posener Turnerbund was a robust association. Its sporting contacts with Jewish gymnasts outside Poznań, among others, in Berlin and Vienna confirm this. It popularised physical culture among the Jewish population, while at the same time cultivating a spirit of nationalism which was to contribute to the preservation and maintenance of ethnic identity.

Many Jews belonged to the Posener Schach-Club. Wilhelm Kornfeld, the club's chairman for many years, was particularly active; he was also an outstanding chess player.[6]

IN INDEPENDENT POLAND (1918–39)

After Poland regained independence in 1918, Poznań acquired special significance within the boundaries of the reviving Polish state; it was transformed from a border town and Prussian military fortress into one of the most important cities in the country. Between 1918 and 1939 it became the capital of a province (*województwo*), a hub of international trade, an important economic, scientific and cultural centre at the centre of the Polish western territories which regarded it as their unofficial capital. The city was quickly re-polonised. Germans and Jews emigrated in large numbers in the early years of independence with the result that its inhabitants were virtually all Polish.

The city's education system also underwent rapid re-polonisation. With the exodus of the German population, the number of students in German schools gradually decreased. In 1922 only one German school remained in Poznań. It was the Public Common School Nr.4 (Publiczna Szkoła Powszechna Nr.4), located in the historic Street of Wielkie Garbary (Great Tannery).[7]

Some of the parents (of the Jewish minority) sent their children to municipal schools, in particular School Nr.4. This school received a good report from the school inspector, Dr Władysław Sperczyński, who visited it in March 1934. He stated that the school building, the sports field and the gymnasium met the hygiene requirements. The physical education curriculum was restricted to extra-curricular games and recreations. No exercise was provided during lesson periods.[8]

On the initiative of the Jewish Popular Council (Żdowska Rada Ludowa) on 1 May 1919, School Nr.14 was created for Jewish children with Polish as the language of instruction. Originally it was located at 10 Szewska Street and then at 3 Noskowski Street. On 18 April 1933 an application was made to the city authorities to obtain a gymnasium. Unfortunately, the Municipal Government (*Zarząd Miejski*) did not accede to this request and at the School's disposal there was only a schoolyard and a garden. The available sources do not make it possible to ascertain how physical education was taught at the school. It is only known that children were sent to summer camps and in winter were provided with supplementary food.

A large number of older children attended state and private grammar schools. The boys most often chose the Berger Grammar School and the private Schiller Grammar School; the girls' primary choice was the

'Dąbrówka'.[9] Physical education classes were part of the curriculum of these schools.

The curriculum made physical education obligatory, and linked it with military training. Different exercises were provided for boys and girls and talks on the subject of hygiene were introduced. From 1932 a clear division was made in the curriculum between balancing exercises with or without the use of gymnastic apparatus, and exercises developing agility. Sports were supplemented with cycling. Of the various gymnastic systems, the Swedish system was adopted.[10]

Among the Jewish gymnastic and sporting organisations, Posener Turnerbund resumed activity. Classes were held in the gymnasium of the Below-Knothe Secondary School. Exercises were held in three groups: women's, men's and youth's. Together with exercises, social afternoon tea meetings were organised.[11] The Sports Club, 'Bar Kochba', operated for some time in the 1930s. In the club, the boxing section was strong, partly due to the fact that it had its own coach.[12]

The setting up of physical culture organisations by the Jews dispersed in diaspora, which took place towards the end of the nineteenth century and in the years after the First World War, contributed on the one hand to the raising of physical fitness, and on the other to the cultivation of spiritual culture and to the preservation of a Jewish identity. All these activities ended tragically in the years of the Second World War. During the Nazi occupation the Jews of Poznań were first forced to discontinue their gymnastic and sporting activity and then shortly afterwards shared the fate of their compatriots from other regions of Poland.

NOTES

1. G. Młodzikowski, *Genealogia społeczna i klasowe funkcje sportu w latach 1860-1928* [Social and Class Genealogy of Sport in the Years 1860–1928] (Warsaw, 1970), p.44.
2. 'Was wir wollen! Gesunder Geist wohnt in Gesunden Körper!', *Jüdische Turnzeitung*, 1 (1900), 2; *Anruf zur Gründung eines varbandes jüdischer Turnvereine!*, *Jüdische Turnzeitung*, 2 (1900), 9; E. Edelstein, 'Die Aufgabe der jüdischen Turner', *Jüdische Turnzeitung*, 7 (1900), 73–5.
3. H. Jałowicz, 'Zum vierten zionisten- Kongress', *Jüdische Turnzeitung*, 4 (1900), 33–4.
4. Achive of the City of Poznań and Its Voivodship (ACPV); Zespół Akt Miast Poznania (Set of Documents of the City of Poznań): *Akten betreffend Ortsverband für Jugendpflege. Satzungen des Posener Turnerbundes. Posener Trunerbund Jahres – Bericht 1910; Rechenschaftsbericht über die Tätigkeit des Jüdischen Turnvereins Posen für das jahr 1913*, archive number 2867, unnumbered page; ACVP, Zespół Akt Miast Poznania (Set of Documents of the City of Poznań): *Akten betreffend Ortverband für Jegendpflege Sonder – Ausschuss I, für Leibesübungen, Posener Turnerbund Jahres – Bericht 1911*, archive number 2863, p. 63.

5. A. Kwilecki, *Szachy w Poznaniu 1839–1988* [Chess Playing in Poznań 1839–1988] (Poznań, 1990), pp.18–20.
6. Z. Dworecki, *Poznań i Poznaniacy w latach Drugiej Rzeczpospolitej 1918–1939* [City of Poznań and Its Inhabitants during the Second Republic of Poland 1918–1939] (Poznań, 1994), pp.402–4.
7. ACPV, *Akta Kuratorium Okręgu szkolnego* Poznańskiego (Documents of the School Curatorium of the Poznań District, DSCP): *Sprawozdanie z wizytacji publicznych szkół powszechnych z niemieckim językiem nauczania. Publiczna Szkoła Powszechna nr 4 (Report from the Visitations to the Common Public Schools with the German Language Teaching. The Common Public School nr 4)*, archive number 65, pp.209–16.
8. ACPV, *Zespół Akt Miast Poznania. Akta dotyczące nowozałożonej szkoły żydowskiej* (Set of Documents of the City of Poznań. Documents Pertaining to the Newly Established Jewish School), archive number 3205, pp.79, 114–42; J. Kowalski, 'Poznańska gmina żydowska w latach II Rzeczpospolitej' (Jewish Community of Poznań in the years of the Second Republic of Poland), *Kronika Miasta Poznania* (Chronicle of the City of Poznań, 1–2 (1992) 91–7.
9. Z. Grot and J. Gaj, *Zarys kultury fizycznej w Wielkopolsce* [An Outline of Physical Culture in Great Poland] (Warsaw-Poznań, 1973), p.228.
10. 'Jüdisch-liberaler Jugendverein Posen', *Posener Jüdische Zeitung*, 1 (1920), 7–8.
11. Z. Dworecki, pp.472–3.
12. (Name of author not given), *Der jüdische Sportplatz* (Berlin, 1920), p.3.

English Elementary Education Revisited and Revised: Drill and Athleticism in Tandem

J.A. MANGAN and COLM HICKEY

In a relatively recent article Stephen Humphries surveyed the current ideological battleground between liberal orthodoxy and Marxist revisionism.[1] In his view, the liberals maintain that the growth of state education was democratic and progressive in both intention and effect. Their Marxist critics argue that this argument fails to set the evolution of state education realistically within a wider framework of social and political mandates. Most importantly, they maintain, such a view fails to acknowledge the bureaucratic response to demands for class control derived from a view of state schooling as a means to maintain and sustain capitalist society.

Two criticisms can be made of the revisionists: they exaggerate the importance of a minority of legislators who were concerned with notions of class control and, as a corollary, they adopt a point of view advanced by Gwyn Williams in which he argues that it was virtually impossible for the working class to resist the dominant culture or to generate independent ideas and actions.[2] This consideration of the ideology of athleticism in selected London elementary schools before the Great War advances an argument that is less simplistic and which reflects more complex working-class reactions and responses to their schooling.

The Education Act of 1870 made provision for the establishment of local school boards throughout England and Wales. They were to be responsible for the organisation of elementary education in their area. Such School Boards quickly mushroomed all over the country. This essay will concentrate on London. Elections for the London School Board were held on Tuesday, 29 November 1870. Its area of responsibility was to be the same as the existing Metropolitan Board of Works, a grand total of 114 square miles. London was divided into ten administrative districts: City, Southwark, Chelsea, Greenwich, Lambeth, Tower Hamlets, Hackney, Westminster, Finsbury and Marylebone. The number of representatives for each area depended on its size and the elections held were significant in two respects: they used the secret ballot and women were allowed to stand as candidates: two were elected, Miss Emily Davies, the female emancipationist, and Dr Elizabeth Garrett (later Garrett-Anderson), the first woman doctor.

The task facing the Board was enormous. London's population was 3,265,005. There were 681,000 children aged between three and thirteen. Some 97,307 were educated at home or attended schools which charged more than 9d. per week, taking them out of the social class for whom elementary schools were meant to cater. Another 9,101 were officially classed as 'inmates of institutions'. Then there were children who were too young to attend school, working at home or abroad, ill, disabled or ineligible for other reasons.[3] This left 454,783 to be educated by the Board.

Faced with this vast undertaking what, therefore, were the aims of the members of the London School Board? David Rubenstein identifies three main points of view held by the Board members.[4] The main preoccupation of the Conservatives was to maintain the status quo. Many Conservatives were suspicious of popular education, believing that if the mental horizons of the working class were enlarged they might get ideas above their station and this would subvert the existing social order. The Conservatives, says Rubenstein, 'initially at least [were] opposed to compulsory education, to free elementary schools, and to advanced, or "higher grade" elementary schools. That they contributed to the introduction of these reforms indicates that their tactics changed in response to pressure; the ends, however, remained constant.'[5] The Conservatives, Rubenstein further asserts, were particularly concerned with the level of the School Board Rate and the position of Anglican schools believing that church schools would 'encourage both working class docility and lower rates'.[6] They also opposed higher grade schools. Lord George Hamilton, a Conservative who was to become Chairman of the London School Board in the 1890s, observed that the function of the School Board should be:

> To give the children of the working mass a sound, a compact and a thorough education in those subjects which children during the limited time they were at school could master ... What ought to be

resolutely fought was any attempt to grasp a secondary system of graded education and applying it to the education of the School Board. Such an education ... would be bad for the children, bad for the teachers and worse for the ratepayers.[7]

The Liberals, although sharing similar social backgrounds to the Conservatives, looked at things rather differently. Liberals and Socialists comprised the Board's Progressive faction. 'The Liberals,' states Rubinstein, 'believed that a well-educated working class was an aim desirable in itself. But additionally, it was also an important means of securing economic advance and social mobility.'[8] E. Lyulph Stanley, vice-chairman of the London School Board and a prominent member of the Progressives, declared at the time:

> We want our lower classes to be educated ... We want them in the schools and in the homes to learn the self respect of citizens, to feel their responsibility as voters, to have the self restraint, the thoughtfulness, the power of judging and weighing evidence, which should discipline them in the exercise of the great power they now wield by their industrial combinations and through their political action.[9]

For their part, the Socialists, while broadly in sympathy with the Liberals, were often prepared to advance what were often unpopular ideas with the Board. The Rev. Stewart Healam, for example, demanded that board school education should make children discontented 'with the evil circumstances that surround them ... not indeed with that state of life into which it shall please God to call them, but with that evil state into which anarchy and monopoly has [*sic*] forced them, so that by their own organised and disciplined effort they may lead fuller lives ... in a more beautiful world.'[10]

The Board was dominated by the Progressives. As mentioned earlier, their aims were the provision of good basic education, the creation of an educational ladder and the 'civilising' of the working classes. The first two of these aims it can be said were widely achieved. The last one is contentious for it raises a whole host of issues concerning the relationship between working-class culture and values of the consumers – the children, and middle-class culture and values of the providers – the School Boards. Physical Education provides an excellent example of how the School Boards approached what in their view was the mutually supportive needs of their children and society and will be the focus of this chapter.

Peter McIntosh believes that the introduction of military drill into the curriculum of Board schools in 1871, which attempted to ensure 'attendance at drill under a competent instructor for not more than two hours a week and twenty weeks in the year', was designed mainly as a disciplinary measure. He writes:

> Four features of this administrative measure are noteworthy. First it was permissive legislation, and no obligation was put upon any school to provide physical education. Secondly, physical education was permitted for boys only ... Thirdly, the permitted physical education took the form of military drill. The Education Department made arrangements with the War Office for instruction by drill sergeants at the rate of sixpence a day and a penny a mile marching money ... Fourthly, the main purpose of this drill was disciplinary. The exercises in the words of the Committee's *Report*, 'would be sufficient to teach the boys habits of sharp obedience, smartness, order and cleanliness'. The fact that the Franco-Prussian War had broken out in the year preceding the issue of the new code may have been partly responsible for the strong military flavour of the regulations.[11]

McIntosh's explanation for the absence of organised games (increasingly popular, of course, in the private schools of the privileged) from the curriculum of Board schools is that it was a widely held view that drill was most suitable for the working classes and games were most suitable for the middle and upper classes. Matthew Arnold appears to have held this view. He endorsed the need for physical education in the elementary school, but advocated gymnastics rather than games because if boys worked long hours then gymnastics would be better for their health than games. 'It suggests,' writes McIntosh quite reasonably, 'that he assumed that there should be one type of physical education for the ruling class and a different one for the masses.'[12] This view, in fact, was made explicit by Wallace MacLaren, who in a preface to a new edition of his father's [Archibald] book on Physical Education in 1895, asserted:

> On the one hand we have to deal with the upper and middle classes, in fact with all that large class who are sent to private and public schools or training colleges for their education, and proceed to the

army, to the universities or to business life. On the other side is the still larger class of those whom the nation still educates, a class which the subject of gymnastics may be thought to touch more nearly, in as much as, after an early age, they have little or no time for recreation like those socially above them, and the gymnasium is therefore to them a vital source of health.[13]

He went on to claim that the physical requirements of the two classes were in themselves distinct, and should be dealt with from altogether different standpoints.[14]

McIntosh paints a bleak picture of games provision in elementary schools in the early twentieth century:

> In 1900 and again in 1906 organised games received tardy recognition as a possible means of physical education and were officially allowed by the Board to be a suitable alternative to Swedish drill or physical exercises. The hard realities of the situation prevented a very large number of children from benefiting from this innovation of policy. As recently as 1895 Her Majesty's Inspector for the Metropolitan Division had estimated that there were 25,000 school children within a mile of Charing Cross who had no playground at all and very few playgrounds worth the name were to be found in the whole of London.[15]

Thus he gives the clear impression that at this time physical education in the shape of games was virtually non-existent in elementary schools, that the schools had very poor facilities and that games were seen by the Board as either unnecessary or unsuitable for elementary school children. As will be shown below, non-existence was not necessarily the case. For one thing playgrounds were not park playing fields! The absence of games has been exaggerated both prior to and after 1900.

The formal introduction of games came about, according to McIntosh, through the appointment of officials to the Board of Education who believed strongly in their educational value: 'Fortunately for physical education Robert Morant, an ardent Old Wykehamist, who became Permanent Secretary of the Board of Education, was as keen on the physical welfare and physical development of children as he was on administrative tidiness.'[16] The man directly responsible for the inclusion of games in curriculum time, according to McIntosh, was A.P. Graves,

HMI, who had written an article in the *Contemporary Review* in 1904, in which he deplored the way in which school playgrounds were so little used and called for the introduction of games into elementary schools. Graves subsequently met Augustine Birrell who had succeeded Lord Londonderry as Head of the Board of Education. Birrell told his Chief HMI, E.G.A. Holmes, to discuss the matter with Graves. He did. In 1906 organised games, namely cricket, hockey and football, were introduced in school hours. There were other crucial reasons rather than a failure to utilise unused space why games were seen as desirable for elementary pupils. The Board now accepted that discipline, *esprit de corps*, and fair play could be acquired through the games field, with the result that a new conception of the content of public elementary education now became *de rigueur*.[17]

McIntosh's explanation for the introduction of games into the elementary school when they arrived, is supported by H. C. Barnard:

> Health education should be not merely palliative, or even preventative, but still more positive. The increasing realisation of this fact has been shown by the development of all kinds of physical activity, designed not merely to strengthen the bodies of pupils, but also as an integral part of the 'education of the whole man'. Here again something is due to the influence of Morant.[18]

McIntosh has neatly summed up the developments in physical education in the years leading up to the First World War in a classic exposition of liberal orthodoxy.

> Between 1900 and 1914 physical education in elementary schools had taken great strides forward. Military drill persisted in many places as a legacy from the past, but military training as official policy had been left in the ditch, and armed with the 1909 syllabus of which nearly 100,000 copies were sold within a year of its publication, inspectors, organisers, and teachers marched along the road to therapeutic physical training. Some even had visions of a more liberal physical education beyond.[19]

McIntosh's belief that the disparity of games provision was a reflection of priorities in society has wider support: 'Games, ostensibly the main means of transmitting the concept of fair play, and until 1900 denied by the state to the elementary school [and afterwards not greatly encouraged there] were part of a definition of selective education, but more than that they were evident symbols of the disparate dispensation of national resources among the classes.'[20]

The general view is that the physical education received by children in elementary schools in curriculum time after 1872 and before 1906 was drill. After 1872 drill, of course, had proved to be a contentious issue. Initially, it was seen as a desirable part of the curriculum. David Smith, for example, has pointed out that 'concentration on drill would obviously be approved by the militarists, and by others who believed that physical training should complement an instrumentary education. They saw the result, the acquisition of the physical equivalent of literacy, as paying dividends in better and more obedient workers, servants and soldiers.'[21] Smith also makes the point that militarists argued that as the upper and middle classes financed elementary schools through the rates, it was only reasonable that the state should obtain a return in the form of drill as basic military preparation. They further argued that discipline would improve: 'A basic belief in the effectiveness of the transfer of training encouraged the view that the way to civilise the "street arabs" and hooligans was to drill them into habits of instant obedience, a training held to be eminently suitable for the character of the recipients.'[22]

In London, the School Board, presumably acting on this belief, in 1872 appointed Regimental Major William Sheffield as Drill Master on a salary of £2.10.0d. per week. Sheffield organised courses in drill for serving teachers who became qualified to teach drill in Board schools. Sheffield died in 1888 and the Board then appointed two men – Allan Broman from Sweden, who had been trained in what was known as the Swedish system of gymnastics, and Thomas Chesterton to oversee the implementation of an 'English' system of drill.

Chesterton's English 'system' was, in fact, little more than a reworking of existing military drill exercises with references to military words and phrases omitted. Indeed Chesterton admitted that much of his system was unoriginal: 'I do not, in any way claim to have originated the whole, the classification and adaptation being the chief points claimed as original.' He continued that his 'system' was 'compiled after the careful and practical test of the whole of the methods taught on the Continent in which I was guided by the experience of twenty years gained in teaching physical culture in all its branches.'[23] Chesterton explicitly stated that his system was not military in flavour. He wrote: 'The various systems in vogue on the Continent, though their primary

object is undoubtedly an educational one, have another object in view –
viz the laying of a foundation for future military service under a system
of conscription ... Hence any Continental system built on these lines is
unsuitable for adoption in its entirety in this country.'[24]

This assertion was quite specious. Although Chesterton maintained
that his system was not military in origin and nature, he was later forced
to admit that in fact it was! When he gave evidence on his own system to
The Royal Commission on Physical Training (Scotland) 1903, he stated
that 'Military drill is indispensable in securing discipline and a ready
response to orders', yet he then went on to say that 'It is erroneous to
suppose ... that the system is a military one although all the exercises
contained in the military system are contained therein.' Questioned by
one of the Commissioners as to why, if he claimed that his drill was for
children, he sometimes referred to it as military drill, he answered
weakly:

> Well, we will call it drill if you like. It is based on military lines ...
> In my book I do not call it 'military drill'; I call it 'drill and military
> exercises', but the drill that I teach is solely military drill, but I
> leave out the word military. It is advisable in many cases to do so.[25]

Chesterton's duplicity on this point is very probably due to the fact that
the London School Board did not allow military drill to be taught
directly in its schools. Indeed, the Board of Education had insisted since
1895 that 'the higher grant for Discipline and Organisation will not be
paid to any school in which provision is not made for instruction in
Swedish or other drill or suitable physical exercises'.[26]

However, the reality as distinct from the theory was made clear in
1901. A committee established to look at the curricula of Training
Colleges commented:

> All the systems that are in use at the present time are founded on
> the army system, but each local instructor wants to make a book to
> sell; it is a laudable desire; and so he pads it up with a certain
> amount that is merely exhibition or decorative or amusing, adds
> pictures and music until the book will sell for three shillings or
> whatever the price may be ...[27]

This distinction between reality and theory, incidentally, is
overlooked by Richard Holt, the historian of British sport, in his too
slight pronouncements on drill in English elementary education.[28] In

addition, he fails to appreciate the commitment to drill, military or otherwise, among politicians, educationists and others at this time.

Chesterton, incidentally, firmly believed in the value of games. In his book *The Theory of Physical Education* published in 1895, he provided the classic Victorian justification for games playing:

> In addition to developing bodily powers, boys' games exercise a powerful influence in forming individual character. They promote good temper, self-control, self-reliance, endurance, patience, courage under defeat, promptness and rapid judgement. Mutual goodwill and the advantages of co-operation are taught by the companionship associated with the performance of games. Much of the success in after life may be attributed to the qualities developed in boyhood, by the healthy, spirited games of school life.[29]

Athleticism, as it was now very well known, was an ideology born and nurtured in the public schools,[30] which by a process of 'reverse social osmosis' steadily permeated the late nineteenth-century and early twentieth-century grammar schools which increasingly emulated the upper middle-class public schools and attempted to distance themselves from the public elementary schools.[31] The explanation, as discussed earlier, for the extensive official non-adoption of athleticism by the elementary schools is that the acquisition of the playing fields necessary for the ideology to flourish fully was beyond the means of the schools and that funds were denied them – as they certainly were – by the state for playing fields after 1872, as a reflection of priorities in public education.

A rather dramatic description of these priorities is provided by Humphries adopting a position 'similar to that of the emerging revisionist school of Marxist sociologists and historians who during the past decade have challenged the method and metaphor upon which the orthodox literature on youth has been based'.[32] Humphries maintains that the state elementary schooling system 'was not designed to impart literacy, skills and knowledge as ends in themselves. Instead learning was conceived as a means to an end – it made the pupil more amenable to a socialisation process, through which his or her character and future lifestyle might be shaped.'[33] He endorses, in short, the classic education for social control thesis. He does concede wisely that games were introduced into elementary schools after 1906 but argues that 'the inclusion of games and sports in the school curriculum was justified in terms of their encouragement of a corporate spirit and their development of the physical strength and moral fibre of working class youth – thus contributing to imperial success and stability'.[34]

In short, with the proletariat controlled in the Metropolis, the natives were to be controlled in the colonies – and the elementary schools were to be part of the process. While there is some truth in this, it is hardly the whole truth. In fact it is a considerable simplification.[35]

At the outset, the term athleticism requires definition. In what is widely recognised as the most authoritative study of the subject, it is described as:

> Physical exercise ... taken, considerably and compulsorily, in the sincere belief of many, however romantic, misplaced or myopic, that it was a highly effective means of inculcating valuable instrumental and impressive educational goals: physical and moral courage, loyalty and cooperation, the capacity to act fairly and take defeat well, the ability to command and obey.[36]

Of course, games had a multiplicity of functions, including control, pleasure, recreation and fitness, but the primary educational purpose was moral – the inculcation of the qualities outlined above.

This was true also of athleticism in elementary education. This is hardly surprising. After 1906 the introduction of athleticism into the elementary schools was state pedagogical policy and this policy was in the hands of public school educated state officials. In addition, for some decades earlier the London (and other) teacher training colleges had increasingly embraced this public school ideology and their products left these institutions imbued with a sense of the moral value of team games and took this moral conviction into the elementary school.[37]

Thus when reference is made below to the introduction and assimilation of athleticism into elementary education earlier than 1906, this is neither casual, nor unfounded, nor surprising. It has however been substantially overlooked. If the complex nature of drill and full significance of drill in the elementary school have been carelessly dismissed by at least one historian of sport,[38] generally the presence prior to 1906 of the influential philosophy and practice of athleticism has also been casually ignored. While it is true that records of elementary schools are in short supply in contrast to those of the public schools, happily sources are being discovered which ensure that the pedagogical history of elementary education is being slowly re-written. Perhaps even more to the point, the presence of the ideology of athleticism in the teacher training colleges is now being revealed along with the presence of public school educated staff who brought their educational precepts and practices to these institutions and widened their pedagogical rationale and activities. Furthermore, the Cross Commission of 1888 lent its weight, both directly and indirectly, to the espousal of athleticism in the Training Colleges – and thus the elementary schools. The ideology faced many difficulties in these schools and it is unlikely that it had the same powerful impact as in the public schools. The reasons for this are obvious and will be set out later, but the point is that the ideology existed, was promulgated and was absorbed in the schools.

Athleticism, therefore, as is now well established, was initially an upper- and middle-class means of coercing and controlling and cajoling large numbers of boys in public schools in the mid-nineteenth century.[39] Once, however, control had been achieved it evolved into an educational rationale to sustain imperial masculinity.[40] In this process, and in time, the ideology spread to the teacher training colleges. How far, and in what ways, did it permeate the elementary schools of England and the hearts and minds of working–class boys? The difficulties in answering these questions are readily apparent. The amount of documentary, or other archival, material that has survived is fragmentary and limited and the material that does survive tends to be a bland record of special events that took place during official school hours like the anodyne one-lined entry 'the School Manager visited today'.[41] Furthermore, days often go unrecorded. In addition, extra–curricular activities are not always recorded in School Log Books. Finally, the overwhelming evidence that does survive tends to have been written by those who were involved in the delivery of education: HMIs, School Board Managers, Headmasters or those who compiled Official Reports and Commissions. This poses an obvious problem. How is it possible to find out how athleticism was received by the children themselves?

There is one thing that can be asserted with confidence: athleticism in the public schools and grammar schools of England and Wales between 1870 and 1914 was not the same as athleticism in elementary schools in London between 1870 and 1914. There are a number of basic reasons for this. Perhaps the most important is that public schools were independent of state control. If a headmaster wanted to introduce athleticism in his school he had far more latitude to do so than an elementary school headmaster answerable to his Manager, the School Board and the Board of Education, who laid down precisely which subjects were to be taught in his school. Then elementary schools dealt with children from the ages of five or six to 14, whereas public and grammar schools contained children from 11 to 19. Many public schools and some grammar schools had a boarding element: elementary schools did not. There is the matter of facilities and their expense: public schools were wealthy schools for wealthy people; grammar schools were comfortable schools for comfortable people; elementary schools were poor schools for poor people. Finally, the matter of facilities affected staff as well as pupils – staff at public schools and many at grammar schools would have had the privilege and advantage of an 'Oxbridge' games–playing education while elementary school teachers would have spent one or two years at a far less privileged residential training college. However, despite these considerable differences, athleticism was so pervasive and dominant an ideology that it was adapted to suit the conditions of the elementary schools and did bring new values and ideals into these schools while at the same time having these ideals and values modified by working class experience.

Athleticism in the elementary schools, this enquiry suggests, went through a number of recognisable phases. The first involved the pioneering efforts of a number of influential headteachers who acted as proselytisers for this new ideology before as well as after 1906. The second involved a period of reinforcement which saw the expansion of schools sports and games organisation. The third saw the growth of a muted rhetoric which sustained the ideology, the fourth and final phase produced the official recognition and legitimisation of the ideology through the inclusion of games playing in the formal curriculum. Of course, it must be appreciated that there was often overlap between these stages.

One point should be laboured. While it is difficult to be precise about when games playing began in the schools and while it is clear that games were not officially allowed in curriculum time until 1906, it is also quite clear that elementary schoolboys were playing games under teacher supervision certainly as early as 1885! Of course, even before this date boys were playing team games outside of school time. F.H. Spencer, for example, who was born into a working-class family in Swindon in 1872, recalled that he had become 'boy secretary of a home-made cricket club which played or attempted to play less primitive cricket'.[42]

The men who were responsible for the introduction of athleticism as an educational ideology into the elementary schools of England before and after 1906, had themselves been exposed to it in their training colleges. In London the early pioneers of this ideology included W.J. Wilson of Oldridge Road Board School, Balham, and J.G. Timms of Rosendale Road Board School, Lambeth. W. J. Wilson is arguably the most significant of this pair. In 1885 he established the South London Schools' Football Association. Wilson used *The Schoolmaster*, the official newspaper of the National Union of Teachers, to promote the Association and to encourage schools to become affiliated. By 1888 the Association had both a senior and junior section and Wilson politely issued their 'invitation' to the Annual General Meeting: 'all teachers [Board and Voluntary] in South London, interested in our popular winter pastime, are kindly requested to attend'.[43]

The following year saw two significant developments. The first was a match between South London Schools and Chatham Schools in Chatham with the money raised going to the Orphanage Fund of the NUT, and the second was the printing of a pamphlet 'How to start and Manage a Football Club', which was distributed at the Annual General Meeting of the Association. The success of the Association can be seen from the fact that by 1891 sixteen schools were regularly members.

TABLE 1
SOUTH LONDON SCHOOLS FOOTBALL ASSOCIATION 1890–91[44]

SENIORS	Played	Won	Drawn	Lost	Points
Nunhead Passage	10	9	0	1	18
Oldridge Road	10	7	1	2	15
Hasselrigge Road	10	5	1	4	11
Goodridge Road	10	5	0	5	10
St. Mary's Balham	10	2	2	6	6
Belle Ville	10	0	0	10	0
JUNIORS					
St. Mathews Brixton	18	17	1	0	35
Hackford Road	18	14	1	3	29
Eltringham Street	17	11	3	3	25
Bellenden Road	17	10	1	6	21
Priory Grove	18	8	5	5	21
Upper Kennington Lane	18	8	1	9	17
Heber Road	18	5	3	10	13
Springfield	18	6	1	11	13
Southwark Park	18	2	0	16	4
St. Thomas	18	0	0	18	0

Wilson proved to be both an energetic Association secretary and a successful headmaster. His school, Oldridge Road, opened on Monday, 26 June 1882 with 85 boys. As a games enthusiast Wilson was soon organising a series of fundraising events for his school teams. A regular feature was an evening's entertainment at which the proceeds went to the sports fund he established. For example, the Log Book for 16 November 1888 reads: 'The Children's Operetta of Golden Hair was repeated on Wednesday for the third time in aid of the funds for the school sports. The first performance was in aid of the Teachers Orphanage and Benevolent Fund. The proceeds of the concerts amounted to over £42.'[45] Wilson's efforts were appreciated by his local Board Manager, W.J. Rogers. In the Government Report of 1888 he noted: 'Cricket, Football and Swimming Clubs exist in connection with this school to the obvious benefit of the boys.'[46]

Whatever else he was, Wilson was certainly an enthusiast. Almost any and every sporting and athletic competition was entered with alacrity and generally no little success. For example, for the Annual Drill Competition at the Albert Hall, Wilson closed the school and entered his boys who 'obtained 89 marks out of 100'.[47] Swimming and drill were both part of the curriculum and regular drill displays were given to parents and friends. Against this background of a commitment to swimming and drill in curriculum time and athletics, cricket and football as extra curricular activities, numbers soared. In October 1891, 456 boys were in attendance with an average attendance rate of 90%; in March 1892, 538 boys had an average attendance rate of 93%. In October 1890, he wrote, 'Every week I am refusing children, who apply for admission, unless they have passed Standard II. The reason for this is that Standards I and II are overfull and as all the rest of the school is nearly full I have no room for these fresh applicants.'[48]

Wilson was driven by a threefold desire to improve the health and fitness of the boys, teach them to enjoy games playing for its own sake and to develop in them a competitive spirit. In an article in *The Schoolmaster*, of the South London Schools' Football Association it was claimed:

> South London Teachers give up a lot of their time to teaching the young idea the art of 'leather hunting'. All matches are played on Saturday mornings, so the attendance of the teachers means the sacrifice of a good portion of the weekly holiday ... Mr Wilson who

is an enthusiastic lover of manly sports is never so happy as when his boys secure a victory, and they have won laurels not only in South London, but at Sheffield, Chatham and elsewhere'.[49]

Wilson was undoubtedly a dedicated and dynamic headmaster. He was a tireless and devoted active member of the influential South London Schools' Football Association – the first elementary schools' football association in the world. However, to what extent was Wilson typical as an elementary school headmaster? This is not known at this moment but he was not alone. It is possible to chart athleticism's progress in the London elementary school by providing a fuller picture of its growth in another school, Rosendale Road, in Lambeth.

Rosendale Road was designed by the London School Board's own architect, Thomas Jerram Bailey. Plans for the construction of an elementary school of 238 boys, 238 girls and 277 infants were approved by the Board on the 29 July 1897. The school was officially opened in 1898 in time for the autumn term, although it was housed in temporary accommodation until the permanent buildings were ready on 8 January 1900. Its first headmaster was John Goddard Timms, who had been trained at Borough Road College from 1883 to 1885. When he graduated he was appointed to Paradise Road Board School, Peckham, where he remained until becoming the Headmaster, first of Priory Grove in 1888, and subsequently Rosendale in 1897.

Timms was a conscientious and devoted headmaster. In 1902 the Board's Inspector wrote that:

> The headmaster has made reports not only in each subject, in each class, but on each subject for each child in addition to ordinary numerical results. This elaboration, however, has not prevented him from doing much actual teaching. No Head Teacher have I oftener found teaching a class.[50]

He was also committed to the ethos easing its way down from public school to elementary public school. From the earliest moments games played an important role in the life of the school. In the first year the Manager's Annual Report noted, 'considerable attention has been paid to cricket and football'.[51]

The earliest surviving Log Book for the school begins in 1903. It is replete with references to games. Between 24 and 29 June, for example, there are five entries relating to games and sports activities, and a detailed and comprehensive record of what had happened during the week. To provide a flavour of Timms' commitment to the period ideology of athleticism these entries require to be quoted in full:

24/06/03   School closed for the South London School Sports. The athletics of the school are flourishing. The Football championship of the South London Schools was nearly secured this season as the boys were the runners up and only succumbed after a good struggle in the final match to a much heavier and stronger team. The boys were winners of the East Lambeth Division section and had a fine record of wins in the football league competition securing medals from the association. The boys were trained by Mr Mingay and in every way did the greatest credit to him and the school. Great pains were taken by the master in securing every benefit possible for the boys from the exercises ...

The cricket club and class organisation in connection with it is in a most flourishing condition and the interest taken by the staff all round is most gratifying.

In each classroom a smaller club is organised and the younger boys are looked after by Mr Huggins and Mr Hill, while in the upper divisions Mr Boait has charge of, and is responsible for, the training of the school team being warmly assisted by Mr Mingay. The boys are playing successfully and a miniature league has been formed in the school with the greatest success. The club is over 120 strong and is doing great work among the boys.

The athletics ... are also in a successful state and for the South London Schools Festival, the school entered this year 120 competitors from 7 years of age to over 14. The boys have been trained for the past few months and their practices in the evening have been much enjoyed. The Head Teacher who has this year personally undertaken the training of the boys has been heartily assisted in every direction by Mr Boait, Mr Mingay, Mr Huggins and Mr Hill, the latter two masters being present at the sports to look after the boys. The boys easily secured the championship of the South London Schools gaining 90½ points in the competition against the next highest 62½ points and bringing up their wins to four out of the last five years.

26/06/03   The children who competed in the sports festival were photographed on this day after the close of the afternoon session.

29/06/03   An outing to Ashstead Woods was decided upon for Saturday July 18th as a reward to the competitors at the sports and to commemorate the winning of the championships at sports.[52]

In 1906 the Board of Education permitted, as noted earlier, games to be played in curriculum time. What was seen by McIntosh as a progressive measure was similarly viewed by members of the London County Council. The Day Schools Sub-Committee reported to the LCC on 29 November 1906: 'We are of the opinion that the educational value of organised games is becoming so generally recognised that the Council should be asked to give its authority for their introduction into schools and to make some provision for the expenditure in connections therewith.'[53]

Rosendale Road took up games playing in school time enthusiastically. On 21 September 1906 Timms recorded:

> The Head Teacher and his assistant supervised the games and kept those poorly equipped physically, or by nature, encouraged. One boy Shambrook was in an unfit state to strip and had his parents communicated with. The scholars appeared to receive great freshness and benefit from these games and thoroughly enjoyed themselves.[54]

A week later Timms noted that an assistant master, Mr Bartlett, took the boys 'in an excellent match of football with properly laid out ground poles, flags etc. and with sides and captains of each team appointed'. With the result that, 'At 4.20 the scholars were brought back looking bright and fresh and having thoroughly entered into the games.'[55] In October HMI Graves visited the school. The Log Book read: 'From 3 p.m. a section of the school took organised games for the lessons on the timetable and under the supervision of their masters the scholars went into the playing fields and played matches in football. His Majesty's Inspector watched the games proceeding under the instruction of the masters.'[56]

Timms had an influence beyond Rosendale. He was a committee member of the influential South London Schools' Football Association and a man whose advice on sport was widely sought. By 1913 he was contributing to a number of sports conferences and events. On 1

December, for example, the Log Book recorded:

> Visit by Head Teacher to various schools in North Lambeth in
> connection with organised games to be played in the Archbishop's
> Park on the afternoons of 8th, 9th, 11th and on one of the
> mornings; also on the morning of Friday 12th December.[57]

How was Timms able to develop games so successfully in his school?
The answer is that he used coercion, rewards and rhetoric to instil into
the boys a belief that games were rewarding both physically and morally.

Discipline at Rosendale Road historically had been severe. In his
autobiography, *A Cab at the Door*, Victor S. Pritchett, the writer and
critic, has recalled rather less than objectively, with a sharp polemic style,
and perhaps sour grapes, his school days at Rosendale:[58]

> Discipline was meant to encourage subservience, and to squash
> rebellion – very undesirable in children who would grow up to
> obey orders from their betters. No child here would enter the
> ruling classes unless he was very gifted and won scholarship after
> scholarship. A great many boys from these schools did so and did
> rise to high places; but they had to slave and crush part of their
> lives, to machine themselves so that they became brain alone. They
> ground away at their lessons, and, for all their boyhood and youth
> and perhaps all their lives, they were in the ingenious torture
> chamber of examination halls. They were brilliant, of course, and
> some when they grew up tended to be obsequious to the ruling
> class and ruthless to the rest, if they were not tired out. Among
> them were many who were emotionally infantile.[59]

However, even Pritchett recognised that under Timms the situation
gradually changed:

> A reaction against this fierce system of education had set in at the
> turn of the century. Socialism and the scientific revolution – which
> Wells had described – had moved many people. New private
> schools for the well-off were beginning to break with the traditions
> of the nineteenth century and a little of the happy influence seeped
> down to ourselves.[60]

Pritchett is making an important distinction here between the harsh
attitudes that existed in many elementary schools in the late nineteenth
century and the more 'liberal' outlook increasingly found in the

twentieth century. Interestingly, he picks out for special praise the new progressive system of active tutorial work employed in his class by Mr Bartlett, the keen football coach and trainer.

> The other teachers hated him and it; we either made so much noise that the rest of the school could hardly get on with their work, or were so silent that teachers would look over the frosted glass of the door to see if we had gone off for a holiday. Mr Bartlett … by some strange magnetism he could silence a class almost without a word. He never used the cane. Since we could make as much noise as we liked, he got silence easily when he wanted it.[61]

Pritchett's account of a more relaxed school is certainly borne out by official statements. The Annual Report of the Inspectors in 1906, for example, commented that, 'Every effort by organised games and by many other means, is made by the staff to maintain a beneficial influence over the scholars outside the ordinary school work.'[62] Such accounts, of course, provide difficulties for historians following Humphries' committed Marxist standpoint. He sees working-class children as being in constant conflict with the teachers:

> The most potent and persistent opposition of working-class children to schooling, however, occurred in the classroom itself. Their enforced confinement in institutions which had little to offer apart from rote learning, rigid discipline and training in manners and morals which were often alien and meaningless, led to a constantly antagonistic atmosphere … This non-cooperative and sometimes openly hostile behaviour of many children, together with the large size of classes and the inadequately trained or equipped teachers, combined to produce a potentially dangerous conflict situation. Elementary schools attempted to resolve this conflict by tightly regulating the learning situation and by resorting to the traditional authoritarian methods of fear, punishment and physical violence.[63]

Humphries is perhaps too handicapped by Marxist views, by inflexible notions of class and control and dominant and subordinate groups. He is perhaps too quick to present elementary schools and elementary teachers in stereotypical ways. In truth there was variety in London's elementary schools, a fact acknowledged by Pritchett who is surely more accurate in his first-hand analysis.

There were and are good and bad elementary schools in London. They are as nearly as much created by their districts and their children as by their teachers. The children at Rosendale Road, which was a large school, were a mixture of working class and a few middles with a few foreigners and colonials – Germans, Portuguese, Australians, French and one or two Indians. It was a mixed school.[64]

One thing is certain – Rosendale did not fit neatly into Humphries' neat stereotypic paradigm. This is made even clearer by what follows below.

Games evolved successfully in Rosendale through a system of rewards for athletic success. Teams were regularly photographed with an often beaming headmaster[65] and outings for successful teams were arranged. Humphries, predictably, is wary of reading too much into the participation of boys in school sport. In his view, although children may have been enthusiastic, this was because 'Many children clearly welcomed games lessons … as a relief from the monotony of the school routine,'[66] but so do children everywhere! This was even more true in the public schools. Humphries is quick to point out that even where children competed in large numbers their 'enthusiastic participation in school sports did not imply automatic development of the specific character traits intended by the school authorities'.[67] Of course, it did not! Only the naive would claim this. Humphries also takes the jaundiced view that the fact that boys embraced the games cult only served to 'illustrate not only the internalisation of the public school ethos by a working-class boy, but also the process by which the corporate and competitive spirit and the hierarchical control that infused school sports, was reproduced in deference to social superiors.'[68] He quotes an elementary school educated man from Bristol:

> I was proud of the school, I used to play football for the school. On Friday afternoons we would 'ave school assembly and whoever was picked for the team, their name was called out and you had to march to the front. The teacher would give you out your 'shirties' as we used to call them. No football knickers or nothing like that … We'd play in the park … The teachers would arrange the teams … We had our own colours, green shirt, 'St Giles for honour, for loyalty, for courage, for courtesy. Play up, play fair, play the game.' When I left school they had one of the finest teams in England.[69]

Is this experience all bad? Perhaps Humphries should reflect a little more deeply and less prejudicially. There is at least one powerful reason to recommend this: games playing, whether it was cricket or football, was not possible within the school curriculum until 1906. Therefore, all training was done in the evenings and all matches were played out of school time and this realistically meant Saturday mornings for St. Giles and all the other schools. Those elementary school children who played games did so in their own leisure time voluntarily and enthusiastically, wholly before, and partially after 1906, and not as a release from the monotonous school curriculum or as an act of deference to social superiors. As remarked earlier, elementary school athleticism, of necessity, was expressed in different ways than in the public and grammar schools.

Athleticism in the elementary school as in public and grammar schools developed its own supportive rhetoric. If Rosendale's Log Book is anything to go by, praise for those selected for sporting competitions – the elementary school 'bloods' – found full expression. And Timms established a Social Club which acted as an Old Scholars Club:

> Meeting of the Social Club and Guild and Reunion of Old Scholars. A successful meeting was held with the sanction of the Board on the evening of Wednesday 24th February from 7.30-9.30 p.m. and was attended nearly 200 past and present scholars of the school.[70]

Then in December 1904 Timms founded a school magazine:

> The first issue of the school quarterly magazine 'Rosebuds' on this date. The programme of the scholars entertainment being printed with it as a supplement and the magazine itself containing a list of school honours, prizes, medal and certificate winners. The Head Teacher places on record his great appreciation of the services and loyal work and co-operation of the members of his staff in organising and bringing to a successful issue the entertainment and distribution of prizes.[71]

Unfortunately no copy of the magazine survives. However, we do have a single copy of another school's home produced magazine for 1893, *The Bellenden*, the magazine of Bellenden Road Board School. The magazine was produced by the boys of Standard VI and edited by them and is full

of articles about the South London Schools' Sports, and it contains this
enthusiastic if ungainly verse:

The Sports

The sports were something lovely
And went off jolly fine
I hope that they will be repeated
Many and many a time
    They cannot be praised too highly
For I'm sure nothing could have been
so highly interesting
For competition was so keen
    Everyone wanted a prize of course
But everyone cannot win
Somebody must be beaten
And to loose [*sic*] is not such a sin
    You fellows are'nt [*sic*] half artful
If there's a chap you want to beat
Take him to the refreshment bar
And stand a jolly good treat
    And when he wants to run
He'l have a pain in his back
And then you'l win the race
Which will be quite exact
    And then if you win a marble clock
Or a nice little watch and chain
You won't need to ask a Policeman
When the time is wanted again
    The prizes were really handsome
But I think that all our mothers
Ought to have raced for the sunlight soap
Presented by Lever Bros.[72]

If anything illustrates the difference between public school and
elementary public school athleticism it is this exceedingly clumsy verse.
The central theme of the poem is how to beat an opponent by 'artful'
means and win useful prizes! Such sentiments are not normally found in
the doggerel in public school magazines in which 'fair play' is celebrated.
    A further way in which the rhetoric of athleticism was sustained was

through school songs. In his autobiography Pritchett recalled one dramatic match:

> The school was beaten by Effra Road Higher Grade – boys stayed until fifteen there and were heavier than we were – on a frosty morning, near the railway arches, one to nil. It was a desperate game. The assistant teacher came with us and sang the school song on the touchline, in his weak, Cockney voice. Roses was pronounced 'Rowsis'.
>
> Roses on the ball, Roses on the ball,
> Never mind the half back line
> The Roses beat them every time.
> Give the ball a swing
> Right over to the wing,
> Roses, Roses, Roses on the ba-a-ll.[73]

Boys, of course, were also influenced by what was said in school lessons and assemblies were especially important. In class they were encouraged to write, stories and verses about games. But whether it was in school time or on Saturday mornings they were nevertheless under teacher supervision. Accordingly, it may be argued – it certainly is by Humphries – that their behaviour was influenced, even determined, by teacher expectations, and then once free from them they would reject the values of the adults. Such a view, again of limited insight, ignores the powerful effect that the public schools' games cult had on young boys through weekly comics and magazines.[74]

Undoubtedly, the two most popular boys' weekly comics were *The Gem* and *The Magnet*, both of which contained stories of life in an imaginary English public school, Greyfriars. The stories about the school were written by Frank Richards, who was born in Ealing on 8 August 1876. His real name was Charles Harold St. John Hamilton, but he came to use, and to regard his pseudonym, as his real name. Richards did not go to a public school and in some respects Greyfriars was rather idiosyncratic – in one respect, discussed below, deliberately so. By 1905, after having had a number of stories accepted by various boys' newspapers, he was invited to write for a new newspaper, *The Gem*. He was so successful that he then was asked to contribute to another paper *The Magnet*, and it was in this paper that on 15 February 1908 Greyfriars School and Billy Bunter were born.

In his book *Happiest Days*, Jeffrey Richards analyses the importance of these two papers in shaping and influencing schoolboy reading and behaviour.[75] A number of features stand out about life in Greyfriars. In the first place games are not compulsory and there are no cadet corps, chapel nor houses.

> Most interesting of all, perhaps, is the fact that the Greyfriars boys play association football and not the rugby so integral to the public school ethos. This clearly points to the intended audience of non-public school boys, for whom soccer was the chief sport, an assumption reinforced by the presence in *The Magnet* of a regular soccer column where readers' queries were answered by the Linesman or the Old Ref.[76]

These papers exerted a powerful influence upon the boys of Rosendale Road. Pritchett relates how he was offered them by a friend of his: 'One page and I was entranced. I gobbled these stories as if I were eating pie or stuffing ... The Japanese-looking boy was called Nott. He had a friend, called Howard, the son of a compositor. *The Gem* and *The Magnet* united us. We called ourselves by Greyfriars' names and jumped about shouting words like "Garoo".'[77] For Pritchett's father, however, the discovery that Victor was reading these papers was an horrific experience:

> 'Good godfathers', said my father not touching the pile... 'I give you your Saturday penny and this is what you're doing with it. Wasting the money I earn. I suppose you think you're so superior because you have a father who has his own business and you spend right and left on muck like this...' 'A man is known by the company he keeps' said my father. And getting up ... he threw the whole lot on the fire.[78]

George Orwell more or less agreed with a reviewer in the *Times Literary Supplement* of 1938 when he wrote that public schoolboys read them till about the age of 12 years; boys at cheap private schools for several more years, but they were certainly read by working-class boys as well.[79] How right he was! *The Gem* and *The Magnet* remained firm favourites at Rosendale Road and other London elementary schools. These weeklies helped shape positive attitudes to the previously middle-class games cult in a way that was very seductive. Coercion, rewards and rhetoric; these then were effective ways in which Timms and his staff promoted athleticism at Rosendale, but as noted above, there were a variety of other factors at work which created the adapted athleticism of the elementary school. As already noted facilities and time were not as readily or fully available to elementary schools as they were to secondary schools – public or grammar.

In passing it should be noted that it was due to the influence of men like Timms that there was a rapid growth in the number of elementary schools football associations well before 1906, as the following table shows:

Finally, it should also be noted that there was one further powerful means by which the ideology of athleticism was promoted in the

TABLE 2

Year of Formation	Association1885
1886	South London Schools FA
1887	
1888	Sheffield Schools FA
1889	
1890	Manchester Schools FA
	Birmingham Schools FA
	Liverpool Schools FA
	Nottingham Schools FA
	West London Schools FA
1892	Brighton Schools FA
1893	
1894	Leyton Schools FA
	Reading Schools FA
	Newcastle Schools FA
	Sunderland Schools FA
	Leicester Schools FA
1895	Northampton Schools FA
	Leeds School FA
	Oldham Schools FA
	Cardiff Schools FA
1897	Blackburn Schools FA
1898	Hull Schools FA

elementary school: diffusion. One influential diffusionist was George Sharples. He was born in Bolton in 1856, and educated as both a pupil and pupil teacher at Holy Trinity National School. In 1875 he entered St. John's Teacher Training College, Battersea. A brilliant scholar he was Latin prize man in both years at college. He was also one of the top twenty prize men in the country in Mathematics, gaining the Committee of Council on Education prize for Euclid in 1876. After leaving college he became Head of All Saints Church School in Bolton and in 1879,

Headmaster of Pikes Lane Board School. By 1881 he had been
appointed Organising Master and Inspector of Board Schools in Bolton.
In 1883 he moved across the Pennines and was appointed Headmaster of
the Spring Grove Board School in Huddersfield. Five years later he
became Headmaster of Leeds Central Higher Grade Board School
before returning to Lancashire to take up the headship of Waterloo Road
Board School, Manchester. Sharples, incidentally, was an excellent
footballer. Apart from representing college he also played for Eagley FC
and ultimately Bolton Wanderers, captaining them in 1882. He retired
from playing in 1885 having represented Lancashire and subsequently
became a football league referee. Sharples had no doubt about the value
of games, believing that the growth of elementary schools' football 'has
done more for the real well-being of the boys of this country than all the
drill and callisthenics exercises yet introduced'.[80] He spread the ideals of
athleticism widely as a 'roving' headmaster.

   Athleticism then gradually developed in the elementary schools of
England and Wales from 1870 onwards. Again, the point must be
laboured, once more, athleticism in these schools was not the athleticism
of the public and grammar schools. The reasons for this have been well
rehearsed and do not require detailed repetition. The way in which the
ideology could be delivered, of necessity, was different. The twin
problems of lack of time and lack of facilities had to be overcome, and
they were up to a point. When government regulations proscribed
games in school time schools promptly played them after school or on
Saturday mornings – a legacy that still survives today. If schools lacked
their own playing fields they simply took to the nearest park. The
teachers negotiated for facilities with representatives of the Royal Parks,
the Archbishop of Canterbury and with local park wardens or
philanthropic private individuals.

   By the time of the First World War, physical education in English
elementary schools had undergone a radical transformation. Originally
introduced into the school timetable as military drill and intended as a
means of instilling discipline, drill had moved first towards a 'non-
military' variety and finally, been assimilated in the early twentieth
century, into a physical education programme reflecting a holistic view
of education. In particular, team games, which were not allowed
originally in the school curriculum or in school time, saw their
significance reassessed until they were formally introduced into the
curriculum in 1906.

While the elementary schools were still denied the games facilities typical of both public schools and grammar schools well into the twentieth century, in fact, by virtue of staff commitment, training college experience and pupil enthusiasm, the English elementary schools well before the twentieth century in some instances, as illustrated here by London Board Schools, had embraced the philosophy and practice of the upper middle class ideology of athleticism. Drill and games went in tandem. If it is unacceptably casual to dismiss drill in the elementary school as a rudimentary exercise for elementary school children, and to fail to be aware of the significance of, and support for, military drill in the late nineteenth and early twentieth centuries,[81] it is equally casual to view the elementary schools as locations simply for the practice of drill-military or 'non-military'. This is to fail to recognise the role of teacher training colleges in the diffusion and dissemination of athleticism in Britain and its empire,[82] and to fail to be aware of the proselytising efforts of its products at home and abroad. W.J. Wilson and J.G. Timms, and in time others, some known and some as yet unknown, are ensuring that the history of English elementary schools is being both revisited and revised.

NOTES

1. S. Humphries, 'Hurrah for England: Schooling and the Working Class in Bristol 1870–1914', *Southern History*, 1 (1979), 171–207.
2. Gwyn Williams, 'The Concept of Egomania in the Thought of Antonio Gramsci', *Journal of the History of Ideas* (1960), 586–99.
3. For a full account of the establishment of the London School Board see S. Maclure, *One Hundred Years of London Education 1870–1970* (London, 1970).
4. David Rubenstein 'Socialization and the London School Board 1870–1904: aims, methods and public opinion', in P. McCann (ed.), *Popular Education and Socialization in the Nineteenth Century* (London, 1977), pp.231–64.
5. Ibid., pp.239–40.
6. Ibid., p.240.
7. *The Times*, 25 November, 1891, 7, quoted in Rubenstein, p.243.
8. Rubenstein, 'Socialization', p.242.
9. E. Lyulph Stanley, *Our National Education* (London, 1899), pp.139–40 quoted in Rubenstein, 'Socialization', p.243.
10. D. Rubenstein, 'Annie Beasant and Stewart Headlam: the London School Board Elections of 1888', *East London Papers*, 13 (Summer 1970), 10–11.
11. P. C. McIntosh, *P.E. in England since 1800* (2nd ed.) (London, 1968), p.109.
12. P. C. McIntosh, 'Games and Gymnastics for Two Nations in One', in P.C. McIntosh (ed.), *Landmarks in the History of Physical Education* (London, 1981), p.202.
13. Ibid., p.202.
14. Ibid., p.202.
15. Ibid., p.209.
16. McIntosh, *P.E.*, p.145.
17. Ibid., pp.146–7.

18. H. C. Barnard, *A History of English Education from 1760* (2nd ed.) (London, 1961), p.226.

19. McIntosh, *P.E.*, pp.168–9.

20. J.A. Mangan, 'Imitating their Betters and Dissociating from their Inferiors: Grammar Schools and the Games Ethic in the Late Nineteenth and Early Twentieth Centuries', *Proceedings of the 1982 Annual Conference of the History of Education Society of Great Britain* (Leicester, 1983), p.22.

21. W. D. Smith, *Stretching their Bodies* (London, 1974), p.88.

22. Ibid., p.90.

23. T. Chesterton, 'Physical Education under the School Board for London', *Special Reports on Educational Subjects* (London, 1898), p.188.

24. Ibid., p.188.

25. *Royal Commission on Physical Training* (Scotland, 1903), p.154.

26. McIntosh, *P.E.*, p.118.

27. PRO *Committee on Training Colleges Courses of Instruction*, 1901, 1, p.184. Ed 24 68B.

28. See Richard Holt, 'Contrasting Nationalisms: Sport, Militarism, and the Unitary State in Britain and France before 1914', in J.A. Mangan (ed.), *Tribal Identities: Nationalism, Europe, Sport* (London, 1996), p.90. Holt states that elementary school drill was brief, basic and by no means uniformly practical. He reveals no awareness of the considerable efforts made by politicians, educationalists and others to promote drill, of the extensive debate on drill and the types of drill for years in the late nineteenth and early twentieth century or of the careful and systematic programmes attempted by educational agencies throughout England at this time. In contrast, for a thorough, detailed and careful consideration of the topic, see Alan Penn, *Targeting the Schools. Militarism, Drill and the Elementary School 1870–1914* (London, forthcoming).

29. T. Chesterton, *The Theory of Physical Education* (London, 1895), pp.94–5.

30. See J.A. Mangan, *Athleticism in the Victorian and Edwardian Public School. The Emergence and Consolidation of an Educational Ideology* (Cambridge, 1981 and Falmer, 1986).

31. See Mangan, 'Imitating their Betters'.

32. S. Humphries, *Hooligans or Rebels? An Oral History of Working Class Childhood and Youth, 1889–1939* (Oxford, 1981), p.2.

33. Ibid., p.31.

34. Ibid., p.41.

35. See J.A. Mangan, *The Games Ethic and Imperialism* (London, 1986) for a more complete analysis of the role of games in British Imperial purpose. See also J.A. Mangan, 'Prologue: Britain's Chief Spiritual Export: Imperial Sport as a Moral Metaphor, Political Symbol and Cultural Bond', in J.A. Mangan (ed.), *The Cultural Bond: Sport, Empire, Society* (London, 1992), pp.1–9.

36. Mangan, *Athleticism*, p.9.

37. See C.F. Hickey, 'Athleticism and the London Training Colleges' (Ph.D. thesis, IRCSSS, University of Strathclyde, to be completed in 1998).

38. Holt, 'Contrasting Nationalisms', passim.

39. Mangan, *Athleticism*, passim.

40. See Mangan, *The Games Ethic and Imperialism*, passim. and J.A. Mangan, 'Duty unto Death: English Masculinity and Militarism in the Age of the New Imperialism', in J. A. Mangan, *Tribal Identities*, pp.10–38.

41. A large number of school Log Books covering this period are housed in the Greater London Record Office. They await systematic and thorough examination.

42. F. H. Spencer, *An Inspector's Testament* (London, 1938), p.31.

43. *The Schoolmaster*, 34, 29 September 1888, 388.

44. *The Schoolmaster*, 39, 21 March 1891, 541.

45. Greater London Record Office (hereafter GLRO), Oldridge Road School Log Book EO/DIV9/OLD/LB/1, 16 November 1888.

46. Ibid., 15 March 1889.

47. Ibid., 30 June 1891.

48. Ibid., 3 October 1890.

49. *The Schoolmaster*, 16 May 1891, 39, p.872.

50. Annual Report of Board Inspector, Rosendale Road School, 1902.
51. GLRO Annual Report of Board Manager, Rosendale Road School, EO/PS/12/R40/1, 1897.
52. GLRO Rosendale Road School Log Book, EO/DIV8/ROS/LB/1, June 24th–29th 1903.
53. GLRO, *London Council Education Committee Minutes*, 2, November 28th 1906, p.3628.
54. GLRO Rosendale Road School Log Book, September 21st 1906.
55. Ibid., 28 September 1906.
56. Ibid., 26 October 1906.
57. Ibid., 1 December 1913.
58. V. S. Pritchett, *A Cab at the Door* (New York, 1967). Pritchett was born into a lower middle-class family in Ipswich in 1900. His father was an unsuccessful salesman and the family was constantly in debt. To avoid creditors and landlords the family was always on the move to the extent that by 1911 Pritchett had moved house 18 times and he had lived in Woodford, Palmers Green, Balham, Uxbridge, Acton, Ealing, Hammersmith, Camberwell, Bromley and Dulwich. After Rosendale Pritchett entered Alleyns Grammar School in 1914 from where he drifted into the leather trade before moving to Paris in 1921 subsequently becoming an author, academic and critic.
59. V. S. Pritchett, *A Cab at the Door*, p.103.
60. Ibid., p.103.
61. Ibid., p.104.
62. Annual Report of Board Inspector Rosendale Road School, 1905.
63. Humphries, 'Hurrah for England', p.190.
64. Pritchett, *A Cab at the Door*, p.102.
65. The Greater London Record Office houses an extensive collection of photographs of all aspects of life in Elementary Schools.
66. Humphries, *Hooligans or Rebels?*, p.41.
67. Ibid., p.42.
68. Ibid.
69. Ibid.
70. GLRO Rosendale Road School Log Book, 24 February 1904.
71. Ibid., 12 December 1904.
72. GLRO The Bellenden, June 1893.
73. Pritchett, *A Cab at the Door*, p.128.
74. See Jeffrey Richards, *Happiest Days: the public schools in English fiction* (Manchester, 1988), and P. W. Musgrave, *From Brown to Bunter* (London, 1985).
75. Jeffrey Richards, *Happiest Days*.
76. Ibid., p.277.
77. Pritchett, *A Cab at the Door*, p.110.
78. Ibid., p.113.
79. George Orwell, 'Boys' Weeklies', *Horizon*, 1, 3 (1940), 174–200, quoted in Musgrave, *From Brown to Bunter*, p. 230.
80. George Sharples, 'The organization of games out of school for the children attending public elementary schools in large industrial centres as voluntarily undertaken by the teachers', in *Special Reports on Educational Subjects*, 2 (London, 1898), pp.159–84.
81. See Holt, 'Contrasting Nationalisms', but see also the discussion of Holt's shallow consideration of drill in the English elementary school in J.A. Mangan, 'Sport in Society: The Nordic World and Other Worlds', in Henrik Meinander and J.A. Mangan (eds.), *The Nordic World: Sport and Society* (London, 1998), pp.189–91.
82. See Colm Hickey, 'Athleticism and the London Training Colleges', especially Chapters 4, 5 and 6, and J. A. Mangan and Colm Hickey, 'A Pioneer of the Proletariat: The Proselytiser Herbert Milnes and the Games Cult in New Zealand', in J.A. Mangan (ed.), *The Australasian World: Sport in Antipodean Society pre-1950* (forthcoming).

Football's Missing Link:
The Real Story of the Evolution of
Modern Football

ADRIAN HARVEY

Conventional accounts of the development of modern football stress the role of the public schools, a view derived in large measure from the most influential of the game's early historians, the Old Harrovian C.W. Alcock. For him, history was progress. This was expressed in the spread of the 'rationalised' football of the public schools throughout the population. Alternative varieties of the game were of no interest to him. For example, he barely even noticed the substantial football culture of Sheffield, despite the fact that until at least 1868 in its organisation it was far bigger than the FA.[1]

The received view of the development of football rests on a fundamental distinction between two types of the game. The first sort was much older and often referred to as 'folk football' and was a 'folk-game' played by the general population. It resembled an extremely violent form of rugby and was 'rough and wild, closer to "real" fighting than modern sport', and was typified by the traditional festival games that were conducted on Shrove Tuesday. By contrast, the second type of football, a more disciplined variety that was well organised and governed by strict rules, could be found only in public schools, where it had been invented. Unlike the traditional game, this variant grew in importance, and, according to the early historians, it was the dissemination of these public-school-derived rules into the wider society that created the modern sports of rugby and soccer. E. Dunning and K. Sheard use this distinction as the basis for a wide-reaching typology consisting of 15 points which distinguished 'folk-games' from 'modern sport', and argue that traditional recreation was transformed into modern sport by the imposition of rational laws.[2]

Historians contended that the growth of industrial and urban society in the years after 1800 led to the steady eradication of the traditional Shrove game until it had become quite rare by 1860. While it was recognised that the Shrove variety was not the only type of football that was conducted outside of the public schools, even the most assiduous researcher, Magouin, was unable to find any examples after 1827 and concluded that it was 'dead'. Modern scholars agree, A. Mason speaking of 'the final nail in the coffin' and Holt suggesting that 'the game survived primarily as a rural pastime which had been in slow decline over a long period'.[3] In the years after 1830 football survived within the public schools, where it 'was reconditioned and made into an effective instrument for modern use'.[4]

While some later historians have offered minor changes to this picture, it has, essentially, remained intact. This essay fully concedes that in the period after 1850 sport generally, and football specifically, became far more organised within the public schools. Indeed, sport became an integral part of the wider reforms that were designed to instil discipline and exert 'social control' over the behaviour of pupils. These reforms were pragmatic innovations initially advanced by George Edward Lynch Cotton (Marlborough) and included the restructuring of a number of facets of school life, notably the house and prefect systems. In sport this manifested itself in the cultivation of an ethic that was generally known as 'fair play'. In time the dissemination of such an ideology helped to create the late-Victorian concept of the athletic English gentleman.[5] Nonetheless, it argues that the importance given to the role of the public schools in the diffusion and codification of association football is exaggerated and based on a failure to appreciate both the extent and sophistication of the football played in the wider community in the years preceding 1863. In contrast to the established history, it contends that popularly played football was governed by rules, achieving a high degree of organisation in certain regions. Similarly, the influence exerted by codes emanating from the public schools is regarded as exaggerated. In essence, this essay contends that an organised football culture would have emerged in the latter half of the nineteenth century even if there had there been no public school model. The study consists of four parts. The first shows that during the nineteenth century there was far more football, particularly of the Shrove variety, than has been generally supposed. The second demonstrates that public school football was unsuited to general diffusion because it was too esoteric. In the third, new evidence reveals that there were a large number of football teams and clubs, completely unrelated to the public schools, functioning between 1830 and 1860. Whereas some scholars have conjectured, on largely theoretical grounds, that ordinary football persisted in the period between 1840 and 1860, this study provides substance to the shadows.[6] Far from being amorphous abstractions, the social composition and background of most of these teams can be discerned as can the type of rules governing their games. Whereas most scholars, for instance Dunning and Sheard, treat the Shrove game as synonymous with the football played outside of the public schools, enquiry reveals that many teams were playing by rules that were effectively as sophisticated as those used within the public schools, and conforming to Dunning and Sheard's classification of modern sport in 11 of the 15 criteria. Part four examines the most substantial football culture that existed in Britain before the 1870s, that of Sheffield. Previous historians have maintained that the Sheffield club's rules were derived from a public school model.[7] In reality they were effectively an internal creation and the game was related to the football that was generally extant outside of the public schools. Part four also considers the public schools' impact on the FA.

The first part of the study considers the extent to which Shrove football and other less formal varieties of the game existed in the nineteenth century. It has been assumed that increasing urbanisation, especially the disciplines of industrial life, meant that the population had less time, space and energy in which to play football. It has also been contended that the authorities attacked the game.[8] This has led historians to maintain that during the first half of the nineteenth century traditional football, particularly events held on Shrove Tuesday, was in decline.[9] This is not supported by the evidence. Between 1540 and 1799 Shrove games were recorded in just 19 places, as compared to 56 in the nineteenth century. Whilst 12 of these were either suppressed or moved, 23 persisted after 1880.[10] Likewise, the significance of everyday football has been overlooked, there being at least 30 examples between 1800 and 1830.[11] Whilst the lack of suitable playing areas was a common problem in the early portion of the nineteenth century, evidence from the Commission on Public Walks reveals that football persisted, even in industrial areas such as Bolton and Blackburn.[12]

In the conventional view the period between 1830 and 1860 witnessed a staggering transformation of the game, in which the original 'folk football' was given a strict code of laws and rendered rational. This was essentially due to the public schools, where, as James Walvin says, 'the game which we now know as football was to evolve'. Each school developed rules that were suitable for their particular circumstances, with skill and fair play replacing the historic violence of the game.[13] A consideration of this point of view forms the second part of this paper.

Before 1850 football at public schools was organised by the boys themselves. The levels of sophistication varied considerably. Two of the most developed games were at Eton, where an annual match between Collegers and Oppidians was established before 1820, and at Harrow, where house championships were conducted from the 1840s. Generally, while there appear to have been rules for football, these could be quite elementary, permitting a substantial degree of violence. The game at Westminster offers a good illustration; being contested by an indefinite number of players, using large goals that were simply imaginary lines. It had no offside law and was rough, scrimmages being 'agonizing'. The first written public school code appeared at Rugby in 1845 and in that year Eton introduced another novelty, the referee. Such innovations did little to curb the violence or resolve disputed interpretations. At Eton, for instance, a variety of football games were played, each peculiar to a particular house, and both the principal types, 'the field' and 'the wall', were incredibly brutal. Despite possessing a well-thought-out code, Rugby School suffered similar problems, the systematic breaking of rules resulting in considerable violence.[14]

The involvement of masters in football resulted in the establishment of written codes, though in the 1850s this did not prevent problems over the infraction of rules, especially in the more violent games found at Rugby and Marlborough.[15] By 1856 most public schools had their codes printed, but only Eton's rules were easily available, appearing in a *Cricket Guide* from 1859. Compilations, such as that produced by Lillywhite in 1861, were some help, but the major breakthrough did not occur until late in 1863 when *The Field* provided a clear explanation of the particular codes. Until then the general public had lacked any guidance when trying to interpret their meaning. However, the public school codes were designed to settle 'disputed points' for those for whom the game was 'too well known to render any explanation necessary'. Thus, as late as 1864, rugby's code, generally regarded as the most considered, was still far from comprehensive. Similarly, even in 1863 major football games, notably those at Eton and Shrewsbury, depended largely on unwritten laws derived from tradition. It was little wonder that in 1861 the football editor of *The Field*, despite spending half an hour puzzling over Eton's rules, conceded that he could not understand them. Contemporaries felt that the laws of public school football needed 'simplifying' because they were too 'obscure' and no effort was made to disseminate them. Public school football became neither codified nor organised until well after 1850, even then remaining largely incomprehensible to outsiders.[16]

The existence of a wide variety of codes, each dependent to a certain degree on the esoteric knowledge peculiar to a particular school, impeded football's dissemination to outsiders. It also prevented footballers from different public schools playing together. However, as early as 1846, undergraduates from every major public school had created a football club at Cambridge University and established a joint set of rules, which formed the basis of codes there in 1848, 1854 and 1858. Yet these rules remained largely unknown, and were absent from a compilation of the various extant football laws issued by Lillywhite in 1861. Some public school boys were not receptive to this fusion and even at Cambridge old boys from Eton, Harrow and Rugby continued to establish clubs devoted exclusively to their respective school football. In many senses fusion was completely anathema to the whole spirit of public school football. Each school was a zealous defender of its unique game. Thus, when, in 1858, some public school men advocated the creation of a committee made up of representatives from all schools in order to establish a common code, suggesting various compromises, their idea was denounced as simply giving rise to a 'mongrel' game. Schools, it was asserted, had distinct cultures and anything which threatened the 'slang' of tradition was certain to arouse prickly displays of feeling. One correspondent summed the whole debate up by declaring that 'prejudices are the very basis of our public school'. Such a tone made reasoned discussion on laws impossible and one can readily agree with the correspondent who discouraged any contact between the public schools on the football field because it just created animosity. The editor of *Bell's Life in London*, who had tried to foster dialogue, was soon forced to curtail letters on the subject because they were 'so mixed up with abuse of each other'. Four years later, in 1863, when *The Field* initiated such a process, the editor expressed similar fears.[17]

The production of a shared code embracing the public schools was obviously impossible. This meant that outsiders were confronted by a bewildering array of different rules, many of which could not be easily understood. According to historians this limitation in the accessibility of printed matter was solved by the initiatives of a number of reformers belonging to privileged social groups, to whom they refer as 'missionaries'. Walvin is quite explicit concerning this, describing it as 'more deliberate and organised attempts by men who had passed through public schools. Though generally this happened via middle class social work in deprived urban areas...'. It was these individuals who were endeavouring to promote healthy leisure pursuits among the lower orders, who disseminated the new rationalised football, which the public schools had created, giving it a discernible impact on those beyond the previously small milieu of practitioners.[18]

While there is some evidence for this from the 1880s, between 1864 and 1872 in England there were only five teams that can plausibly be described as the product of such a process; Pennard (1864), Bradfield (1865), Edmonton (1860s), Turton (1870s), Darwen (1872).[19] More usually in this period there was little social mixing at football, clubs remaining a strict preserve of the upper and middle class. After 1875 an increasing number of teams appear with a significant working–class input. However, the extent to which they were the product of missionaries remains unclear.

Given the lack of 'missionaries' scholars are unclear as to their influence, but with little to replace them with, simply assert that football existed outside the public schools between 1840 and 1860, though at a level which did not attract attention.[20] It is hard to understand how such an attenuated football culture could blossom so rapidly after 1870.

In fact, as the third part of this study will show, there is an abundance of evidence of organised football activity between 1835 and 1859, stemming in the main from a previously overlooked source, *Bell's Life in London*. For most of the period between 1822 and 1863 it was the third best selling stamped weekly. Despite being quite costly, many pubs and clubs held copies. With the onset of the penny post in 1840, its columns filled with letters from readers from all classes and from a wide geographical area. Some of those from footballers provide a wealth of information. While it is obviously impossible to assess the level of activity of the teams mentioned, the information demonstrates organised activity. There follows a list of teams, arranged geographically, with the dates when their activity commenced.

Scotland
(1) Blairdrummond Estate (1835) (2) Deanston Cotton Mill (1835)
(3) Edinburgh Gentlemen's Servants (1841)

(4) Edinburgh Chairmen (1841) (5) Edinburgh Waiters (1841)
(6) Edinburgh 93rd Highlanders (1851) (7) Edinburgh University FC
     (1851) (8) Academical Club (1858)
(9) Glasgow Celtic Society (1859)

Cumbria
(10) Ulverstone Leathermen (1839)
(11) Ulverstone other trades (1839)

Yorkshire
(12) Thurlstone (1843–5) (13) Tottley (1843)
(14) Thurstoneland (1843) (15) Bilkerstone(1844)
(16) Denby (1844) (17) Foolstone (1844) (18) Hoylandswaine (1844) (19)
     Penistone (1844) (20) Thurlstone Upper End (1844) (21) Southouse
     (1845) (22) Holmfirth (1845) (23) Hebworth (1845) (24) Holmfirth
     (1852)
(25) Sheffield Football Club (1857)
(26) Hallam Football Club (1857)

Lancashire
(27) Sidney Smith's Tavern (1841)
(28) Bolton Rifle Brigade (1841) (29) Four Lanes End (1841)
(30) Drovers Inn (1841)
(31) Cronkeysham Champions Society (1841) – They were renamed
     Fieldhead Lads in 1842.
(32) Bodyguards Club (1841–2) (33) Fear-noughts (1841–2)
(34) Orrel (1841) (35) Whitford Lads (1842)
(36) Bolton (1844) (37) Kings Guards (1844) (38) Charlestown (1846)
     (39) Boston (1846)
(40) Manchester Athenaeum (1849)
(41) Liverpool Football Club (1858)

Derbyshire
(42) Derby (1838) (43) Ashbourne Upwards (1846)
(44) Ashbourne Downwards (1846) (45) Eggington (1849)
(46) Willington (1849)

West Midlands
(47) Barley Mow (1839) (48) White Lion (1839)

(49) Birmingham Athenic Institution (1842)

Leicestershire
(50) Leicester (1838) (51) Blaby Youth (1852)
(52) Enderby (1852) (53) Whetstone (1852)
(54) Wigston (1852)

Northamptonshire
(55) Staverton (1849)

Warwickshire
(56) Bickinhill (1842) (57) Hampton-in-Arden (1842)
(58) Flecknoe (1843) (59) Grandbigh (1843)
(60) Rugby Tailors (1845) (61) Flecknoe (1849)

Berkshire
(62) East Isley (1843) (63) West Isley (1843)

London Area
(64) Forest Football Club (1859)

Surrey
(65) Light Dragoons (Hampton Court) (1844)
(66) Surrey Football Club (1849)

Hampshire
(67) Southampton Club (1852) (68) Winchester (1852).[21]

Of the 68 teams, eight appeared in the 1830s, 45 from the 1840s and 15 in the 1850s. During this period football was played at 28 educational institutions that were not established public schools. When analysed the 68 teams can be divided into five categories based on their membership: clubs, rural divisions, pubs, occupations, military. However, what is less easy to ascertain is the founding members and their association with public schools. It is possible, and this is recognised, that the schools may have had a direct influence on the creation and maintenance of clubs. This is an issue that certainly merits investigation.

In the early 1840s three teams from Rochdale referred to themselves as 'clubs'. They were based in pubs and probably made up of local operatives. Christian Chartists at Birmingham had founded the Athenic Institution, which offered a mixture of physical and intellectual recreations, including, by 1842, football. In 1849 the game was given increased prominence by the Manchester Athenaeum's Gymnastic Society, which commenced regular football on Saturday afternoons. This was part of the middle-class institution's effort to increase its membership. The Glasgow Celtic Society also played football, though it usually concentrated on shinty. The first side to call themselves a Football Club were Surrey. They were created in 1849 and had written rules. From these it is clear that only members of Oval-based cricket clubs could join, by paying five shillings a year. The money was used to pay for balls and ropes and an attendant to look after them. They played on Wednesday and Saturday afternoons from October until the end of April. Edinburgh University started a football club in 1851 and a year later the Southampton club began. Towards the end of the 1850s football clubs became more common. Both Liverpool and Forest were created by old public schoolboys, from Rugby and Harrow respectively. Both used their old school's rules, though the latter soon switched to the code drawn up at Cambridge University in 1856. Both clubs at Sheffield and Hallam were the enthusiastic outcomes of efforts by a number of individuals who met regularly to compete in a range of athletic sports.[22]

Throughout the 1840s teams in rural areas were often based on parish boundaries, especially in Warwickshire. At both Ashbourne and Isley, two ends of a parish would compete. On only one occasion, in Leicestershire in 1852, did two villages play. There appear to be no teams divided according to marital status, a pervasive distinction in Shrove games. In Derbyshire, however, participation was restricted to 'single men'.[23]

The involvement of pubs in football was multifaceted. In 1839 a match at Duffery occurred between two pubs. At Bolton, the noted athlete Ben Hart was proprietor of the Sidney Smith Tavern, and had his pub team.[24] Publicans, especially in the Manchester area, often sponsored events by providing prizes. More usually, they acted as stakeholders, a practice that was especially common in Yorkshire and Lancashire. Relationships could be bilateral. Cronkeysham Champions changed their name to Fieldhead Lads, the pub where they were based, while Ashbourne had its 'Football Inn'.[25]

The spread of industrial and urban developments in the 1840s is supposed to have destroyed the traditional game. Walvin states that 'in the new cities of the midlands and the north, football ... similarly disappeared'.[26] A close examination of the evidence, however, reveals that, on the contrary, it was precisely those regions, notably Lancashire, which enjoyed the most organised activity. Although some historians stress the debilitating effect of early industrial life, a number of teams that were created were clearly based on their members' occupations. In parts of Scotland agricultural workers played. Teams of operatives from cotton mills existed in Perthshire and Rochdale. In Edinburgh, men from various service industries, waiters, chairmen and gentlemen's servants, formed sides. Skilled members of various trades in Ulverstone, especially shoemakers, created teams, as did Rugby's tailors.[27]

In 1846 troops were used to suppress the Shrovetide game at Derby. More usually, the military were keen footballers, perhaps the most persistent of the adult players during this period, especially after the Crimean War when their activity increased dramatically.[28] It does not appear that they played any specific variety of the game, and most of the sides were made up of officers from a particular public school, such as Eton or Winchester, some of whom would make regular visits back to play the current first team. It appears to have been rare for the ranks to mix, such an event only occurring in 1851 when the 93rd Highlanders were unable to raise a team made up of officers. Their contact with outsiders was similarly limited, and most army football was internal and often had a strong element of conviviality. During the Crimean War the game appears to have been part of a programme of convalescence given to troops recuperating on the Isle of Wight.[29]

The orthodox view is that one chief reason for traditional football's disappearance was the shortage of leisure hours available to the working class. Some instances support the former. In 1841 Whitford Lads were unable to arrange a match against Fieldhead Lads because the latter already had a game organised for that day, and they thus had to wait a whole year to play them. Yet generally the evidence, though patchy, refutes such notions. There are a total of 42 games mentioned in sources during this period which are not related to either traditional Shrove matches or school football. Eleven were staged on days which can be described as likely holiday times, but the other 30 were not, a fact that suggests that football was generally played independently of established holidays. Matches were distributed throughout every day of the week, including Sundays, the most popular being Monday (7) and Saturday

(6). The latter was the principal day for middle-class institutions such as the Manchester Athenaeum, Surrey FC and Edinburgh University FC.

Orthodoxy offers another main reason for football's demise. This cannot be sustained. In Manchester, one of the period's more built-up areas, grounds were provided by at least four pubs. Other places, such as Newton Common and the Stretford Road, had ample available space. Although players were deprived of access to green fields, even a team from heavily urbanised Rochdale clearly regarded the availability of a playing area as an insignificant problem, suggesting to prospective opponents that they 'toss for choice of grounds'. In Yorkshire's urban areas, Doncaster Race Course and Sheffield's Hyde Park were accessible venues. Edinburgh's hotels had land where teams made up of servants could play. Whilst some playing areas were clearly far from perfect, afflicted by 'dense browd' and 'loose yard dogs', others had goals pitched and were laid out to an agreed size. Rural areas contained even more space, games being played in fields. The principal difficulty experienced by many teams related to travel. Some solved this problem by meeting opponents half way. Another solution was to offer to 'give or take reasonable expenses'. This practice persisted in rural areas, as did that of meeting half way, until the expansion of the availability of railway travel. Before then it was rare for a team to play outside its locality. Rugby's tailors, who challenged any team within five miles, were probably typical. By 1852 the growth of transport meant that Winchester were willing to journey up to 50 miles for a match.[30]

There are many indications that football was a well-organised sport that was capable of attracting substantial popular attention. Far from being informal improvisations, matches were arranged well in advance, often having been initiated by challenges in *Bell's Life in London*. Rules would be drawn up and strict preparations made. Inclusion in a team depended on ability for 'only those selected may play'. The players would practise for weeks beforehand and were even given specific roles, as at Ashton Under Lyne, where both sides had a 'Backguardsman'. In the Shrove game at Scone in 1836, a revival involving a match against Perth, both teams were captained by local dignitaries, who were active participants. Matches would draw large, socially mixed crowds, sometimes numbering 'thousands'.[31] Publicans clearly regarded football as a commercial venture, offering prizes or free food in order to attract entrants.

The players and their backers also appear to have been aware of the financial opportunities that football provided. Betting occurred in at least two matches and virtually every fixture had stakes or prizes, ranging from gold medals to barrels of wine. On six occasions the stakes were clearly sociable – the teams dining together afterwards with the losers paying. More usually, the stakes were for money, as this table shows.

Sums	£1	£2	£3	£5	£10	£20	£25	£50
	1	1	1	6	5	3	2	1

It seems likely that this engine created a climate in which efforts were made to ensure the enforcement of agreed rules. These were far more sophisticated than has been generally understood, quite refuting those who portray it as lawless.[32] Every single one of the 30 ordinary matches detailed for the period between 1835 and 1859 was contested by fixed, equal sides. These break down as follows:

Numbers a side												
1	2	3	4	6	8	10	11	12	15	20	22	24	30
1	1	1	1	2	3	3	4	6	2	4	1	1	1

By co-ordinating the various match reports with accounts provided by nineteenth-century writers on recreation, the rules of some of the football games that were played outside the public schools before 1860 can be uncovered. Of the 68 teams listed only Forest and Liverpool derived their rules from public school influence. For the rest, the situation is unclear. However, there are six reasons for assuming, at least in the case of those sides formed before 1850, that they were not derived from public school influences.

Firstly, there are a number of examples prior to the nineteenth century, and from geographically diffuse areas, of football matches conducted by teams consisting of even sides: Durham (1683), Lancashire (1755), Suffolk (1759) and Surrey (1790s). Secondly, as noted earlier, before 1850 both the extent and the level of organisation of the football in public schools is unclear. Thirdly, during the first half of the nineteenth century there is little evidence of interaction between different social classes in sport. Consequently, it is unlikely that the public school game was transmitted to outsiders. Fourthly, the various match reports describe games similar to those found in the accounts of antiquarians relating to parish football, which long preceded the public school varieties. Fifthly, the vocabulary of football terms is devoid of such public school phrases as 'rouge' and 'bully', containing instead local colloquialisms, notably 'hail', 'bye', 'headland'. Finally, there are only two of the early football teams for which we possess substantial information, Surrey and Sheffield. In both cases we have strong reasons for believing that their games were derived independently of any public school influence.[33]

It is clear that rules were very important and before commencing a match teams would agree details. In some cases these negotiations would result in contracts being signed by representatives of both sides, concerning the length of pitch, size of goals and such like, as occurred in Warwickshire and Hampshire. Of an altogether different order were the rules created by the Surrey Football Club in 1849. These consisted of six laws and were the very first example of a non-public school team the issuing a code. The first three points concern the administration of the club but the rest are worth citing because they show that basic laws were being outlined. Naturally, as with early public school codes, no attempt was made to give a comprehensive exposition of the game, such knowledge being assumed. There are two reasons for rejecting any public school involvement in this venture. Firstly, it is clear that at the initial meeting of the club the chairman, William Denison, was referring to a detailed record of the history of football in Surrey, devoting the bulk of his speech to the deeds of the Gymnastic Society, a club that disbanded in the 1790s. Denison advocates a 'revival' of the game, and it seems likely that this historical record provided the source for the rules that he sets out, particularly as Surrey advocated matches involving 22 players a side, precisely the same number used by the Gymnastic society. Secondly, the Surrey club's rules were 'drawn up by Denison'. An examination of public school registers showed that Denison was never a pupil at either Charterhouse, Eton, Harrow, Rugby, Westminster or Winchester.

Rules of Surrey Football Club

4. That the side shall consist of not more than twenty-two each, but if less than to be arranged by those present.

5. Wilful kicking shall not be allowed.

6. Ball shall be tossed up in centre of the ground, and the game be determined in favour of that side which shall first kick the ball over 'goal rope' of their opponents. Should the ball be kicked over the fence on either side of the ground, then the ball, when

regained, shall be tossed up in the centre of the ground, in a line with the place where it went out.[34]

Referees were used extensively in football games. The football-style game, camping, was commenced by a neutral man throwing the ball up. Beyond this he had no further role. By contrast, even the supposedly lawless street football at Derby and the Shrove-match at Scone used to have 'men of both sides attend to see fair play'. These cases long precede the first employment of officials to supervise football rules in public schools, which occurred at Eton in 1845. Although P. Young claimed that this was an important innovation, it had been anticipated three years earlier, in 1842, in a match between two Rochdale teams, The Bodyguards and Fearnoughts, where the umpire's role was startling, as the following quote reveals: 'one of the Bodyguards (being tired) putting another person not connected with the game to kick for him, and their own umpire declaring it foul play according to the rules agreed to by both parties, decided the game'. The umpire had declared that his own team had broken the rules and thus awarded victory to the other side. Four years later, at Ashton Under Lyne, the level of sophistication had developed still further, referees and umpires officiated who were unrelated to either team. By the early 1850s the use of referees and umpires was common place in Edinburgh.[35]

There were basically four types of goal that were used in football games:

1. Objects. Shrove-type games would often utilise some landmark as a goal, such as a church.

2. Two markers in the ground. In many games these were indicated by simple symbols such as the discarded clothes of the players. In 1801 Strutt described two stakes in the ground, two or three feet apart.

3. Two posts linked by a crossbar indicating the goal's height. Our most accurate idea of goal size comes from Warwickshire in 1842: ten feet wide and six feet high. At Surrey FC a goal was scored by kicking the ball over a rope.

4. A piece of ground. This was widely used in both England, where it was referred to as the 'boundary' or 'bounds', and Scotland, 'the hailing point' or 'hail'. They were situated in the two far corners of the pitch, diagonally opposite one another. They would sometimes be

indicated by flags but were often simply imaginary lines. The object was to get the ball beyond this area. This was the only type of goal in Scotland until the 1850s and was widely used throughout England until at least 1856.

Information on the length of pitches varies enormously, probably due to the numbers of players involved and the type of game played. In the game camping, which was predominantly played with the hands, pitches were between 150 and 200 yards long. Our two most detailed reports of football matches, from Deanston and Hampton-in-Arden, display a similar ratio of playing area to number of competitors; 20 a side on a 620 yard pitch, six a side on a 200 yard pitch. The most common figure, related in three general accounts that were independent of one another, was 100 yards. We have very little information concerning the width of pitches and it is probably safe to assume that generally, as in Scotland, such boundaries as there were stemmed from natural obstacles. At Surrey FC touchlines were defined by fences running along either side of the pitch.[36]

The aim of footballers was to score a goal, also known as a 'game' or 'hail'. Usually matches defined the amount of goals required for victory, with no limitation on time. There were a variety of agreed objectives, ranging from the scoring of a single goal, up to 11. The most common, occurring on eight occasions, was for matches for the best of three, the team scoring two goals first winning. Having no fixed time limit, their length varied widely. The quickest was about three hours but some were six or eight hours. Occasionally, as at Lancashire in 1846, a strict time limit was employed, the rules specifying that the team with the most goals was then the winner. In the early 1850s at Edinburgh, matches were played with twin objectives. The victor would be the first team to score three goals, or should that not be achieved, the side with the most goals at the end of the three-hour match.[37]

There were three different ways of starting the game:

1. A place kick from the middle of the pitch by one of the teams. Stonehenge's account states that 'ball is then placed on the ground and the captain gives the first kick towards the opponents bounds'.

2. The ball was placed in the centre and at a given signal both teams, separated by an equal distance, raced for it. This was recorded three times, the last occasion being in 1862.

3. The ball was thrown up in the middle by a neutral person, usually the referee, between the teams, which were an equal distance apart: this was common in variants such as camping or hard ball, and was also found as late as 1849 in football games.[38]

There was certainly more handling than one would see today in soccer, but the emphasis was on kicking rather than throwing the ball, though as Stonehenge's account makes clear, players could do either. Cartwright believed that the practice of running holding the ball was a later development and in some games, such as that at Scone, it was compulsory. The football-variant game, camping, was occasionally played with a football, and involved a great deal of running with the ball. In many Scottish football games, a player making a 'fair catch', that is catching the ball before it touched the ground, was entitled to a 'free kick'. No one was allowed to interfere with this until he had struck the ball. Such rules appear to have been used by both sides in a match held in Edinburgh in 1851 between English and Scottish students belonging to the local football club. The component of handling in the football games played in Scotland expanded, generally, as the century wore on. This was due, principally, to the spread of rugby, a game that was first taken up by the Edinburgh Academy in 1851, and relied heavily on players who had 'learnt the drop kick in England'.[39]

Historians often emphasise the violence of popular football, yet on only three occasions, all from traditional Shrove games, was there evidence of sustained animosity.[40] More usually, as at Wigton in 1830, the atmosphere was convivial. Shrove games could also be full of tactics, as a report from Derby in 1827 made clear. Throughout the entire period there were only two examples of ordinary matches containing gratuitous violence. The first ever football club, the Gymnastics Society, pursued football and wrestling. The latter sport was certainly a part of some football games and between 1789 and 1858 was recorded in a number of diverse geographical locations. Commentators rarely considered this as brutal and bruised shins were regarded, almost universally, as the only real difficulty. There appears to have been very little animosity and teams often dined together afterwards. Skill was the main element in football as many reports made quite clear. Teams might play 'toughly', but were 'outmanœuvred' by their 'more scientific opponents'. In Scotland, 'hacking and collaring' were unknown and the game described as 'less hazardous than shinty'. Just ten years earlier an Old Etonian had assessed his school's game as being more violent than hockey. There is certainly no reason for believing that football in public schools was any less violent or more scientific than the popularly played version in the years before 1860.

This essay will now examine the first major football culture that emerged outside the public schools for which there is detailed information, that of Sheffield.[41] From at least 1831 organised football matches were played in Sheffield's Hyde Park. In 1855 a group began playing a variety of sports, including football, in the Sheffield area. Football was quite informal, there was no limit as to time to be played, or numbers of players on each side. There were no crossbars to the goals, and these goals were as wide as the sides agreed on. In 1857 these players decided to create a club, issuing a code of rules in October 1858. The origin of these laws has been a matter of dispute, the competing interpretations stemming from the various histories of the club provided by some of the early members as part of the jubilee celebrations of 1907. There are two histories in the club's archive and it is apparent that they were never completed. Even those in typescript are covered in handwritten revisions and the documents contain a number of significant factual errors. They are also mutually contradictory, resulting in four different explanations concerning the origin of the club's laws.

Two views regard them as stemming from codes that were learnt by the members before the club was formed. One maintains that the members were old public school boys and that the club's laws were an amalgam of their experiences. The other view was that the bulk of the team comprised former pupils of the Sheffield Collegiate School who had been taught a brand of public school football by a master who had himself been to public school. Both suggestions can be dismissed. Only one of the club's initial 57 members had been to public school. While 17 players hailed from the Collegiate school, an institution that could provide 'pleasure grounds of three broad acres' in which to play, only one teacher in the relevant period, Reverend Sandford, had belonged to a public school. He had left Shrewsbury in 1836, a time long before its football had become standardised, and there is no indication of any sporting ability on his part.

The other two views regard the rules as the creation of a club committee. In one account, they were derived by a careful study of various public school codes, from which the best rules were selected. The other makes no mention of this, simply describing the laws as 'half rugby and half association'.[42] A speech given in 1907, at the club's jubilee dinner, by its chief founder, N. Creswick, provides an interesting insight into the origin of the club's laws. He stated that when the club was set up on a permanent footing it was decided to write to all the leading public schools requesting copies of their codes. He was sarcastic concerning the result, declaring 'and a lot of different rules they obtained'. He then laughed and, after ridiculing one of the rules he received, went on to describe the type of game played by the club in its first few years of existence. It was very basic, 'there being no limit as to players or time', suggesting that nothing had changed.[43] Nowhere does he state that the various public school codes were studied. On the contrary, the impression which he gives is that they were unintelligible to him. As we saw earlier, such an experience was pervasive among those outsiders who endeavoured to understand public school codes. It appears likely that the Sheffield committee was unable to derive much assistance from the various public school laws and that the first set of laws were principally of local origin. They appeared in writing on 21 October 1858 and were as follows:

1. Kick off from the middle must be a place kick.

2. Kick out must not be from more than twenty-five yards out of goal.

3. Fair catch is a catch direct from the foot of the opposite side and entitles a free kick.

4. Charging is fair in case of a place kick with the exception of kick off as soon as player offer to kick, but may always draw back unless he has actually touched the ball with his foot.

5. No pushing with the hands or hacking, or tripping up is fair under any circumstances whatsoever.

6. Knocking or pushing on the ball is altogether disallowed. The side breaking the rule forfeits a free kick to the opposite side.

7. No player may be held or pulled over.

8. It is not lawful to take the ball off the ground, except in touch, for any purpose whatsoever.

9. If the ball be bouncing it may be stopped by the hand, not pushed or hit, but if rolling it may not be stopped except by the foot.

10. No goal may be kicked from touch, nor by free kick from a fair catch.

11. A ball in touch is dead. Consequently the side that touches it down, must bring it to the edge of touch, and throw it straight out at least five yards from touch.

It may be noted that laws 3, 5, 6, 9 and 10 had parts of them crossed out and were amended at the meeting, laws 6 and 9 being struck out altogether. The resulting product became the first printed code of the Sheffield FC.[44]

Only three of the laws, 3, 4 and 7, have been linked to any public school model.[45] Far more striking than these tenuous suggestions was the absence of any offside rule. This was a fundamental in all public school games and a crucial element distinguishing them from those played outside. Not only that, Sheffield's sixth law, punishing illegal play with a free kick, was completely unknown in any public school code. In fact, though the evidence only offers a very fragmentary insight into the rules used by the various popularly played football games, the code produced at Sheffield in 1858 resembles them far more closely than any supposed public school model. The game played at Glasgow College, from 1820 until 1870, had rules resembling those of 3,4,5,6 and 7. The code created by Surrey FC in 1849 laws 5 and 11. Rules 3 and 8 might have been anticipated by those used at Edinburgh University FC. Rule 1 was referred to in Stonehenge's account from 1856, and rule 6 in the earlier cited game from Rochdale in 1842. In essence, only laws 2 and 10 lack any popularly played prototype, and no one has claimed a public school derivation for either.

In the years before the formation of Sheffield FC there were at least ten teams and three schools playing football in Yorkshire. During this period an association-type game was played at another Yorkshire institution with a similar middle-class intake, Richmond Grammar School, despite the fact that the master in charge of football was Tate, a noted Old Rugbeian. It may well be that the boys at Sheffield Collegiate played a game similar to those existing elsewhere and used it as the basis for the very rudimentary code they established in 1858. They clearly regarded it as a first step and made persistent adjustments. As their understanding of the various public school games increased they began to introduce refinements, with committees, such as that set up in 1859, developing their own code. By 1860 the idea of 'rouge's' had been borrowed from the Eton game. These were expansions of four yards on either side of the goal which provided an additional mode of scoring. Far from being a slavish adherence to a public school model, this was adopted in response to a particular problem, the proliferation of goalless draws due to the fact that Sheffield's goals were only four yards wide. In 1862 a series of meetings discussing the club's laws resulted in the production of a detailed code which they referred to as 'The Sheffield Rules', declaring that these would be the only ones they would use. Soon this code was adopted throughout the area, though adaptations and revisions were made on a regular basis in order to accommodate emerging problems and iron 'defects' out. Sheffield's rules were a code created by committees responding to a variety of influences, of which the public schools appear to have been a relatively minor component. In 1867 the Sheffield Football Association was formed: it had more clubs and players than the FA.[46]

Arguments claiming the paternity of the public schools for modern football rest on the assumption that they were primarily responsible for providing the game with an organised set of rules. As we have seen, there is substantial evidence that quite sophisticated rules, including the use of referees, were being utilised outside of the public schools long before 1860. Similarly, both Surrey and Sheffield football clubs produced written codes. Public school football became organised far later than has been generally believed and the codes which they produced were almost completely inaccessible to those outside and therefore of limited use. The result was that the general public confronted a bewildering spectrum of football games belonging to prestigious bodies that were jealous of their own status. Whilst the intricacies of these codes were not understood, their existence fragmented the game, preventing it developing at an organised level. In fact, as late as 1862, an attempt by Thring to establish a simple, national code, failed for this reason.[47] The fragmenting effect that the public school models had on football can be clearly seen. Only two non-public school clubs were able to emerge before 1860, at Surrey and Sheffield, both growing out of organisations established for other sports. In the period after 1870 football enjoyed an astonishingly rapid growth, demonstrating that the public had an immense appetite for the game. This receptivity was surely present but was impeded by the lack of uniform rules. It required the substantial press attention of the 1860s to fuse this sentiment into the creation of clubs.

The movement that led to the creation of the FA stemmed, principally, from the London press, especially *The Times*. The FA's early meetings attracted few delegates – the public schools, either implicitly or overtly, refused to co-operate – and the resulting laws were regarded as poor and soon scrapped, replaced by those just created at Cambridge

University Football Club. These were printed and made available to the public cheaply, though their adoption brought about a schism in the FA, which eventually induced those who favoured a rugby-style game to leave. Despite the fact that most of the creators of the Cambridge rules were 'old boys', the FA's code gained few adherents in the public schools. An editorial in *The Field* confessed that the FA had solved nothing and there were many appeals over the next few years for the public schools and universities to take a lead. Few clubs adopted the FA's code, many, such as Lincoln and Louth, rejecting them after a season as unsatisfactory. Generally, the provinces seem to have gone their own way, a match such as that in 1865 between Sheffield and Nottingham, in which neither understood the other's code, being typical. By 1867 the FA's membership had shrunk to just ten clubs and public school hostility was regarded as so disruptive that some observers urged the FA to adopt one of the most popular public school codes as their own in an effort to standardise rules.[48]

Given the obstructive attitude of the public schools towards the FA, it is ironic that they have been credited with the creation of modern football. The code adopted by the FA in 1863 owed a great deal to both public school laws and former public school boys. However, it was not a success. The FA only became a significant national force with the accession of new teams, especially from the provinces. Dialogue with these clubs resulted in a virtual transformation of the code, there being 12 significant changes in the rules between 1863 and 1870, eight of these stemming from the Sheffield area. Of 16 public schools, only Charterhouse and Westminster joined the FA, and although old boys, notably the old Harrovian C.W. Alcock, played an important role on the committee, contemporaries regarded the conscious opposition of Eton, Harrow and Rugby as impeding the code's acceptance.[49]

It is unlikely that the various popularly played football games discussed above bore a significant resemblance to what we now know as Association football. What is clear, however, is that many, if not all of the elements that were to constitute the modern game, such as equal sides, restrictions on the level of violence, use of referees, goal size and such like, were present. The only important exception was the offside law. However, popular football introduced an idea unknown in public school games: punishment for infringing rules. Of course, the various football games conducted outside the public schools were essentially local and lacked the national organisations that were eventually established to administer both rugby and Association football. However, as we shall see, even in the 1860s both of these games, despite the involvement of influential former public school boys, were in a largely embryonic condition.

The process of segregating what came to be known as rugby from Association football was much slower than has been generally appreciated. As we have seen, elements that were later to be distinctive constituents of either rugby or Association football often existed side-by-side in games both inside and outside public schools. Until the 1860s it would be anachronistic to distinguish between the Association and rugby varieties of the game because contemporaries, even at Rugby School, referred to them as 'football'.[50] The first major attempt to define and create what later came to be known as Association occurred at one of the early meetings of the FA in 1863. There, attempts were made to exclude hacking, an important element of rugby-type games. This prompted protests from Blackheath's delegate and in response to this the issue was left in abeyance, Blackheath remaining in the FA. In January 1864 a game was conducted under the FA's auspices which permitted both catching and running holding the ball. For the next few years it was common for clubs, such as Lincoln and Colchester, to use a mixture of Association and rugby rules. Instructively, early in 1867 there was a match between the FA and the Sheffield FA, in which the latter objected to the amount of hacking by the Southern players.[51] Clearly, as late as 1867 the Association game contained elements that would come to be regarded as distinctively belonging to rugby. The establishment of a single code regulating Association football was a long process and even in 1873 of the 110 clubs that were recorded as playing Association football, 39, that is over a third, did not use the FA's code.[52]

Unlike Association football, rugby remained much closer to its public school laws. However, significant changes did occur, particularly relating to the levels of acceptable violence. In Rugby School there were many disputes about the interpretation of fundamental rules until at least the 1860s. Such difficulties were compounded in matches between schools playing rugby football, culminating in a match of legendary violence between Clifton and Marlborough in 1864.[53]

As the above has demonstrated, the rules governing both the Association and rugby varieties of football required significant development in the 1860s. Evidence indicates that the major influence on rugby stemmed from the public schools. With regard to the

Association game, however, it is difficult to assess precisely the public schools' contribution. While persistently nourishing divisions, they also produced some useful laws. However, as we have seen, there is considerable evidence that football was conducted in the wider society between 1830 and 1860 according to rules that were similar in terms of their sophistication to those found in public schools. The example of Sheffield demonstrates that a rationalised football culture could develop without significant public school involvement. Evidence suggests that the existence of a number of public school codes may well have impeded the wider creation of more organised non-public school clubs. In turn, as was clearly apparent in the early stages of the FA, public school laws obstructed the development of a national code. It is therefore possible that football might have developed a national code before 1863 had there been a complete vacuum in terms of codified rules. It is certainly the case that after 1863 it was predominantly an essentially non-public school influence that created and established what came later to be known as association football.

The notion that in the years after 1850 traditional recreation was transformed into modern sport by the imposition of rational laws is a popular one.[54] In the case of football, as we have seen, it is highly inaccurate. The 'civilising process' experienced by popular football was very slight because the game was essentially skilful. Thus, the transition between the 'traditional' and 'modern' game has been exaggerated. The construction of a national code involved the neutralising of rivals rather than the introduction of 'civilised' modes of playing. As regards football, the public schools were one of a number of influences in the creation of the modern game – a game that would have developed as a rationalised sport in the latter half of the nineteenth century had there been no pubic school model whatsoever.

Finally, what the development of nineteenth-century football illustrates is the polyphylenic nature of the growth of modern sport and the complexity of the processes of continuity and change in this growth. At times both existed in parallel, at times both overlapped, both experienced accretions at different moments at different places, on occasion they were held in initial balance, on other occasions one diminished while the other expanded. Recent requests for greater sophistication of analysis in the study of the growth of modern sport can only gain from this analysis of the real story of the evolution of modern British football.

NOTES

I would like to thank Dr John Goldthorpe (Nuffield College) and Dr John Stevenson (Worcester College) for their advice on this study.

1. C. Alcock, 'Association Football' *English Illustrated Magazine* Vol.8 (1890–91), 282.
2. E. Dunning and K. Sheard, *Barbarians, Gentlemen and Players* (London, 1979), pp.30, 33–4.
3. R. Holt, *Sport and the British: A Modern History* (Oxford, 1989), p.40. F. Magouin, *History of Football* (Bochum-Langendreer, 1938), pp.70–1, 96. A. Mason, *Association Football and British Society 1863–1915* (London, 1980), p.10.
4. A. Mason, p.14. P. Young, *A History of British Football* (London, 1968), p.62.
5. J.A. Mangan, *Athleticism in the Victorian and Edwardian Public School: The Emergence and Consolidation of an Educational Ideology* (Cambridge, 1981), pp.22, 28, 34.
6. H. Cunningham, *Leisure in the Industrial Revolution 1780–1880* (London, 1980), p.127.
7. A. Mason, p.22. R.Holt, p.84. J.Walvin, *The People's Game* (London, 1975), p.40.
8. D. Reid, 'Folk football, the aristocracy and culture change: A critique of Dunning and Sheard', *International Journal of the History of Sport*, 5, 2 (1988), 230.
9. Magouin, p.149.
10. Magouin, pp.134–5.
11. W. Andrews *Old Church Lore* (Hull, 1891), p.96. *Annals of Sporting and Fancy Gazette*, July 1825, 57. B. Barton, *History of the Borough of Bury and its Neighbourhood in the County of Lancashire* (Bury, 1874), p.41. *Bell's Life In London*, 26 Feb. 1826; 7 March 1830; 30 Jan. 1831; 7 Sept. 1834; 28 Aug. 1836; 4 Feb. 1838; 22 Aug. 1841; 14 Jan. 1849. *RC. on Children in Mines and Manufactories, 1st Report* (PP 1842, xv, 123. *Devon And Cornwall Notes And Queries*, Vol.10 (1918–19), 113. A. Hine *A History of Hitchin* (London, 1929), p.266. H. Kendall Phillips, in R. Cashman and M. McKernan (eds.), *Sport, Money, Morality and the Media* (New South Wales, 1980), p.289. Magouin, pp.69–70. *Manchester Examiner and Times*, 1 June 1850. *Manchester Mercury*, 11 Nov.1800. *New Statistical Account of Scotland* (1845) Vol.3 ,pp.87, 324, Vol.10, pp.268–9. *Notes and Queries* (Jan./June 1904), 331. *Reliquary*, 9 (1868), 93–96, 252. *The Sporting Magazine* (May 1802), 77,114; (June 1815), 138; (Jan.1816), 244; (July 1831), 171.
12. *Report From The Select Committee On Public Walks* (1833), pp.391 393.
13. A. Fabian and G. Green (eds.), *Association Football*, Vol.1 (London, 1960), p.139. Walvin, p.29.
14. *Eton College Magazine* Vol.7 (1832), 283. A.J. Lawrence *The Origins of Rugby Football* (Rugby, 1897). *Westminster School, Town Boy Ledger 1815–62* (Westminster School archive) I am grateful to the following people for their help concerning public school football: S. Bailey (Winchester), J. Field (Westminster), P. Hatfield (Eton), A. Hawkyard (Harrow).
15. *Bell's Life in London*, 2 April 1854, 30 Nov. 1856, 31 Oct. 1858.
16. *Bell's Life in London*, 2 April 1854, 7 Sept. 1856, 9 March 1862. *Field*, 14, 21 Dec. 1861; 10 Oct. 1863. *Football Records of Rugby School 1823–1929* Rugby (1930), p.21.
17. *Bell's* 16, 23 Jan.1859; 5 Nov. 1864. *Field*, 14 Nov. 1863.
18. Holt, pp.137–9. Mason, pp.14–15. Walvin, p.44.
19. T. Arnold, *Windsor Magazine* (Dec.1901/May 1902), 656–7. *Field*, 17 Sept.1864, 1 April 1865. Mason, 24. N. Jackson, *Sporting Days and Sporting Ways* (London, 1932), pp.21–2. P. Young, *Bolton Wanderers* (London, 1961), pp.14, 18.
20. Cunningham; Mason, pp.26, 30, 33; Walvin, p.46.
21. *Athenaeum Gazette*, 19 Oct. 1849. *Bell's*, 25 March 1838; 13 Jan., 31 March 1839; 11, 25 April; 5, 12, 26 Dec.1841; 2 Jan., 25 Sept., 2, 23 Oct, 28 Nov, 25 Dec. 1842; 12, 26 Feb., 7 May, 31 Dec. 1843. 15 Dec. 1844. 26 Jan., 2 Feb., 21 Dec. 1845. 8 Feb., 21 Dec. 1846. 26 Dec. 1847. 4 March, 22 April, 7 Oct. 1849. 2 Feb., 9 March, April 6 1851.11 Jan., 29 Feb., 21, 28 March 1852. 31 Jan. 1858. *Field*, 26 Feb. 1859. Holt, p.43. *Stirling Journal*, 6 Nov. 1835.
22. *Athenaeum Gazette*, 19 Oct. 1849. *Bell's*, 7 Oct. 1849, 9 March 1851, 31 Jan. 1858. *Field*, 26 Feb. 1859. *Manchester Examiner and Times*, 29 Dec. 1849.
23. *Bell's*, 13 Nov. 1842; 26 Feb., 7 May 1843; 21 Dec. 1845; 8 Feb. 1846; 4 March 1849; 29 Feb.1852.
24. *Bell's*, 5 Dec. 1841.
25. *Bell's*, 31 March 1839; 5, 26 Dec. 1841; 20 Nov. 1842; 8 Feb. 1846.

26. Walvin, pp.26–7.
27. *Bell's*, 13 Jan. 1839; 11, 25 April 1841; 15 Dec. 1844; 21 Dec.1845. *Stirling Journal*, 6 Nov. 1835.
28. *Bell's*, 25 Nov., 2 Dec. 1855; 16 Oct., 16 Nov., 23 Nov., 21 Dec. 1856; 8 Nov. 1857.
29. *Bell's*, 16 Feb. 1851; 23 Nov. 1856; 30 Oct. 1859. *Northern Examiner*, 3 March 1855.
30. *Bell's*, 12 Dec. 1841; 2 Jan., 20 Nov. 1842; 26 Feb., 7 May 1843; 31 March 1844; 4 March 1849. *Manchester and Salford Advertiser*, 24 April 1841.
31. *Bell's*, 29 Feb. 1852.
32. E. Dunning and K. Sheard.
33. *Bell's*, 13 Jan. 1839; 2 Jan. 1842, 13 Nov. 1842; 9 March 1851. *Chambers Journal*, 84 (1842), 544. A. Harvey, 'The Evolution of Modern British Sporting Culture 1793–1850' (D.Phil, Oxford, 1995), pp.396–7. *Ipswich Journal*, 19 Oct. 1754. John Johnson Collection, Box 7, Sports (Bodleian Library, Oxford). Magouin, p.57. *Scottish National Dictionary* (Edinburgh, 1956), p.363. Stonehenge, *Manual of British Rural Sports* (London, 1856), p.499. *Stirling Journal*, 6 Nov. 1835. S. Williams *The Boys' Treasury of Sports, Pastimes and Recreations* (London, 1847), p.25.
34. *Bell's*, 7 Oct. 1849.
35. *Bell's*, 12 Dec. 1841. 2 Jan. 1842; 20 Dec. 1846; 9 March 1851. P. Young, p.67.
36. *Bell's*, 13 Jan. 1839; 2 Jan. 1842; 7 Oct. 1849. *Chambers Journal*. E. Moor, *Suffolk Words and Phrases* (London, 1823), p.64. D. Murray, *Memories of the Old College of Glasgow* (Glasgow, 1927), p.445. Stonehenge, *Manual*. J. Strutt, *Sports and Pastimes of the People of England* XII, p.92.
37. *Bell's*, 10 April 1825; 20 Dec. 1846; 22 April, 7 Oct. 1849; 2 Feb., 9 March, 6 April 1851. Murray, *Memories*, p.445.
38. *Bell's*, 13 Jan. 1839; 2 Jan. 1842. *Field*, 11 Jan. 1862. E. Moor, *Suffolk*, p.64. Stonehenge, *Manual*, p.499.
39. C. Alcock. *The Football Annual* (London, 1874), pp.65–100. *Bell's*, 9 March 1851; 24 Jan. 1858. *Field*, 24 Oct. 1863. W. Hone *The Everyday Book* Vol.1 (1827), p.259. E. Moor. D. Murray, p.444.
40. Dunning and Sheard, p.25.
41. *Bell's*, 13 Jan. 1839; 4 March 1841; 17 March 1844. *Chambers Journal*. *Derby Mercury*, 28 Feb. 1827. W. Hone, *The Everyday Book* Vol.1, p.259. Vol.2 (1827), p.374. D. Murray. G. Lyttleton, *Eton College Magazine*, Vol.7 (1832), 283. Stonehenge, *Manual*, p.499.
42. *Bell's*, 30 Jan.1831. *Football Club Records* (FCR1) in Sheffield City Archives. *The Sheffield Collegiate School* (London, 1852). F. Walters, *History of Sheffield Football Club* (Sheffield 1957).
43. *Sheffield Daily Telegraph*, 5 Nov. 1907.
44. FCR 2. FCR 10.
45. P.M.Young, *Football in Sheffield* (London, 1962), pp.17–18.
46. *Bell's*, 19 March 1854; 2 March 1867. *Field*, 26 Dec.1863; 9 Feb., 20 April 1867. *Sheffield and Rotherham Independent*, 15 Oct. 1859; 25 Jan., 10 Oct. 1862.
47. *Bell's*, 5 Oct., 16 Nov. 1862.
48. *Bell's*, 16 Nov. 1862; 31 Oct. 1863; 2 Jan.1864; 6 April 1865. J. Catton; *The Real Football* (London, 1900), p.16. *Field*, 29 Oct. 1864. *FA Minute Books 1863–1874*, 10,17, 24 Nov, 10 Dec. 1863. (Held at Lancaster Gate). *Sportsman*, 8 Oct., 2 Nov. 1867. *Times*, 5, 27 Oct. 1863.
49. *Bell's*, 23 Jan. 1864. A. Fabian and G. Green, *Association Football*, Vol.1 (London 1960), pp.151, 153. *Field*, 24 Feb. 1866, 2 March 1867. *FA Minute Book 1863–1874*, 24 Feb., 13 March 1866; 12 Feb. 1867. R. Graham, 'The Early History of the FA', *Badminton Magazine*, 8 (1899) 79, 82. G. West *Football Calendar* (London, 1876–7), p.32.
50. *Bell's*, 10 Oct. 1852.
51. *Bell's*, 12 Dec. 1863; 29 Dec. 1866. *Field*, 30 Jan., 29 Oct. 1864; 10 Feb. 1866; 12 Jan. 1867.
52. C. Alcock, *The Football Annual* (London, 1873).
53. *English Illustrated Magazine*, Vol.7 (1889–90) 432. *Field*, 24,31 Dec.1864. *Notes and Queries*, 10th Series Vol.11 (1909), 257–8, 315–6, 355.
54. See J.A. Mangan, 'Nordic Worlds and Other Worlds', in Henrik Meinander and J.A. Mangan (eds.), *The Nordic World: Sport in Society* (London 1998), passim.

'Touched Pitch and Been Shockingly Defiled': Football, Class, Social Darwinism and Decadence in England, 1880–1914

R.W. LEWIS

Association football is one of the most important sports in the world today, crossing nearly every form of national and racial boundary; indeed, it could be said to be 'the only global idiom apart from science'.[1] In its professional form, many millions watch the game every week, and it has come to symbolise much more than a mere recreation. The social and psychological significance of football, however, is not merely a modern phenomenon; the game first emerged as an arena for cultural struggle as it evolved from the 1860s onwards. Football was 're-invented' in the nineteenth-century English public-school system, changing from a traditional, unruly pastime to a sport with rules and organisation.

The fledgling English Football Association first met on 26 October 1863 in London, when a number of metropolitan and suburban clubs tried to unify the game by initiating consistent rules and a controlling authority. Once further local associations were formed in the 1860s and 1870s, the way was open for the rapid spread of the new codified game, especially with the establishment of the FA Cup in 1871–72. However, the early dominance of the public school-derived clubs ceased by the early 1880s, when northern and midlands clubs containing working-class players gained ascendancy. This was achieved by the introduction of professional players and 'importations' from other areas, chiefly Scotland. Professionalisation, at first clandestine, was openly legalised by 1885, and further strengthened by the foundation in 1888 of the Football League.[2]

Despite the rapid growth of professional football, the middle and upper classes did not surrender control of 'their' game without a struggle. Their resentment at working-class infiltration became apparent in writings on the subject, as did their detestation of playing for pay, the buying and selling of players, and the corruption of money generally, combined with the professional game's emphasis on spectatorship rather than participation. Of course, some of the privileged classes could, and did, reach a form of accommodation with professional football, as did some of the 'nouveaux-riches' middle classes who financed professional clubs. However, this essay will be concerned with the ideological opposition to professionalism, seeking to relate this to the wider concerns of these groups in the late Victorian/early Edwardian period. Some criticism of professional football is redolent of middle- and upper-class opinion on imperialism, Social Darwinism, economic individualism, class bias and snobbery, athleticism, 'degeneracy' and the like. It should be viewed as an aspect of the wider intellectual picture of the period, not merely confined to the side-galleries of sports history, with the unfairly pejorative connotations that implies.

A brief outline of a number of fields of intellectual debate should put this ideological struggle into context. Athleticism as a dominant creed in the English public-school system was established by reformist headmasters and teachers following on from Arnold's reforms at Rugby, including G.E.L. Cotton (Marlborough), Henry Walford (Lancing), Edward Thring (Uppingham) and H.H. Almond (Loretto). According to this philosophy, a game was played for its own sake, not for reward; no unfair advantage was to be taken, but within the rules no mercy should be expected; self should be subordinated to team effort; cowardice or surrender would not be tolerated. Such qualities of manliness and leadership would help pupils throughout their later lives. This became linked to the other main ideological thread running through the public schools, that of service to the Empire. Team games prepared boys to be men who would serve the imperial community and shoulder the 'white man's burden' with honour. Manliness on the football field could be used to advantage on the battlefield or in dealing with large numbers of unruly natives.[3]

Such imperialism was connected to the post-1850 infatuation with Darwin's theories of evolution, and in this context, their development into the sometimes distorted theories of 'Social Darwinism'. Social Darwinism developed mainly from the ideas of Herbert Spencer, some of which predated Darwin, having first been published in the *Westminster Review* in 1852. Spencer's principal use of Darwin was to defend competitive individualism and *laissez-faire* capitalism, the economic liberalism of the nineteenth century. The struggle for the 'survival of the fittest' enabled others to assert that training to be the fittest, whether by education or other means, had, therefore, an important role to play in the struggle of life. The 'unfit' should not be helped by the fit, since this could lead to 'degeneracy' of the race if the former were allowed to over-breed. August Comte's 'Social Physics', the study of the progress of civilisation through evolutionism, also contributed to the Social Darwinist canon. The combination of such ideas gave birth to Francis Galton's 'Eugenics' movement from the 1860s onwards; those who survived and prospered were nature's elect.

From this kind of philosophy, the two main themes imported into the public schools were the 'survival of the fittest', and the tendency of the evolutionary process towards a better state. This in turn led to a morality which often owed more to a secular morality governed by Social Darwinism than to 'Muscular Christianity'. Typical was H.H. Almond at Loretto, who practised a form of what J.A. Mangan has termed 'Spencerian functionalism', more like stoicism with Christian trappings. Harsh discipline and even bullying could be defended as preparing pupils for the struggle of life. Influenced by Social Darwinism and Eugenics, such a philosophy could be used to justify the superiority of the white race over others, and of the upper classes over the lower classes within Britain, and was effectively spread as an ideology throughout British society by the public schools and their agents.

These somewhat disparate elements fitted together rather well as a justifying ideology for the dominant forces in English society from around 1860 to 1914, and possibly after. They were given an additional boost by the 'fin-de-siècle' philosophy of the 1890s, the so-called 'degeneracy' of the times. Max Nordau's famous text on 'Degeneration' was published in England in 1895, and immediately linked with a number of feelings prevalent at the time concerning the slow decline and decay of society. It could be characterised by wide-ranging concerns over moral decline, the failure of marriage, the rise of agnosticism, the Aesthetic Movement, Oscar Wilde and the *Yellow Book*, the rights of women, and 'degeneracy' in art and literature as typified by Ibsen, Wagner, Tolstoy, Nietzsche and the French Impressionists amongst many other themes. Nordau was seen by critics to be part of that intellectual current as defined by Spencer, Comte, Krafft-Ebing, Morel, Charcot, Lombroso and others. Apart from Wilde, British writers condemned as 'decadent' included Arthur Symons, Walter Pater,

George Moore and Algernon Swinburne. As an antidote to such morbid indolence, what could be better than a manly team game played in a competitive spirit out in the open fields? The simplistic 'games ideology' was, however, linked with wider, intellectual criticism by its more intelligent proponents, yet ultimately it failed to dominate Association football, a team game which, along with cricket, had originally been the character-forming game *par excellence*.

What happened in Association football to make upper- and middle-class hegemony fail? One reason was that the middle classes, at least, were disunited. Some favoured accommodation with the new spirit of professionalism, as it appeared to them to make good economic sense, and it appealed to their burgeoning local pride, especially as civic rivalries became increasingly important in the later nineteenth century. Many others exclusively supported amateurism for the reasons given above. Tensions between amateurs and those advocating professionalism grew from the late 1870s onwards, the two sides reflecting conflicting ideologies. Arguments used to justify the advantages of athleticism included the use of football as one means of inculcating the Social-Darwinist view of the 'improvement' of mankind by exercise and moral training. These concerns were wide-ranging, and many were reflected in the ideological conflicts outlined above.[4] Let us examine in detail some of the issues involved.

The threatened split of the Football Association between amateur and professional interests in the 1880s was avoided, although some amateurs formed a breakaway Amateur Football Association from 1907 to 1914. Despite the increasing marginalisation of the amateurs, there was considerable sniping from the wings, particularly over the 'evils' of professionalism and the spread of the game to the working classes. Commentators writing for the 'gentleman's magazines' of the time were often highly critical of these developments for a number of reasons, although not all 'gentlemen' were completely opposed to professionalism. Did this form part of the struggle over the control of the game? Analysis of a number of articles illustrates such criticism, as do the replies on behalf of professionalism. An attempt will be made to put this into context. Lancashire being the originator of professionalism, most of these replies have been taken from the local press. Eric Dunning and other Eliasian sociologists make use of the criticism of professionalism to prove the supposed high incidence of crowd trouble and 'football hooliganism' before 1914. It will be argued that this is a misreading of the true intentions of these critics, and an over-simplification of their arguments. In essence, the debate ranged far wider than mere concern for supposed hooligan crowd behaviour, involving a number of important issues.[5]

However, it is necessary at the outset to outline the Dunning argument to illustrate its defects. Maguire compares different 'images of manliness' of various classes, concluding that these represented 'competing ways of living' in the period 1880–1914. Dunning and he contrast the public schools where 'more civilised conceptions of violence control and manly conduct were emerging', finding expression in the newly codified football games of the 1860s. Reformed football was then seen as 'rational recreation' and recommended by reforming elements. However, we are told, this is not what the working classes identified with; they went for 'the continued stress on masculinity, group loyalty and ruggedness', at variance with the gentlemanly ideals of chivalry and fair play. According to this argument, the middle and upper classes had become involved in reformed versions of what had been originally rough working-class games, only to retreat from them because of increasing class conflict and fear of the latent power of the working classes from 1880 onwards, hence their criticism of professionalism and working-class involvement. Comments on the crowd supposedly show middle- and upper-class concern about 'hooligan behaviour'. Is this a true reflection of the period?

Contemporary writers' concerns can be described more accurately as follows:

1. The physical aspect of football was lost by the emphasis placed on spectatorship rather than participation. This was linked to the late nineteenth- and early twentieth-century anxiety over the physical condition of the nation.

2. There was concern over the corrupting influence of money, which was thought to be 'immoral', undermining the ideals of amateurism, and promoting a win-at-all-costs attitude.

3. Unsportsmanlike attitudes were felt to be invading the game due to professionalism. Even Cups and medals were felt to sustain the idea that winning, not merely taking part, was the aim of matches.

4. The loss of control of the FA to the representatives of professionalism was anathema to men who felt that only amateur

players should control the game; preoccupation with money was felt to impose a different agenda.

5. An attitude of class bias, sometimes conscious, sometimes unconscious, was displayed, typified by the 'man–master' relationship. Public school men resented the take-over of 'their' game by the masses.

6. Spectatorship and 'partisanship' were criticised, as were biased crowds who only wanted to watch their side win.

It is proposed to deal with each of these in turn.

THE PHYSICAL CONDITION OF THE NATION

H.F. Abell, a 'traveller and sketcher' in an article on 'Football Fever' in 1904, thought that 'a hearty, wholesome national pastime' had degenerated into 'an indirect source of national danger'; the danger was, however, not from football hooligans, but from poor physical specimens who would not provide good workers or soldiers. Spectatorship was passive rather than active, and fear of war meant 'there was so much necessity for solving this problem of the improvement of physique of the class upon which we shall have to rely so largely in the hour of need'; if spectatorship were not curtailed, the country would be 'sowing the seeds of such a crop of weeds as ... the future will be unable to eradicate'. There are hints here of Social Darwinism and eugenics, as in other writers.[6]

H.H. Almond, headmaster of Loretto, had very similar concerns in 1893. He stated, 'Recreations may have very far-reaching effects on national character', but physical degeneracy meant the emphasis had to be placed on active involvement, even though he did acknowledge that manual workers would appreciate the open air and excitement of a football match even if they were not participating. An anonymous article on 'Sport and Decadence' in 1909 boldly stated: 'Race suicide is possible ... it may be brought about by popular tendencies towards effeminacy and self-indulgence.' Typical symptoms of national decline included being unwilling or incapable of defending one's country or providing for its own needs, or 'to indulge in recreation except vicariously'. G.B. Pollock Hodsall, the Corinthian footballer, felt in 1907 that 'the 'gates consist mostly of young men ... the majority of whom might ... be walking, cycling, or possibly even rifle shooting, and so qualifying themselves to perform some modicum of duty towards their country'. Robert J. Sturdee, a divine, was particularly concerned in 1903 with military considerations: 'Anything that will strengthen the physique of a nation is worthy of strong support.' He also felt that 'the efficacy of a sport is destroyed when it degenerates into a mere spectacular performance', although he also had some sympathy with working men predominantly involved in physical labour.[7]

H. MacFarlane, a general journalist writing in 1906, echoed these concerns, quoting Admiral Charles Beresford on football: 'Anything which makes men get into condition is for the good of the nation.' Lord Baden-Powell, an Old Carthusian, displayed the most extreme form of this attitude: 'Five million Englishmen paying to look on reminds me forcibly of the Ancient Romans who got into the way of paying other people to play their games for them and eventually fighting their battles for them,' equating the growth of football spectatorship with the fall of the Roman Empire. MacFarlane dissociated himself from such extremes, but had some sympathy with this attitude.[8] Clearly such views reflect concerns with the physical condition of the male population, fears of racial degeneracy and decadence, and external threats of possible war, all significant issues in the 1890s and 1900s, rather than concerns about increasing class conflict or football hooliganism.

The Lancashire response reflects the indignation felt against writers who were generally ignorant of the professional game and distorted certain features of it to prove a political or intellectual point. 'A London Monthly' quoted in the *Football Field* (Bolton) in 1899 criticised spectators in a similar manner: 'There you have twenty-two fellows getting all the exercise and ten thousand foolish youths hanging around, betting on the result … and going off to spend the evening on the streets and in the gin palaces'. *Football Field* felt this was 'positively untrue', since 'visitors to football matches are as sober and well-behaved as any other class of men, and they should not be libelled in this reckless manner'.

An attack on the 'Ethics of Football' quoted above stated: 'There is much more play than these critics are aware of. There is hardly a bit of spare land anywhere that is not used as a football ground … like other ill-informed critics, Mr Ethics bolsters up his weak arguments by trotting out the gambling bogey', even though there was very little evidence of betting on grounds by 1903.[9] Amateur football was strong in areas of professionalism, albeit in works, pub, or church teams, so this criticism was incorrect; perhaps it was because such amateurism was not of the public school type.

Similarly, 'Olympian' in the *Football Field* attacked Abell, this time writing in *Blackwood's Magazine* in 1904, 'the most Imperialist of all the magazines'. Abell's account was said to display 'bigotry', was 'exaggerated', and attacked non-existent 'evils', with 'not a shred of sympathy for a pastime that attracts tens of thousands'. In the same year another exaggerated account was criticised: I. Maclaren of Liverpool at the Annual Meeting of the Evangelical Free Churches ranted about 'undersized and white-faced creatures' watching 'hirelings playing to win money for the spectators who will riot like savages if they be disappointed'. It is a distortion for Dunning and his sympathisers to describe such accounts as accurate, objective descriptions of professional football.[31] We must accept them as criticisms based much more on militaristic or Social Darwinist opinions.

THE 'CORRUPTING INFLUENCE' OF MONEY
AND PROFESSIONALISM

Nineteenth-century critics were also deeply concerned about the taint of money on a game which they believed should be strictly amateur for 'moral' reasons: 'During the past thirty years football has changed – degraded some of us would say – from a pastime into an industry'; 'money, they say, is the root of all evil, and without asserting that professional football is an evil, its origin may be safely ascribed to money'; 'what was ten or fifteen years ago the recreation of a few has now become the pursuit of thousands ... there are many old football fogies who recall ... the days when football had not grown to be so important as to make umpires necessary and the "gate" the first object of consideration'. W.E. Hodgson, a journalist writing in 1891, stated: 'The recreations of the British people have become subject to [an] evil ... leaven ... Football is now as sordid a concern of commerce as Pears' Soap ... All the teams strive after 'big gates' as the highest good they can achieve ... '. N.L. Jackson, another Corinthian footballer and prominent amateur spokesman, condemned monetary influences: 'the introduction of professionalism supplants a sport promoted for the pleasure of those who participate in it by a spectacle arranged for the enjoyment of those who pay to look on'.[11]

In 1913 'W.H.C.' argued: 'Ten years ago, professional football was a game which was played for the glory of victory: today it can only be regarded as a business'. Whether such a distinction can be made between 1903 and 1913 is debatable, but this does illustrate a continuing concern that the game had been lost to monied interests. The sporting nature of football was felt to be undermined by playing for money, since a 'win-at-all-costs' philosophy would predominate. 'An Old Player' wrote in 1902: 'It is because the men who promote and who play professional football are bound to place their own personal gain before any consideration of sport ... that I deplore modern developments.' Pollock Hodsall felt much the same: 'the development of what, of football as a national pastime or of the game as a public entertainment?' G.O. Smith, amateur England international and another Corinthian, feared such commercial attitudes as much as any man brought up in the public school traditions of the nineteenth century, although he did accept the impetus that professionalism had given the game. In 1897 he wrote: 'the true game must be that which is played simply and solely for itself and not for money'.[12]

One aspect which struck amateurs as particularly degrading and unfair was the buying and selling of players as assets; middle-class entrepreneurs at the professional clubs treated players as they might treat their machinery in a mill or factory. The future of the game in 1888 was seen thus: 'Enterprising speculators will hire a team of professionals, paying wages which will secure the best talent, so as to attract large crowds of spectators, and bring in profitable returns by way of Gate Money. There will be eager competition among rival leagues in snapping up promising players.' This perceptive comment was an accurate prediction of the future of the professional game, but one can detect a resentful tone. The game had become too serious to paid players: 'Everyone of these youths ... is playing for bread and butter; in order to "keep his situation", not for pleasure.'[13]

Although such players might enjoy the 'dignity of labour', to the middle- and upper-class amateurs they were treated like slaves in a Roman market, ready for the amphitheatres of football stadiums. There were many complaints against the 'sale and purchase of "cracks" for all the world as if they were human chattels'. Captain Trevor, an army officer and sportswriter, thought in 1899 that both importation and the transfer system were unfair competition in maintaining a good team; he criticised 'questionable business methods', and the big clubs retaining 'a "local habitation and a name" which has long lost all significance', since they played imported players. The transfer system meant players were 'bought, sold and manipulated', and that 'the balance of sportsmanship probably lies with the Romans'. In the end, 'the largest purse must win the day', G.O. Smith complained.[14]

However, smaller town teams once in the Football League combined in a cartel to limit this domination and equalise competition to some extent. This was made possible by the institution of the maximum wage in 1901–2, by which players could not be paid more than a certain sum, and the 'retain and transfer' system, whereby a club could claim a fee for transferring the registration of a talented player. The Football League also tended to maintain the status quo regarding its membership. Although the transfer system was also disliked by the players, the clubs combined to retain a modified system when challenged by leading amateur sympathisers in the the FA. Again Lancashire was at the forefront of the struggle for the acceptance of professionalism, pushing for its legalisation at meetings of the FA in 1884–5. The northern clubs chiefly defended the rights of working-class players to be paid to play as a vocation, and fought for independence from metropolitan amateur dominance in the administration of the game, although, as we have seen, there were some amateurs who were more realistic and voted for compromise.

PROFESSIONALISM AND UNSPORTSMANLIKE ATTITUDES

Attitudes towards professional play were shaped by the public school 'fair-play' ideal of amateur critics. They perceived alternative behaviour as unsportsmanlike. G.O. Smith thought that professionals could be an asset to the game, 'but do they ... play the game in the highest and most sportsmanlike way? ... I am afraid this is not entirely the case'. Inducements other than money, such as cups and medals, were also a danger as 'an extra bribe'. Trevor agreed: 'Whatever may be said in favour of such decorations ... where there is an all absorbing desire to secure a thing, it requires a man to be possessed of fine strains of honour to avoid employing questionable tactics'. Presumably he did not think professionals who were chiefly working class were capable of such 'fine strains of honour'.[15]

For some, this started with the attitude of the clubs, including appealing unnecessarily against decisions or results: 'It is not this spirit that most of us were taught at School to take a beating in a manly English game.' Jackson also thought there was no need for rewards of any kind: 'Every man will play the game, taking no mean advantage, guilty of no dishonourable trick … receiving and giving his knocks with good humour and a sportsmanlike manner. This, indeed, is real football; no howling and ignorant crowd to irritate the players and fluster the officials.' Although physical contact had always been part of the game, it became less significant in the professional game, since injury could mean a player losing his livelihood. The game lost some of its 'keen enjoyment' and 'delightful enthusiasm'. Rough charging and the charge in the back, previously allowed, became fouls; Smith considered them 'an essential of football', but condemned 'underhand tricks' like deliberate handling and time-wasting. 'To win at any cost is the maxim that is followed … it is perfectly legal to do this, but it is a sort of legality that would hardly recommend itself to sportsmen.'[16] The implication here is that professionals were not 'sportsmen'.

The introduction of the penalty kick was thought to be a particularly severe blow to football sportsmanship. It implied that there was 'a disposition to break the laws wilfully and deliberately, or in other words, to cheat their antagonists'. Class bias is evident as well in some commentaries; the professional 'elbows, hacks, trips, shoves and treads on the heels of his foes' and has perfected 'the reduction of chicanery to a fine art'. Another 'unfair' method by which professionals could beat amateurs was by serious training. Amateurs could not do this; they were merely 'earnest for success by reason of their love for the game'. H.C. Lowther, another Old Carthusian, condemned training as 'unfair', making 'competition on the part of the amateurs almost impossible'. The fear of being beaten by one's inferiors therefore played a not insignificant part in the retreat of amateurs from Association football.[17]

Professional apologists claimed that football became more skilful and less physical under professionalism: 'It depends for success less on brilliancy and dash than on skilful combination and dextrous passing.' O.R. Coote, a well-known Irish sportsman, thought that 'to popularize a game one must give the best possible exhibition thereof … in most branches of sport the professional is a superior performer to the amateur'. Billy Meredith believed that professionalism had 'raised the standard of football'. However, it was only when gentleman 'found that they were unable to hold their own in leading events that exception was taken … on account of their social status'. Lancashire felt that the

opposition to professionalism 'savours of a "dog in the manger" policy.
Some of the leading lights appear to resent working men not only
playing, but playing better than themselves.'[18] Another commentator
claimed the amateurs insinuated that 'professionals make a game rough.
This argument evidently comes from one who has not played against
some of our amateur teams'. He also commented about training: 'This is
the real trouble ... because they fear to be beaten.'[19]

Criticism from Lancashire clubs began to be directed against
amateurs, because of the latter's questionable tactics:

> *Liverpool Ramblers v. Southport* (1884)
> 'I believe the game was a good one, as both teams are "strictly
> amateur". Every charge and foul was probably followed by a
> profuse apology.'

> *Preston North End v. Corinthians* (1889)
> 'The vigorous play of the visitors gave dissatisfaction to the
> spectators, and some of the Corinthian supporters on the reserve
> stand were very noisy and demonstrative.'

It was also stated that

> 'unbiased spectators ... aver that the amateurs were unmerciful in
> their charging, and knocked the North End team about like
> ninepins ... if any professional team had played like the amateurs
> did ... some of them would have been reported to the Football
> Association. It's a misnomer to style these southern amateurs
> gentle, they believe in heavy charging ... These Corinthians have
> yet to learn that all the great professional teams endeavour to play
> the most gentlemanly of football, the tremendous crowds who see
> the game in the large towns would not tolerate anything else'.[20]

Defenders of professionalism in Lancashire argued that the game
had become more civilised and scientific because: 'It was urged by many
that ... [it] would ruin the game ... on account of the roughness which
it would import ... in the first place actual experience proves the
contrary ... Amateurs would not have stood the stringent rules as "pros"
have done.'[21] However, amateur ex-public school players would have
argued that the 'true' sportsmanship of a game played for its own sake
had disappeared, to be replaced by a game which reflected the more
mercenary attitudes of the working-classes and parvenu middle-class
entrepreneurs.

THE LOSS OF CONTROL OF THE GAME
TO PROFESSIONALISM

Not only did gentlemen amateurs fail to stem the tide of professional attitudes typified by Lancashire critics, they also lost direct control of 'their' game by the take-over of the FA by professional clubs' representatives, and the institution of the Football League in 1888: 'The Football Association ... has a majority composed of members whose direct interest ... in professionalism involves a corresponding hostility to amateurism. They are men whose pleasure (and business) it is to cater for the unathletic population of the manufacturing towns.' It was argued that the FA should represent the amateur players, or they should form 'a new association which shall exist only to encourage amateurs ... like Rugby Union', with its own Cup. N.L. Jackson agreed: 'The game as a sport was almost forgotten at headquarters so much had the authorities to do in promoting the business of football ... thus it comes about that the rules of the Association and the laws of the game ... are remodelled, not by the players for the benefit of the sport, but by the spectators.'

It was true that the FA Committee had been taken over by professional interests, but it was because the amateur game had been marginalised by the mid-1880s and it was only a matter of time before professional clubs took over the administration of the FA almost completely. By 1890 they had the best teams, the best players, and were watched by many thousands of spectators. It was only natural that more commercial considerations came to the fore, as seen in Lancashire's moves to have professionalism legalised, and the threat to form a breakaway British Football Association in 1885 if this did not occur. This would have meant totally separate administrations for the amateur and professional game. The fact that professionalism won this struggle by 1885 showed how much the balance of power had shifted.

The desire by certain Lancashire clubs to have professionalism legalised led to further conflict between the Lancashire professional clubs and amateur clubs, mainly those in and around the South East. In 1884, while the struggle for professionalism was continuing, a number of Lancashire clubs attempted to form a breakaway 'Northern Association', later rather grandly retitled the British Football Association. The Lancashire professional clubs would have completely dominated this breakaway group, but the move was curtailed by the rapid recognition of professionalism in 1885. Lancashire clubs generally wanted to legalise professionalism, and would not surrender this struggle to the other English Associations who were consistently opposing them, in particular those of London, Sheffield and Birmingham, the three most powerful of these organizations apart from the Lancashire FA. The concessions granted to the professional clubs to prevent such a breakaway led to the increasing dominance of professional representatives on the committees of the national FA, eventually leading to an almost complete control of important positions so that amateur representatives afterwards had very little influence in most major policy decisions regarding English football.

The importance of the formation of the Football League to the demise of amateur-gentleman hegemony in football cannot be overstated. The instigation of a competition with regular home and away games between a fixed group of clubs, with a championship at the end, focused interest on certain professional clubs, dramatically raising the stakes. This improved on the increasingly chaotic fixture scene just before 1888, when flagging interest was caused by short-notice cancellations of fixtures. Teams were turning up late, or fielding a weakened team because they were playing two matches at the same time and so on. The new intensified competition brought increased crowds, and hence more revenue, making it essential for the professional clubs to control the Football Association as the law-giving body of the sport. Naturally, opponents claimed the League had been established purely as a matter of commercial self-interest, and would lead to the dominance of the game by a small number of professional clubs. In this they were right, although the League continually expanded its numbers as more professional clubs came to the game. The operation of the League as a cartel, which has been widely recognized, also enabled the clubs within it to marginalise those outside, chiefly the smaller professional clubs, and, of course, the principal amateur clubs dominated by the public school-educated upper and middle classes.[22]

CLASS BIAS AND THE MAN–MASTER RELATIONSHIP

Class bias is evident in some of the above comments on professionalism, but occasionally, such snobbery became quite blatant. One writer in 1888 commented: 'Football reached the classes from which the professional element in any sport is naturally drawn.' In 1899 Trevor thought the same: 'legalised professionalism has made no converts in the sportsmanlike elements of society'. Lack of respect for social differences was of more importance than supposed threats of working-class domination in society as proposed by Dunning. N.L. Jackson pointed out important differences between football and cricket or golf: 'Generally the professional cricketer is a good fellow ... rarely failing to show due respect to his employers'; in golf there existed 'cordial friendship': 'This is due to the fact that the professional is so truly the servant of the game and the distinction between him and his employer so clearly accepted, that he never forgets his position'. Footballers perhaps forget their position more often than cricketers or golfers, but there was little threat of open rebellion in football, despite the achievements of football unionism, which were significant, but not overwhelming, as professionals were still denied freedom of contract, being tied to clubs by the 'retain and transfer' system and the maximum wage.[23]

Players were tied to their clubs, then bought and sold: 'But while binding the professional hand and foot to his masters, the Football Association is endeavouring to remove all those social distinctions between amateurs and professionals which obtain in other sports'; it would 'drive the better class, or public school, element from the game'. Jackson was a supporter 'of the good fellowship which makes all classes equal on the cricket and football field'; he was willing to allow some professionals, 'but ... do not let the distinctly lower element override the whole of the game'. At one time, 'A young man leaving Charterhouse or Westminster' would have returned North and played football for his local team, but later 'the young amateur is left out in the cold and takes to playing golf or perhaps learns Rugby rules. That is the class for whom professionalism has absolutely and completely ruined football.' Indeed, 'Gentlemen can now only play Association Football with each other for they cannot risk plunging into the moral slough.'[24]

Class bias was obvious in other comments: 'The employment of the scum of the Scottish villages has tended, in no small degree, to brutalize the game.' As we have seen, this is untrue, but it does indicate the distaste with which working-class players were viewed. Defenders of professionalism attempted to point out that snobbery was behind of these attacks. The *Athletic News* objected to the Gentlemen versus Players match in 1886, saying that the FA 'did their best to make the pro's look like pro's', since 'dark blue jerseys savour more of the collier than anything else, and the Gentlemen were clad in spotless white shirts'. The first professional to play for England, J.H. Forrest of Blackburn Rovers in 1886, had to wear a different shirt from the amateurs, since the Scots had objected (Scotland being nominally amateur at the time). Despite professionals being generally better players, amateurs found it easier to get into the England team up to 1900, probably due to selectors' bias. Despite the overwhelming evidence that professional players were superior, the first professional captain of England was Bob Crompton in 1900. On one international journey, the (presumably amateur) captain 'did not recognise his men on a long railway journey ... speak to them in any way ... [travelled] in a separate compartment [and dined] away from them at the hotel'. N.L. Jackson commented that the classes would naturally remain separate, as servants did not dine with their masters.[25] This attitude clearly annoyed Lancashire commentators; describing another Gentleman versus Players match, the *Football Field* described the gentlemen as 'swells' saying 'of course they took little if any notice of the "low pro's" and the preliminary conversation generally observed between competing teams was conspicuous by its absence ... the amateurs dined after the match, but the pro's got 5s. instead ... The Major [Marindin] has an idea that professional footballers are hardly worthy to be treated as gentlemen.'[26]

However, the flavour of such criticism is a distaste, and not a fear, as argued by Dunning and colleagues. Can we see here a fear of the new unionism and the militancy of the working classes in the 1880s and 1890s? Were the working classes in football really threatening middle-class control of society? This is doubtful, despite the obvious snobbery and class bias of the commentators.[27] Professionalism and working–class involvement in football did not threaten middle–class hegemony except in terms of the ideological struggle over the control of the game.

SPECTATORSHIP AND PARTISANSHIP

Condemnation of spectatorship was rife in the early days of professionalism. We have seen spectatorship being criticised as passive. Others were a little less judgmental: 'There is ... a germ of British sportsmanship in the mere desire to take part in a contest, even as a spectator ... but for the most part the stream of professionalism has swept sportsmanship away.' Why did commentators condemn spectatorship? Despite attempts by Dunning and his supporters to link partisanship in spectating to modern football hooliganism, there were other reasons to denigrate it apart from its passive nature or its tendency to promote hostility.[28]

One was the Protestant work ethic. Professional football was condemned for distracting the population from its economic duties: 'The most important business affairs are hurried through or postponed for the sake of a great game ... it is no uncommon occurrence for the men of a large business concern to strike work.' Abell commented: 'Large establishments occasionally closed in mid-week because the whole body of workmen took time off to attend the match.' Trevor agreed: 'a league match in the neighbourhood will seriously deplete [the] workshops for half or the whole of the day'. This was an important 'moral' reason for disliking the 'Football Fever' since it diverted the masses' attention from the work ethic, and again implied a class-based criticism of 'men' by 'masters'.[29]

Bias displayed itself in other ways, particularly a distaste when forced to experience the working classes *en masse*. N.L. Jackson commented in 1894: 'These pampered members of society, the British lower classes, can apparently only regard any form of sport as long as it assists them to make money. It was an ill day for the game when the Northern labourer diverted his attention from quoits and rabbit coursing and pigeon flying and turned it to football.' C. Edwardes, a journalist, commented in 1892 that visitors to a match would 'need to suspend ... their sense of smell. The multitude flock to the fields in their workaday dirt, and with their workaday adjectives very loose on their tongues ... the lower classes may be divided into two sets: Fabians and Footballers, and ... it's difficult to say which is the greater nuisance to the other members of society.'[30]

Some aspects of crowd behaviour did attract attention. These usually concerned the amount of drinking and betting that occurred at matches, rather than the violent conduct of spectators: 'the extra drinking, the quarrelling and the opportunities for gambling' brought charges of 'immorality'. There was some betting in the early days, but this was generally confined to a minority as was heavy drinking. According to Abell, football became 'a direct incentive to idling, gambling, drinking and quarrelling, and the fascination of it should keep so many of our fellow country men away from recreations of real value'. Edwardes felt the same: 'The New Football is a far more effective arousal of the unregenerate passions of mankind than either a political gathering or a race meeting ... you are jubilant, while your neighbour uses language not be to found in grammars ... it all depends ... whether there is or is not a good deal of fighting after the match. Of drinking it may be taken for granted that there is an abundance.' Edwardes does not actually cite any evidence for his assertions, but Dunning and colleagues take them at face value.[31]

Others saw the crowd differently. G.O. Smith could see some advantage in attendance: 'People who otherwise would spend their afternoon in the public house, to the detriment of their pocket' would go to the match instead, although he felt that football had promoted betting. Sturdee felt it 'better to be an idle spectator under these conditions that remain idle in the slums'; however, there was still 'much drinking and betting'. MacFarlane also mentioned the 'evils' of drink, but particularly emphasised betting, which 'possibly ... has much do with the moral deterioration of football'.

However, one of the main criticisms of the crowd was its lack of 'sportsmanship'. Middle- and upper-class writers were unable to comprehend partisanship as a quite natural extension of local loyalties. These built upon rivalries between communities evident during the middle ages, and were typified by fights at local fairs, traditional football matches, rushcart competitions and many other similar manifestations.[32] Abell missed the point entirely: 'When the game is quiet the vulpine and sodden faces are eager, but not happy, when an exciting phase occurs the general expression is one of malignant anxiety ... There is enthusiasm ... but it is an ungenerous one-sided expression without a spark of chivalry or appreciation of alien worth in it.' N.L. Jackson felt, 'As a rule they do not got to see football; they got to see their own side win.' F. Ensor thought that in the North, football 'was passionately adopted by that people whose warped sporting instincts are so difficult to understand', contrasting it with rugby: 'The reason why Rugby remained an amateur game so much longer ... is that it was always performed by better classes of athletes ... Association has touched pitch and been shockingly defiled.' Additionally, 'men go in their thousands not to study and admire skill or endurance, but to see their team gain two points or pass into the next round'. However, it is arguable that the 'fair play' ideal of the public schools, along with the whole of their games ideology, was in fact a nineteenth-century 'invented tradition', and as such was an artificial credo instigated with the particular intention of training young men physically and morally for service to the Empire and survival through life.[33]

'W.H.C.' condemned partisanship: 'There is no sportsmanship in a football crowd ... it has been educated in the wrong school. Partisanship has dulled its idea of sport and warped its moral sense.' Pollock Hodsall stated: 'There is no real local interest to excuse the partisan frenzy of the mob, since the players come from all over the kingdom ... yet doubtful tactics by the home team are applauded to the echo, while the same actions by opponents are met with hooting and groans.' Sturdee bemoaned 'the rapid and extensive growth of professional sport [which has] corrupted the public conception of sportsmanship'. Such statements miss the point about local loyalties, which are to the club, not individual players, whose origin is actually irrelevant. It is interesting that these comments do not mention violent conduct or hooliganism in the crowd, despite the criticism of behaviour.[34]

Lancashire critics condemned these articles as distorted nonsense penned by ignorant writers who failed entirely to understand the phenomenon. An article in the *Saturday Review* in 1898 describing players as 'brutal', spectators as 'blackguards' and directors as 'bloodsuckers' was criticised thus: 'It must have been palpable to every footballer who read the article that its author knew nothing of the game.' The *Football Field* condemned Ensor: 'Mr. Ensor's article has already been so completely exposed and pulverised that the contention in the *New Century Review* seems almost like beating a dead dog.' Hugh W. Strong claimed he had 'attended league matches and test matches, cup matches and "friendlies" for many years past', unlike Ensor,

> who has mostly got his information at second hand ... putting aside the leaven of ruffianism ... the conduct of the great football crowds that assemble week by week is by no means discreditable. There is shouting, of course, and clapping of hands ... I have been at test matches when, practically, the life of the clubs engaged was at stake, and I have seen the home club beaten and the home spectators accept the defeat with a quiet manliness ... I have seen matches of the first importance won by the most glaring luck, and I have seen the defeated accept the inevitable with nothing more that a good-humoured murmur. I have seen referees perpetrate the most glaring errors of judgement ... with no other punishment than a chorus of harmless hoots ... I have never once seen a referee interfered with other than by hisses; I have never seen a single case of personal violence on the part of the spectators ... Mr. Ensor's picture ... is, in short, a figment of the imagination. His

indictment is but the irresponsible invective of ignorant intolerance.[35]

An article in a 'London paper' on 'The Decadence of Football' in 1899 was justified in some ways, the *Football Field* claimed,

> but to assert that the game is going to the dogs and tending to produce degradation and deterioration is to absurdly exaggerate the situation ... as the game is played now it takes thousands from that which would be infinitely less desirable and that is has put a period to forms of sport which formerly attracted great crowds and which were in themselves objectionable to the worst degree ... [Such] degradations ... exist only in their own imaginations: Referee baiting, wicked cruelty, gambling other than that which takes place wherever the general public congregate, grossly unsportsmanlike conduct – these have no real existence so far as first class, or for the matter of fact, second or third class football ... referees are too well protected to get into trouble except on little grounds ... so far from tending to become worse, the conditions under which the game is played are greatly improving. There is less roughness than there was, there is less of betting ... there is less of the doubtful element.

A criticism of professionalism in the *London Daily Chronicle* in 1899 after a 'riot' at Port Glasgow versus Greenock Morton, concluded that there was 'a very tolerable imitation of the rough element which used to assist at prize fighting', with 'brutal exhibitions of violence ... There is no reason why professionalism in games should degenerate into licensed ruffianism, but this has certainly become the case in professional football as played by the onlookers.' Again, such exaggerations were criticised: 'I venture to say that there is no more connection between this riot and professionalism than there is between Manchester Town Hall and Timbuktu.' In England, grounds had been closed for 'infinitely less than this'. It was 'a travesty of common sense', an 'absolute distortion of the facts', since this incident was 'purely local ... yet it is sought to deal with the question as though it sprang from something inherent in the game and common to every district'.[36]

Critics of professional football tended to be conservative journalists, churchmen, or amateur gentlemen footballers who still resented losing the exclusivity of public school football. An article in the *Christian*

Budget for 1899 in the 'Road to Ruin' series claimed that professional football was rife with bribery and corruption: 'The national winter game is being ruined by professional gamblers.' A Lancashire critic countered: 'A good deal ... is a hash up of the Ensor nonsense ... It is charitable to assume that the editor knows less of the game than the man who penned the farrago of baseless insinuations.' The article claimed that gambling 'has made football crowds the roughest and fiercest gatherings in this country. The football mob sticks at nothing from hunting a referee or doing violence to a losing team, to wrecking a house ... in the North, where football is most popular, it is a weekly occurrence for referee to be mobbed.' This kind of second-hand criticism from biased commentators with various types of axe to grind was condemned as the 'clear nonsense' it undoubtedly was. A writer in the *Football Field* made the point that comments were based upon hearsay: 'I venture to say that 75 per cent of the so-called criticism of the game from those who misuse their positions in this way is founded on the same inadequate basis.' It would appear that certain writers were creating a 'moral panic' about professional football for their own ends, and, although the defenders of professional football had their biases as well, and journalists in the sports newspapers and local press could be said to have been acting in self-interest, their accounts appear to be more accurate, and are corroborated by other evidence.[37]

Even towards the end of this period such unfair criticism was still being directed against football. A Mr Walker at the Liverpool Referees Society referred to a speech by Dr Chavasse, Bishop of Liverpool, in 1911, in which the latter criticised professional football for interfering with work, stating that professionals were perfectly acceptable in cricket and golf, but not football. Walker condemned this as based on prejudice and misconception, stating that professional players were more disciplined, and '[football] hadn't the odious caste distinctions which were witnessed in cricket'. He claimed there was more misconduct in amateur than professional football. Another article in a London newspaper in 1911 by 'Robertus' condemned the 'tired desolate crowd for whose benefit various enterprising profit-mongers run music halls and picture palaces as well as football'; such commercialism was contrasted with cricket again, but the whole article was condemned as a 'diatribe'. C.B. Fry became an immoderate critic of professionalism by 1911, even though earlier he had played alongside professionals as an amateur for Southampton. He condemned the 'immorality' of it; due to 'mob rule' and 'professionalism undiluted', 'huge crowds of uneducated people' were encouraging players to trip others and handle the ball wilfully. What caused his change of mind is unknown, but the *Football Field* claimed his earlier comments in 1903 were more accurate. Then the crowd was 'no place ... for your cynic, pale and bloodless'. Spectators were 'simple hearted fellows' who enjoyed football. The average crowd member was 'a bit rough ... but he loves sport ... The cynic who sneers, the sceptic who disbelieves, the aesthete who dislikes, they simply do not understand.' The players showed 'skill acquired not without hard trying and much self-denial' and were 'clean men with clean blood'. This seems a much more balanced view of professional football from one who was admittedly an outsider, and less distorted and second-hand than many others cited.[38]

CONCLUSION

The views of various writers on the professionalisation of Association football in the late nineteenth and early nineteenth century reflect a number of concerns. Although these comments range over a period of roughly 20 years, we have seen that there are common themes in their arguments. What, then, are we to make of claims by Dunning and others that such critics were directly or indirectly referring to football hooliganism before 1914? These writers appear not to have perceived their arguments in such terms. Maguire claims that the above criticism was part of a national concern about the behaviour of working-class youth forcing the middle and upper classes to confront this threat of violence. However, there appears to be no fear of violent revolution inspired by professional football. Spectator misbehaviour was not perceived as a serious problem, hence the lack of concern about 'football hooliganism'. There were many contemporary investigations into the social conditions and behaviour of the working classes, but nothing concerning football crowd misbehaviour. The Victorians and Edwardians were much given to such investigations; if they were really concerned, official and unofficial inquiries would have been instituted.

Nor was this due to a greater tolerance of violence within society at the time. Violent crime was declining throughout this period, and any investigations do not link violent behaviour with football. What we do have are several biased denunciations of professional football covering the period 1880–1914. Dunning and his supporters seem aware only of

Edwardes and Ensor, demonstrating their lack of research in this topic. The criticism of attitudes of working-class players and spectators was limited to the power struggle concerning the control of football and its ultimate destiny as a game; it would be overstating the case to link it with a generalised 'fear' of the working classes as is presented in the Dunning scenario. Rather it was a struggle of competing ideals or philosophies which were class-based, and which reflected general class attitudes. One aspect of the struggle involved writings about professional football, although apologists for professionalism were generally middle-class allies articulating working-class opinions rather than the latter expressing their own feelings. Nevertheless, we can reasonably assume they are an accurate reflection of the 'committed supporter' ideal of the working-class spectator. Similarly, the attitudes of the professional footballer cannot be reduced merely to a win-at-all-costs philosophy; such issues are more complex, and deny the obvious enjoyment of the game shown by many professionals.

In contrast, ideals of 'fair play' and athleticism were an 'invented tradition' formulated in the public schools of the nineteenth century. These ideas were to some extent artificial, and were never completely accepted by the working-class player or spectator. There is, however, a distinction between the biased partisanship of the supporter and the hostility and violence of the football hooligan, which Dunning and his associates seem unwilling to make. Hence they use general criticism of professional football and its crowds to justify a concern about football crowd behaviour and violence in the period.

As we have seen, critics were concerned with the physical condition of the working classes, as British imperialism was being challenged by the expansionism of France and Germany; the British ruling classes were worried, to some extent, by fear of armed insurrection within Britain. However, fear of foreign wars supposedly prescribed more active forms of recreation. Edward Malins, a Birmingham doctor called as a witness before the Inter-Departmental Committee on Physical Deterioration in 1904, connected the growth in football crowds with the decline in physical fitness by a series of leading questions:

'Do you think really the lower-classes, especially in larger towns, would themselves go in for outdoor games now?'
'No.'
'As much as their fore fathers did?'

'I don't think they would as much.'

'They go to look at others?'

'Yes, and do not participate.'

In 1909 an article claimed that football had contributed towards Britain's decline; the country was in the 'downward grade' when its population was 'incapable of defending' the mother country.[39] Such concerns form part of a more general interest in the increasing physical degeneracy of the typical working-class Briton, linked to forms of Social Darwinist philosophy.

Other 'moral' concerns were the corrupting influence of money on football, creating an undesirable urge for increased wages and gates, players competing for prizes and rewards rather than playing for a pure love of the game. Indirectly, this would also supposedly have an effect on the crowds supporting their local teams. 'Unsportsmanlike' attitudes which distorted the ideals of fair play and amateurism were another serious issue, amateur commentators bemoaning deliberate foul play, hand-ball and time-wasting tactics. Such issues may have been undesirable side-effects of professionalism, but they have no direct relevance to hooliganism. The attitudes of committed spectators may have been more partisan and less concerned with general 'fair play', but this did not mean they were predisposed to violence. If interpreted by less biased authors, such attitudes could be described as patriotic and loyal, and honest about motives for watching the game.

In general, Association football functioned as an arena for the diffusion of a dominant ideology, that of the English upper and middle classes. The ideals of athleticism were originally reflected in the public school version of football with its emphasis on team spirit, courage, manliness, fairness and devotion to a cause. As the quintessential team game, it was felt to be the ideal training for the burdens of Empire, which many of its participants would serve in the future. However, there was a reverse side to these virtues; an emphasis on imperialism, the superiority of the white race over others, and the superiority of the upper classes, genetically more fitted to rule over the 'inferior' specimens of the working classes. The doctrines of Social Darwinism, its connections to the pseudo-science of eugenics, and the latter's implications of racial fitness and unfitness, selective breeding and the improvement of 'the race', underlay much of what might be termed the liberal and biologically-individualist philosophy of the time. Late nineteenth-century obsession with the concept of 'degeneration', decay in moral standards, and the corruption of art and literature, convinced some that a fightback was necessary by those who wanted to uphold the status quo in society and spread ideas of duty, morality and correctness supposedly implicit in the upper echelons of the white race.

All these preoccupations were displayed by the critics of professional football, whether consciously or unconsciously. The reformed version of Association football had been conceived, in a way, as an ideal form of enjoyable training for the privileged young men of the British Empire. Now it was thought to be corrupted by an influx of money, and its virtue stained by extensive contact with the lower classes and their supposedly dubious morality. The feeling grew throughout the 1880s and 1890s, and continued up to 1914, while resistance to the professional take-over was urged by critics such as N.L. Jackson. However, as resistance was overcome by superior numbers and influence, the middle and upper classes withdrew to more socially exclusive sports such as golf, tennis and rugby union. As a consequence, these writers did indeed believe their game had been 'shockingly defiled' by the hordes of workers who flocked to play and watch this exciting new entertainment. The game's real purpose had been betrayed, and as such it was no longer worthy of serious consideration or support by the majority of the middle and upper classes, a situation which still pertains today. Association football's decline in respectability can be traced directly to the conflicts over the interpretation and control of the game from the 1880s to the outbreak of the First World War.

NOTES

1. L. Kitchen, 'The Contenders', *Listener*, 27 October 1966.
2. G. Green, *History of the Football Association* (London, 1953), Chs.2, 3, 4; T. Mason, *Association Football and English Society 1863–1915* (Brighton, 1980), Chs.1, 2, 3.
3. J.A. Mangan, *The Games Ethic and Imperialism: Aspects of the Diffusion of an Ideal* (Harmondsworth, 1986); J.A. Mangan, *Athleticism in the Victorian and Edwardian Public School* (Cambridge, 1981).
4. J.C. Greene, *Science, Ideology and World View: Essays in the History of Evolutionary Ideas* (Berkeley, California, 1981); G. Jones, *Social Darwinism and English Thought: the Interaction Between Biological and Social Theory* (Brighton, 1980); H.L. Kaye, *The Social Meaning of Modern Biology; From Social Darwinism to Sociology* (New Haven, Connecticut, 1986); J. Stokes, *In the Nineties* (Hemel Hampstead, 1989); S.A. Barnett, *Biology and Freedom: an Essay on the Implications of Human Ethnology* (Cambridge, 1988); L. Dowling, *Language and Decadence in the Victorian Fin-de-Siècle* (Princeton, New Jersey, 1986); J.A. Mangan, 'Social Darwinism and Upper Class Education in Late Victorian and Edwardian England', in J.A. Mangan and J. Walvin (eds.), 'Manliness and Morality: Middle-class Masculinity in Britain and

American, 1800–1940 (Manchester, 1987), Ch.7, pp.135–59; J. Walvin, 'Symbols of Moral Superiority: Slavery, Sport and the Changing World Order, 1800–1950', in J.A. Mangan and J. Walvin (eds.), *Manliness and Masculinity*, Ch.12, pp.242–60.

5. G. Green, pp.217–29; E. Dunning, P. Murphy and J. Williams, *The Roots of Football Hooliganism* (London, 1988), pp.42–4; J.A. Maguire, 'The Limits of Decent Partisanship: a Sociogenetic Investigation of the Emergence of Football Spectating as a Social Problem' (Leicester University Ph.D. Thesis, 1985), 228; E. Dunning and K. Sheard, *Barbarians, Gentlemen and Players* (Oxford, 1979), pp.196–7; J.A. Maguire, 'Images of Manliness and Competing Ways of Living in Late Victorian and Edwardian Britain', *British Journal of Sports History*, III (1986), 265–8; R.W. Lewis, 'The Development of Professional Football in Lancashire, 1870–1914' (Lancaster University Ph.D. Thesis, 1994), Ch.7; R.W. Lewis 'Football Hooliganism in England before 1914: A Critique of the Dunning Thesis', *International Journal of the History of Sport*, 13, 3 (Dec. 1996), 310–39.

6. H.F. Abell, 'The Football Fever', *Macmillan's Magazine*, LXXXIX (Nov. 1903–April 1904), 276–7, 279–80, 282; Biographical descriptions from W.E. Houghton (ed.), *Wellesley Index to Victorian Periodicals 1824–1900*, 4 volumes (Toronto, 1966–1987).

7. H.H. Almond, 'Football as a Moral Agent', *Nineteenth Century*, XXXIV (July–Dec. 1893), 900, 903–4, 906–7; 'Sport and Decadence', *Quarterly Review*, CCXI, 421, Oct. 1909, 487,489, 495; G.B. Pollock Hodsall, 'Football: Amateur and Professional', *C.B. Fry's Magazine*, VI (Oct. 1906–March 1907), 90; R.J. Sturdee, 'Ethics of Football', *Westminster Review*, CLIX, 1903, 180–3.

8. H. MacFarlane, 'Football of Yesterday and Today – a Comparison', *Monthly Review* (Oct. 1906), 132–3; Baden-Powell quoted 133.

9. *Football Field* (*FF*), 30 Sept. 1899, 21 Feb. 1903.

10. *FF*, 20 Feb., 12 March 1904.

11. P.C.W. Trevor, 'Football', *Badminton Magazine*, XII, 67 (Feb. 1901), 214; N.L. Jackson, *Association Football* (2nd ed., London, 1900), p.210; C.W. Alcock writing c.1880–81, quoted in Jackson, *Association Football*, pp.58–9; W.E. Hodgson, 'The Degradation of British Sport', *National Review*, XVII (1891), 784–7; N.L.Jackson, 'Professionalism and Sport', *Fortnightly Review*, VII (1900), 154.

12. "W.H.C.", 'The Case Against Professional Football', *C.B. Fry's Magazine*, XX, 2 Nov. 1913, 197; "An Old Player", 'The World's Play: Football: The Game and the Business', *World's Work* (Dec. 1902), 76, 79; Pollock Hodsall, 89; G.O. Smith, 'Football', *Pall Mall Magazine*, XIII, 56 (1897), 569.

13. 'Professionals in English Sports', *Saturday Review*, 14 April 1888, 437–8; Hodgson, 788.

14. 'Sport and Decadence', 499; P.C.W. Trevor, 'The Season's Football', *Badminton Magazine*, VIII (1899), 424; G.O. Smith in M. Shearman, *Football* (London, 1899), p.183; Lewis, Thesis, Chs.3, 4, 6 for a fuller explanation.

15. Smith, 'Football', 570; Trevor, 'Season's Football', 428.

16. Trevor, 'Season's Football', 424; Jackson, 'Professionalism', 159; Smith in Shearman, pp.174–7, 180, 184.

17. Jackson, *Association Football*, p.121; 'Association Football: a Retrospect and a Lament', *Saturday Review*, 3 March 1890, 261; Trevor, 'Football', 214; McFarlane, 135.

18. *Sporting Mirror*, II (Aug. 1881–Jan. 1882), 165, quoted in T. Mason, p.74; *Athletic News*, 23 Dec. 1889, quoted in S. Tischler, *Footballers and Businessmen* (London, 1981), p.45.

19. *FF*, 20 Sept. 1884.

20. *FF*, 22 Nov. 1884; 28 Dec. 1889; 4 Jan. 1890.

21. *FF*, 11 Jan. 1890.

22. 'Association Football: a Retrospect'; Jackson, *Association Football*, pp.108, 111–2, 139–40; Lewis, Thesis Ch.3; R.W. Lewis, 'The Genesis of Professional Football: Bolton – Blackburn – Darwen, the Centre of Innovation, 1878–85', *International Journal of the History of Sport*, 14, 1 (April 1997), 1, 21–54.

23. 'Professionals in English Sports', *Saturday Review*, 14 April 1888, 437–8; Trevor, 'Football', 214; Lewis, Thesis, Ch.6.

24. Jackson, 'Professionalism', 157; "Creston", 'Football' *Fortnightly Review*, V (Jan.–June 1894), 38; F. Ensor, 'The Football Madness', *Contemporary Review*, LXIV (Nov. 1898), 760.

25. *Athletic News*, N.D. 1886; 11 April 1892; 15 Jan. 1900, quoted in Mason, pp.76–7; *The Athlete*, 29 Sept. 1884, quoted in Tischler, p.44; E. Needham, *Association Football 1900–1901* (London, 1901), p.52; C. Francis, *History of Blackburn Rovers Football Club* (Blackburn, 1925), p.198.
26. *FF*, 27 Dec. 1886.
27. Dunning and Sheard, pp.182–94.
28. Trevor, 'Season's Football', 423.
29. Abell, 277, 281; Trevor, 'Season's Football', 423.
30. "Creston", 30; C. Edwardes, 'The New Football Mania', *Nineteenth Century*, XXXII (1892), 627, 630.
31. Abell, 279, 282; Edwardes, 622, 629; Lewis, Thesis, Ch.7.
32. Smith, 'Football', 570; Sturdee, 181; MacFarlane, 136; Lewis, Thesis, Ch.2.
33. Abell, 278; "Creston", 33–7; Ensor, 754, 757–8; Lewis, Thesis, Ch.2, Ch.3.
34. "W.H.C.", 201; Pollock Hodsall, 90; Sturdee, 182.
35. *FF*, 10 Dec. 1898; 11 Feb. 1899.
36. *FF*, 8, 15 April 1899.
37. *FF*, 4 Nov. 1899, 22 Nov. 1902; Lewis, Thesis, Ch.7.
38. *FF*, 21 Jan., 1 April, 23 Sept., 11 Nov. 1911.
39. J. Hargreaves, *Sport, Power and Culture* (Cambridge, 1986) pp.60, 62, 64; Interdepartmental Committee on Physical Deterioration, Parliamentary Papers, 1904, Vol.32, p.139, quoted in Tischler, p.130; 'Sport and Decadence', 489.

Organised Memories:
The Construction of Sporting Traditions in
the German Democratic Republic

TARA MAGDALINSKI

Whoever does not know the past, does not know the present and cannot master the future.[1]

In recent years, a great deal of research within sports studies has focused on the role of sport in generating and maintaining national identities, yet much of this research has concentrated on elite sport. There has been little examination, however, of sport on a regional and local level, and the role of sports history in the process of creating identities remains virtually unexplored. Although the process of identity formation varies from state to state and institution to institution, generally elites maintain a vested interest in articulating and sustaining appropriate meanings about identity in order to establish and preserve their preferred ideology. In emerging states with new or radical ideologies to promote, this process is particularly complex and requires a conscious effort to remove residual forms of identification that pre-date the new regime. Identity formation regularly involves organised forgetting and remembering. This essay explores the ways in which meanings about national identity were generated by the state in the German Democratic Republic (GDR) during the 1970s. The process of identity formation was crucial to the success of the socialist regime and involved creating a culture of political and social legitimation at a time of national social disorientation. Lyn Spillman suggests that 'The formulation and inculcation of national identities is always a matter of cultural production – but the question is where and how that production ... occurs.'[2] This study specifically examines the complex role and cultural significance of history, and in particular sports history, in the construction of a national identity. The role of history in identity formation cannot be underestimated, as history imparts to the citizenry an understanding of a state and its development, which encourages a sense of ownership of, and responsibility for, the nation. This essay is not concerned with discussing whether the state successfully instilled a new national identity into the citizens, but rather the paper remains on a theoretical level and identifies the mechanisms employed by the state to communicate a preferred vision of history.[3] This paper is less concerned, however, with the implementation of these mechanisms within the community, and is not an attempt to discuss whether measures were *actually* successful in creating a national identity within the population. Thus, this essay remains focused on the aims, objectives and strategies rather than on material, measurable outcomes. This approach is necessary as it gives insight into strategies used by elites in their efforts to secure consensus for ideology. Some examples are necessary to provide context for the paper, though these are simply illustrations rather than specific evidence of the success of the regime's strategies.

From the outset it should be stated that the GDR is not a unique case as all states use history to attract loyalty to the state. Tales of heroic battles, famous explorers and adventurers and political insurrections are all demarcated as milestones in the development of a nation and the celebration and commemoration of such events are often used as opportunities for national self-reflection. The role of sports history was also of particular significance in the GDR. Generally, sport in its modern form is regarded publicly as an apolitical, if not trivial, part of society, and sports history is not usually considered to be an important educational tool. In the GDR, however, sport was considered by educators to be a valuable part of the educational process that was responsible for communicating state ideology. Like history in general, sports history was not considered to be simply an esoteric cultural venture, but was integrated into the overall political education of citizens. Political ideology, officials believed, could be just as effectively transmitted through the history of sport, as through other avenues of education. It is important to point out, however, that the value of sport and sports history in transmitting political ideology was not overemphasised. In the West, there has been a tendency to inflate the significance of sport in the GDR without viewing it in its broad social context. Sport, it is important to stress, was not more or less important than other areas of society when it came to education, but was certainly not rejected as an apolitical activity that had no place in the ideological education of citizens.

It is also important to understand that the GDR is not the only country to have used sports history to communicate a politically expedient version of the past. The recent Ken Burns baseball series in the United States, for example, provided an excellent means by which Americans could revel in nostalgia for a sanitised national past that shored up contemporary feelings about the United States. In Australia, in preparation for the Olympics, citizens are regularly reminded of Australia's proud Olympic tradition harking back to a triumphant Melbourne Olympics in 1956, reinforced by ageing 'star' athletes who are trotted out at major sporting events across the country. The above examples do not link sports history directly to the state, which suggests that the significance of the East German case lies in the fact that sports history was a part of the official state strategy to develop a national identity.

Research on eastern Europe and the Soviet Union has focused largely on the role of elite sport in generating an international profile and on legitimisation of states through international sporting success. Mass sport, by contrast, is usually reduced to simply part of the feeder system for elite sport.[4] Though important, this approach often neglects to consider sport as a useful means of political socialisation, and does not take into account the means by which other activities associated with sports participation are incorporated into the educational process. In the GDR, mass participation in sport itself was not necessarily responsible for politically educating the youth, but rather clubs and sports groups provided social opportunities for political education. Within sports clubs and collectives, activities were encouraged that drew on a new understanding of national history, and these played an important part in forging a new national identity.

HISTORICAL CONSCIOUSNESS AND NATIONAL IDENTITY

In order to inculcate popular support, newer states rely on the development of a mass historical consciousness. In order to invoke popular support, established states appropriate history to establish an 'objective' justification of the regime. The state maintains a preferred view of history by employing a number of processes, including the routine celebration and commemoration of selected 'historical moments'. This is part of a process of reorganising and reappropriating the past that characterises all modern nation states. Of greatest importance in this process is the 'organised remembering' of the national past, through the selection of key events and figures for celebration. As Kate Darian-Smith and Paula Hamilton point out, 'collective memories are both reflected and reinforced through culturally and temporally specific activities and behaviour, such as rituals, commemorative ceremonies and bodily practices'.[5]

New regimes that differ radically from their predecessors are particularly active in the reorganisation of their nation's past, as the effective foundation of a new state usually demands an 'overthrow' of all that has gone before. Christel Lane argues that this reconstruction occurs on both political and social levels and suggests that a cultural revolution must immediately follow political revolution.[6] States must 'stage manage' cultural and social resources, in addition to economic and political assets, in order to celebrate, legitimate and eventually support and maintain the new society.[7]

Yet, despite rejecting 'all that came before', a complete denial of history does not benefit the new state. It is paradoxical that the more radical the upheaval in political and social organisations, the more reliant a new state is on the past for its stabilility. Although paradoxical, it should not be a surprise, as Paul Connerton points out: 'All beginnings contain an element of recollection' and this 'is particularly so when a social group makes a concerted effort to begin a wholly new start'.[8] National celebrations become increasingly significant during times of rapid social change, as the society or state must 'project themselves into the future' while at the same time 'grappling' with the 'legacy of the past'.[9] On a national scale, public recollection demands an encompassing revival and analysis of the past, as the 'reassuring presence of the past allows the society to move into the future with confidence'.[10] The radical change in political philosophy after 1945 meant that the German past could only be remembered in specific ways, namely those that foregrounded the workers' historic struggle against capitalism. History certainly could not be remembered and honoured in its entirety for fear of aligning the new revolutionary age with the National Socialist state, a system diametrically opposed to the new communist state.

Politically desirable versions of the past are regularly presented publicly through rituals, ceremonies and commemorations. More specifically, 'traditions' are employed to augment the process of political socialisation. As traditions strengthen claims of historical 'continuity', they contribute to the construction of collective identity by linking the future through the present to the past. In order to include the nation's past in contemporary celebrations, positive elements from that past are designated as events to be venerated. The past is thus transformed into a 'myth of destiny'.[11] Links between historical events are made and personalities are chosen and analysed, and both are then presented as conclusive evidence or 'proof' of the historical inevitability of the new state. More specifically, 'foundation events are selected from the past and strung together in a sequence that simulates historical progression'.[12] Public endorsement of a new political or social order requires this kind of 'blood-line' or ancestry. Arbitrary claims to power or leadership are typically viewed sceptically, whereas demonstration of the political and social heritage of the party or political ideology convinces and later reinforces to most citizens the 'divine nature' of its claims to authority. Thus, East Germany was presented through historical traditions as the logical culmination of those forces that had historically agitated for political, social and economic revolution. In order to reconstruct a national history that clearly demonstrated this, historians selected suitable historical moments that were gradually forged into state traditions.

Although these processes were already in place soon after the foundation of the GDR, it was during the 1970s that the East German government placed greater emphasis on reconceptualising state history, as this decade marked a turning point in the development of the GDR. During this decade the East German state was formally recognised by the United Nations, the Federal Republic of Germany and other Western nations, as well as international sporting organisations such as the International Olympic Committee, and this international recognition of the state led to a greater need to establish a wholly independent identity. Although the process of selecting an appropriate historical narrative had begun soon after the establishment of the state, by the 1970s there was a more concerted effort to communicate this narrative to a broad population where many of the adults identified with potentially conflicting versions of the national past. Although national history can be transmitted passively through mechanisms such as school history lessons or visiting museums, educators and historians thought that active participation in the construction and commemoration of historical events was a more effective means of developing an organised and sanctioned historical consciousness in the GDR. Holidays, memorials and celebrations of historically and politically important events took place regularly which persistently exposed citizens to their state's history. Educational institutions, youth organisations, sports clubs, parents, families, teachers, veterans, museum and archival workers were all involved in developing historical consciousness, and many of these efforts were directed specifically at the young.[13] In this way, the repetition of so-called 'traditional' commemorations became more and more politically significant.

Traditionspflege

By the late 1960s, the East German state had institutionalised the process of constructing traditions through a complex process called *Traditionspflege*[14] that encompassed the selection or production, maintenance and promotion of historical 'traditions'. East German and other socialist theorists considered traditions to be modifiable and adaptable entities, thus *Traditionspflege* was a process of cultivating and refining traditions based on a material or dialectic (re)interpretation of German history. It is important to understand that *Traditionspflege* was not responsible for *creating* or *inventing* new East German traditions, but rather emphasised the importance of those historical events that demonstrated socialist trends throughout German history. In addition to selected German traditions, international socialist traditions were crucial to the restructuring of East German identity and the emergence of a state that had secured international legitimacy.

Traditionspflege was incorporated into all areas of society including the educational system, science and culture,[15] as educationalists recognised that moments of intensive political and ideological education could be linked closely to significant historical and commemorative events.[16] Sports historian Siegfried Forbrig recognised that 'the closer the emotional links to the event, the higher the educational effects', so efforts were made to ensure emotional experiences were well combined with historical propaganda.[17] 'Historical propaganda', it was reasoned, stimulated both the intellect and the emotions simultaneously.[18]

Historical knowledge was transmitted in a variety of contexts. Teachers, veterans, former resistance fighters and historians were responsible for inculcating an historical awareness into the population, especially into the youth.[19] Historical consciousness was furthered on the mass level by the daily national newspaper, *Neues Deutschland*. Almost every issue throughout the 1970s contained references and feature articles focusing on local, regional, national and international commemorations, historical events and traditions.[20] The persistent reports dealing with memorials and historical events reinforced the historical origins of the GDR and helped establish a 'calendar of remembering' amongst citizens.

PRESENTING THE PAST THROUGH MUSEUMS

One of the most extensive means of presenting national history was the elaborate system of museums that developed in the GDR. Museums have legitimacy amongst the public, as they are regarded as an objective measure of 'how it was' in the past. Indeed, museums actively seek to retain an aura of objectivity. Museums typically try to 'replicate' the real world in a confined space, yet they inevitably reproduce a version of the world that is acceptable to social elites. In other words, museums highlight an ideal, 'natural order' of society that is ultimately highly politicised.[21] The presence of particular exhibitions in museums is, of course, a selective process that, from the outset, privileges particular historical figures and events above others. Museums, however, rarely advertise that their exhibitions are only one version of history, and Tony Bennett recognises that 'few museums draw attention to the assumptions which have informed their choice of what to preserve or the principles which govern the organisation of their exhibits'.[22]

Mike Crang suggests that museums 'encapsulate time', that they 'represent [time] in terms of periodized displays'.[23] He further argues that time is 'manipulated in terms of the amount and organization of the space accorded to historical events'.[24] By organising displays in contrasting spatial territories, significance is added to or detracted from particular displays and, by implication, periods of time. The preponderance of formal and informal regional and local museums in the GDR clearly demonstrated the state's efforts to develop both historical and national consciousness from a regional or local level. Approaching history from this level meant that history became more relevant to, and potentially more acceptable to, the population. Ultimately, regional and local histories were used as examples of wider and therefore stronger historical traditions that ultimately enabled the state to cultivate a commitment to the nation and to national interests. The allocation of space and resources to displays primarily depicting the development of the GDR since its foundation is further evidence of the importance of East Germany's own history for the development of historical and national consciousness. Memorials functioned in a similar manner to museums, although they each utilised different means to reach the common end of inculcating an historical consciousness into citizens.[25] Whereas memorials assumed the quasi-religious function of a place of worship or praise in the form of commemorations, museums displayed the history of East Germany and provided a constructed and, therefore, politically acceptable, lineage of the nation.

While museums and memorials were crucial in efforts to confront all citizens with official history, schools and sports clubs were encouraged to play a key role in attempts to instil national identity in the youth. Margot Honecker, long-time Minister of Education, suggested in 1979 that all areas of society directly affecting youth, including schools, sports, Free German Youth (FDJ) and Pioneer organisations, were to be responsible for teaching the history of East Germany and the development of state-sanctioned traditions.[26] Educators recognised schools to be important gatherers and disseminators of historical information and students were encouraged to develop research projects focusing on regional and local history, and on worker movements in the area.[27] Within this context, the construction of sporting traditions was a significant part of *Traditionspflege* and the sporting past was well integrated into other aspects of East German interpretations of German history.

THE SOCIAL CONSTRUCTION OF SPORTING TRADITIONS

All educational procedures aimed to instil a 'love of the homeland' into young citizens, and sport was therefore considered a part of this process.[28] As physical education classes and extracurricular sport provided a useful means of political-ideological education, sport was thus integral to the generation of an East German national identity. Simply participating in sport, however, was not considered an effective means of instilling political awareness in the youth. Instead, the political significance of sport needed to be conveyed, and the celebration of sporting traditions was regarded as an effective mechanism of achieving this outcome. Thus, *Traditionspflege* within the sports movement was earmarked as a productive means of increasing political awareness and national devotion.[29] Through the celebration of selected historical moments such as the National Day, it was expected that participants would increase their historical consciousness through participation in thematically and politically relevant and interesting traditions. Sporting traditions were responsible for raising an awareness of the national and regional past of particular sports as well as of political revolutionaries involved in sport. The preservation of German sporting traditions, and in particular revolutionary worker sporting traditions, therefore, formed a basis of political-ideological education.[30]

The three main tasks of *Traditionspflege* within sport were to encourage the citizens to take a positive attitude towards sport; to identify with the moral characteristics of revolutionaries; and to develop political and ideological convictions.[31] These tasks were incorporated into the three main sections of sports *Traditionspflege*. The first area concentrated on instilling a general historical consciousness in students within physical education classes. The second aspect aimed to increase the commitment to the state through *Traditionspflege* in sports clubs and collectives, including the FDJ. The final aim of the political-moral position of athletes in sports schools and colleges was secured by *Traditionspflege*. Although *Traditionspflege* had largely political or ideological tasks to fulfil, another important task in sport education was to encourage an interest in sport and a commitment to a healthy lifestyle.[32]

The most important outcome of sports *Traditionspflege* was, of course, the development of socialist patriotism and proletarian internationalism, both seen as crucial elements of national identity.[33] As a result, ideological education through selected historical propaganda and *Traditionspflege* within sport were critical for the successful emergence of an East German identity.[34] Although, small regional and local collectives and associations maintained revolutionary socialist traditions at the grass-roots level, these programmes were co-ordinated nationally by the German Gymnastics and Sport Federation (DTSB). The DTSB actively encouraged *Traditionspflege* and guaranteed that within all areas, the progressive, revolutionary and socialist traditions of sport in East Germany would be maintained and used within the organisation for the political-ideological education of athletes.[35] Indeed, the statute of the DTSB stated that one of its tasks was to maintain and protect the heritage of the nation's best athletes as well as respecting the patriotic and national achievements of historical figures such as Friedrich Ludwig Jahn, Johann Christoph GutsMuths and August Schärttner. Anti-Fascist resistance fighters and athletes such as Werner Seelenbinder, Katja Niederkirchner and Ernst Grube were honoured by the DTSB as the founders of the progressive German sports movement.[36]

As a political organisation, the DTSB was committed to raising historical consciousness and to the production of socialist personalities amongst its members. According to DTSB President Manfred Ewald, a fundamental method of generating socialist modes of behaviour was the maintenance of the 'rich' traditions of the socialist sports organisation.[37] Ewald further suggested that 'by concerning ourselves with the progressive heritage of our history, we contribute to the conveyance of a true socialist view of history'.[38] Historical consciousness, according to GDR sports historian Willi Schröder, further led to an understanding and appreciation of society's achievements, as well as instilling courage and a desire to work towards the future.[39] He suggested that without an historical consciousness or without a knowledge of the historical processes within society, a passionate commitment to developing the GDR would be impossible.[40]

MECHANISMS OF *TRADITIONSPFLEGE*

Given the stated importance of *Traditionspflege*, attention was paid to the details of the forms and methods of this movement. Each parameter that affected *Traditionspflege's* ability to influence purposefully and effectively the political and ideological convictions of the citizens was carefully surveyed and guidelines for the successful implementation of *Traditionspflege* programmes were devised. In 1985 the DTSB (Propaganda Section) publication *Wir pflegen Traditionen* outlined the preferred methods of *Traditionspflege* that were to be implemented in sports collectives.[41] Overall, there were three main considerations that were essential to the successful implementation of *Traditionspflege*. First, the forms of *Traditionspflege* had to contain significant traditions. Second, the forms of *Traditionspflege* had to be conducive to application in collectives. Third, it was to be remembered that the forms of *Traditionspflege* did not function independently, but in conjunction with other educational processes. Specifically, 12 forms of *Traditionspflege* that could contribute to overall political-ideological education within sports clubs were detailed and several of the main forms are worth discussing in detail.

One of the most important aspects of *Traditionspflege* in sport was the concept of role models. Role models were historical figures who were considered to possess 'socialist personalities' and who provided examples of ideal socialist behaviour. Role models became 'guides' for both political behaviour and moral beliefs and personified the past in general and the history of the socialist struggle in particular so that children could easily link their life to the past and vice versa.[42] Role models were presented as friends, whom children could trust, by using first names and continually referring to, for example, Karl Liebknecht and Rosa Luxemburg as 'Karl' and 'Rosa', Ho Chi Min as 'Uncle Ho', or Angela Davis as 'Comrade Angela'.[43] Children from the age of five were gradually introduced to the heroes of the national and international workers' movement through the use of picture books, cartoons and stories, thereby familiarising them with Uncle Ho, Karl and Rosa and other important revolutionaries.[44] By adopting a particular historical figure, usually an anti-Fascist resistance fighter, members of a collective were able to gain personal insight into the motivations for the development of the nation, in addition to learning valuable political, ideological, behavioural and moral lessons. The citizens' attention was focused on the achievements and personalities of various role models, such as Werner Seelenbinder or Katja Niederkirchner.[45] Schools, collectives, factories and sports clubs went through an official process of selecting a significant role model, usually from the region, after whom their organisation would be named. On some occasions, groups applied to carry the names of nationally significant role models, such as Karl Marx or Ernst Thälmann; however, the allocation of such role models was restricted. Within sport, former worker athletes were favoured role models and they had the dual function of sanctioning ideologically appropriate behaviour and of encouraging the adoption of a healthy lifestyle and commitment to regular physical activity.[46] The most popular role model in the GDR was Werner Seelenbinder, a wrestler and worker activist who died in a concentration camp in 1944. Many clubs, organisations, stadiums and tournaments were named in his honour, and collectives were entrusted with the responsibility of researching his life and disseminating this information.

The second component of *Traditionspflege*, traditional sporting competitions, was an important feature of the regular commemoration of people and events. Sports events were often organised to coincide with important regional and national holidays and remembrance days, though gradually they took on their own significance. Significantly, these events were not exclusively for elite athletes, but rather were mass participatory events. Examples of such commemorative events include the *Willi-Sänger-Lauf*, which was similar to a 'fun run', and the innumerable tournaments in diverse sports ranging from badminton to wrestling that were named after Werner Seelenbinder. Although these events often only commemorated regional traditions or people, on occasion they developed into significant national traditions that existed along side other mass sporting displays, such as Spartakiads.

Third, establishing cross-generational links was crucial to the process of ideological education. Veterans of the workers' sports movement and so-called 'activists of the first hour' (early GDR history in the 1940s and 1950s) provided informative links to the past. Veterans were asked to communicate their experiences in the resistance movement, thereby providing personal illustration of the broader struggle for a socialist German state. The life stories of activists and anti-Fascists were not simply interesting accounts of days past, but were of the highest educational value in making East German history 'alive' for the young. Willi Zeidler, a veteran who joined Karl Liebknecht and Rosa Luxemburg's German Communist Party, found that children, in particular, were eager to hear his stories, and that the young paid more attention to events and episodes recounted from his life than to the same episodes reported in a book.[47] Ultimately, veterans were a living reminder of the German past and were regularly invited to participate in physical activities, memorials, informal education meetings and forums. From discussions with veterans, and in conjunction with their club or school's role model, young people were also expected to learn ideal patterns of behaviour and to use the biographical details of veterans to support their own revolutionary behaviour.[48]

Fourth, elite sport was a useful tool for maintaining pride in the nation as well as strengthening the state and class consciousness of the citizens. Success in international sport stimulated national pride and evoked a sense of patriotism. Elite sport was also viewed as an encouragement for people, especially children, to strive to achieve their best in all areas of life, not just sport, thereby developing their socialist personalities.[49] Elite athletes were role models who provided living examples of how to behave although they were not as widely 'used' in political-ideological education as former athletes such as Gustav Schur, or deceased athletes such as Werner Seelenbinder.[50] Elite sport also provided a mechanism that encouraged children, in particular, to take up sport and play sport throughout their lives,[51] and in terms of generating

short-term identification with the state, elite athletes were invaluable.
Physical education within schools was another important site of
political and ideological socialisation, and physical education teachers,
although primarily responsible for the physical development of their
students, were also accountable for the students' political and ideological
education. Physical education in the early 1970s, however, was far from
an ideal context for political socialisation. Sports and physical education
classes had diverse educational tasks and as a result the political-
ideological training of students occurred sporadically, with teachers only
briefly discussing historical developments in German sport, or quickly
referring to famous worker athletes.[52] Pleas subsequently went out for
greater attention to be devoted to the historical education of school
children in all school subjects, including sport. Various sports historians
and educationalists devised methods of bringing sports *Traditionspflege*
effectively into the sports lesson, bearing in mind that, in order to be
educationally effective, *Traditionspflege* could not be fragmented into
specific classes, but needed to occur in conjunction with other forms of
political-ideological training.[53] Sports clubs and school-based collectives
had more time to devote to *Traditionspflege* and regular meetings would
take place within sports collectives to discuss political and ideological
matters, as well as to further the interest of the members in the historical
development of the local workers' movement as well as the workers'
sports movement.[54]

An effective form of *Traditionspflege* was the commemoration of
sports-related memorial or remembrance days such as the annual
Seelenbinder memorial day.[55] National and international celebrations
were also incorporated into the sports *Traditionspflege* movement, and
sporting clubs and organisations responded by allocating time and
resources to researching important dates and anniversaries such as the
GDR's national day or May Day, nationally significant moments in
Soviet history such as the 50th anniversary of the Soviet Union in 1972[56]
and the anniversaries of the birth or death of important East German
revolutionaries or resistance fighters such as Katja Niederkirchner or
Ernst Grube.[57] Initially, members of a collective would be required to
research and produce a small chronicle or display that would outline the
significance of the event for the development of East Germany, as well
as to nominate aspects within the history that could assist citizens in the
future. As such, regional, national and international remembrance days
formed an important part of the overall political-ideological education of

members. For example, prior to the celebration of the GDR's 30th anniversary in 1979, it was reported at the executive meeting of the DTSB that the preparation of the celebrations for the anniversary proved that the historical propaganda and *Traditionspflege* within the DTSB continued to make strong contributions to the overall understanding of the great historical development of the GDR and in encouraging a committed socialist perspective within athletes, as well as a commitment to the state.[58]

Probably the most widespread method of introducing sports history into sports clubs was the 'traditions cabinet'. A traditions cabinet was essentially a small display of politically, regionally and historically significant sports memorabilia and included historical documents such as letters and diaries, old sporting equipment, trophies and books. Most sports clubs and collectives erected 'traditions cabinets' to commemorate their own achievements and history, and to situate the club in wider East German history. Often, the cabinet was extended to include an entire room, which essentially became a small museum. The displays in the 'traditions cabinets' provided a constant reminder of the sports collective's evolution and a permanent exhibition of its link to the socialist German state. Although many sports clubs around the world, both professional and grassroots, adopt similar strategies of creating a visible history for their members by presenting club and sports memorabilia, the process in the GDR was deliberately political, as displays necessarily were linked to the evolution of the GDR state as a political and social entity. The displays were not simply isolated and did not function as a reminder of simply the club's past, but rather were more explicitly concerned with developing within members an understanding of, and commitment to, the state.

In addition to 'traditions cabinets', sports museums were established, and where no sports museum existed, other smaller local and regional museums often contained materials that documented the development and significance of sport in the area.[59] These initiatives, however, were not all co-ordinated and, despite the perceived importance of the *Traditionspflege* movement within sport, an overall co-ordinating body was not envisaged until the late 1980s, when it was expected that the Sports Museum of the GDR in Berlin would be opened.[60]

Encouraging an understanding of the historical processes present in society required innovative strategies to consolidate history within daily life. Incorporating historical knowledge into cultural and physical activities was emphasised as an effective, yet unobtrusive, method of imparting an appreciation of the nation's past. Excursions to sports-related memorials could provide evidence for the anti-Fascist resistance, and thus contribute to an understanding of the history of the nation, region and local area. Points of interest, such as battle sites or remnants of resistance hideouts or worker meeting places were often incorporated into physical activities such as running races or hikes around the local forests.

Germans have a strong *Wander* or hiking tradition that was incorporated into *Traditionspflege*. Hikes through nature parks and forests that contained historical landmarks provided a relaxing introduction to local and regional history.[61] Trails transversed old battlefields, passed by secret meeting places and led the participant through historical towns and villages, where important buildings were identified by plaques. Regional history groups were encouraged by various historical societies to discover important historical sites in their area and to construct walks and paths around them. Youth hostels were named after important role models and particular walks had different themes. One such path in Sachsen, *Lehrpfad Hohnstein*, began and ended at the youth hostel 'Ernst Thälmann' and had the regional anti-Fascist struggle as its theme.[62] Schools and sports clubs often went on excursions to these sites and incorporated orienteering into the *Wanderung*.[63] Celebrations of anniversaries on occasion involved physically retracing the steps of famous events or people. Marches along particular routes, such as routes that concentration camp victims were forced to walk or the routes that famous artists wandered were re-enacted while stopping to pay homage at memorials along the way or to lay memorial stones.[64] In total, hundreds of such 'history paths' existed in the GDR, each one planned and maintained by local community groups. Such activities assisted with the strengthening of historical consciousness, while simultaneously promoting physical activity.

To further strengthen the collective or community spirit within villages and towns, collectives organised and participated in activities, such as maintaining sports facilities or commemorative sites. Participation in such communal activities was essential for the development of socialist personalities, one of the main aims of political-ideological education. As citizens contributed to the collective good of the community, collective identity could be further developed. Other sporting and cultural activities such as the preservation of history and customs of the region, were also actively maintained. Indeed, regional customs and traditions became increasingly important, as it was recognised that the bonds to the *Heimat* or homeland could strengthen the bonds to the state, and as a result, the state adopted or incorporated powerful local and regional symbols into national or state life, as a means of legitimising the GDR and locating it in the context of a broader German history. East German officials clearly harnessed the strength of local and regional traditions and symbols of the past in their efforts to generate new identities that could replace former collective identities such as a broader German national identity.

CONCLUSION

Because of the important role that traditions played in East Germany, they were not isolated but were incorporated into a national process, *Traditionspflege*. *Traditionspflege* was responsible for generating a preferred past, based on selected historical events and issues. It operated successfully on several different levels, including collective, regional and local levels, and this made it crucial to the development of identities across these levels. The workplace, schools, social and sporting clubs were all incorporated into the *Traditionspflege* movement and each of these locations became responsible for disseminating historical knowledge and encouraging an understanding of the GDR's historical development. Political-ideological education in the GDR did not remain the preserve of educational institutions. Additionally, historical knowledge, as a key component of political-ideological education, did not remain solely in the classroom. Youth groups and sporting clubs, as well as work collectives and interest-based social collectives were all involved in the inculcation of a preferred historical assessment. Civic commemorations were also an important part of the development of historical consciousness and made the national celebration of significant anniversaries and events accessible for the public. It was through these repeated references to history and to the historical basis of the GDR that the state effectively reinforced its claims to legitimacy, thereby enhancing the construction of a national identity. Specifically, the *Traditionspflege* movement encompassed the layering of identities through the generation of socialist personalities, the promotion of socialist role models, the collection and dissemination of local and regional histories, commemorative events and international connections with the Soviet Union, other socialist states and the international workers' movement. Within the entire political-ideological educational movement, sport and physical education were crucial, though not exclusive agents and carriers of significance and meaning.

NOTES

1. Karl Leibknecht, quoted in *Neues Deutschland*, 12 May 1978, 64. *Neues Deutschland*, 29/30 May 1976; *Neues Deutschland*, 26 Aug. 1977; *Neues Deutschland*, 20/21 May 1978.
2. L. Spillman, *Nation and Commemoration. Creating National Identities in the United States and Australia* (Cambridge, 1997), p. 20.
3. Any qualitative research into feelings about a past state or personal perceptions of an East German national identity are necessarily clouded by the fact that nearly decade has passed since the decline of that nation. Revelations about the presence of a 'national identity' within an individual is mediated by the 'success' or 'failure' of that individual in the new regime. Thus, any real examination of whether a 'national identity' existed may be fundamentally flawed.
4. J. Tampke, 'Politics Only? Sport in the German Democratic Republic', in R. Cashman and M. McKernan (eds.). *Sport in History. The Making of Modern Sporting History* (St Lucia, 1979), pp.86–98; J. Riordan , 'Soviet-style Sport in Eastern Europe: The End of an Era', in L. Allison (ed.), *The Changing Politics of Sport* (Manchester, 1993), pp.37–57; G. Carr, 'The Use of Sport in the German Democratic Republic for the Promotion of National Consciousness and International Prestige', *Journal of Sport History*, 1, 2 (1974), 123–36; J. Riordan, *Sport, Politics and Communism* (Manchester, 1991), p.54; K. Hardman, 'The Development of Physical Education in the German Democratic Republic', *Physical Education Review*, 3, 2 (1980), 121–36; C. Vogel and L. Würsch, *Staats-Sport. Am Beispiel der Deutschen Demokratischen Republik* (Zurich, 1993).
5. K. Darian-Smith and P. Hamilton (eds.), *Memory and History in Twentieth-Century Australia* (Melbourne, 1994), p.2.
6. C. Lane, *The Rites of Rulers. Ritual in Industrial Society – The Soviet Case* (Cambridge, 1981), p.1.
7. Ibid.
8. Paul Connerton, *How Societies Remember* (New York, 1989), p.6.
9. J. von Geldern, *Bolshevik Festivals, 1917–1920* (Berkeley, 1993), p.5.
10. Ibid. p.140.
11. Ibid., p.12.
12. Ibid., p.55.
13. *Neues Deutschland*, 4/5 Dec. 1976; *Neues Deutschland*, 11 Jan. 1977; *Neues Deutschland*, 5 Jan. 1979; S. Forbrig, 'Sporthistorische Traditionspflege', *Körpererziehung*, 35, 6 (1985), 239.
14. *Traditionspflege* is simply defined as the cultivation or maintenance of traditions.
15. W. Schröder, 'Historisches Erbe, Traditionen und Traditionspflege in der sozialistischen Körperkultur der DDR', in G. Wonneberger (ed.), *Körperkultur und Sport in der entwickelten sozialistischen Gesellschaft der DDR*, (Berlin, 1978), p.29.
16. Stiftung Archiv der Parteien und Massenorganisationen der DDR im Bundesarchiv (SAPM) File: FDJ-A 10 521: Tagung der Zentralleitung des Komitees der Antifaschistischen Widerstandskämpfer der DDR am 02.02.1978, Diskussionsbeitrag, Günter Schneider, p.4.
17. S. Forbrig, 'Zur erzieherischen Nutzung progressiver Traditionen aus der Turn- und Sportgeschichte', in M. Reichenbach and H. Schwidtmann (eds.), *Sozialistische Erziehung im Schulsport. Ausgewählte Beiträge zur Erziehungsarbeit im Sportunterricht und im außerunterrichtlichen Sport* (Berlin, 1976), p.91.
18. SAPM: FDJ-A 10 509: Auftrag des Sekretariats des Zentralrates der FDJ an die Arbeitsgemeinschaft zur Erforschung der Geschichte der deutschen Jugendbewegung, Egon Krenz, p.1; D. Riesenberger, *Geschichte und Geschichtsunterricht in der DDR. Aspekte und Tendenzen* (Göttingen, 1973), pp.59–61.

19. *Neues Deutschland*, 17 Oct. 1978.
20. The following are examples of the kinds of articles that appeared in the daily press that were part of the process of conveying an interest in, and an appreciation of, East German history to the citizenry: 'Kompromißloser Kampf gegen die Feinde des Friedens und des Sozialismus. Zum 20. Jahrestag des Ministeriums für Staatssicherheit', *Neues Deutschland*, 8 Feb. 1970; 'Einheit – wie sie Lenin uns lehrte', *Neues Deutschland*, 21 April 1970; 'Jubiläumsausstellung der Deutschen Volkspolizei', *Neues Deutschland*, 29 June 1970; 'Kranzniederlegung zum 10. Todestag von Wilhelm Pieck', *Neues Deutschland*, 8 Sept. 1970; '"Ich will dem Volk den Weg bereiten und seines Glückes Hüter sein". Zum 80. Geburtstag von Ernst Schneller, einem der großen revolutionären Führer der KPD', *Neues Deutschland*, 7 Nov. 1970; 'Gedanken am Pioniergeburtstag', *Neues Deutschland*, 13 Dec. 1970; 'Altfriedland feiert 700jähriges Bestehen', *Neues Deutschland*, 2 July 1971; 'Glückwünsche zu Jubiläen der Städte Remda und Lebus', *Neues Deutschland*, 31 May 1976; 'Glückwünsche zum 750jährigen Jubiläum von Grevesmühlen', *Neues Deutschland*, 3/4 July 1976; 'Grüße zum 1000jährigen Stadtjubiläum von Altenburg', *Neues Deutschland*, 9 July 1976; 'Nebra beging seinen 1100. Geburtstag', *Neues Deutschland*, 10/11 July 1976; 'Harzgemeinde pflegt alte Schützengebräuche', *Neues Deutschland*, 13 June 1978; 'Lehrlinge gestalten Moden der Vergangenheit', *Neues Deutschland*, 10 Aug. 1978; 'Traditionsreiches Hammerfest', *Neues Deutschland*, 16 Aug. 1978; 'Flurnamen erinnern an die Zeit der Backofen', *Neues Deutschland*, 26/27 Aug. 1978; 'Weshalb die Mönchs-Uhr noch heute sieben Minuten vorgeht. Görlitzer pflegen die revolutionären Traditionen ihrer Stadt', *Neues Deutschland*, 23/24 Sept. 1978; 'Alte Weisen erklingen. Vielseitige Pflege der Folklore der Thüringer Waldes', *Neues Deutschland*, 21 Nov. 1978; 'Singakademie an der Oder pflegt Musiktraditionen', *Neues Deutschland*, 11 Jan. 1979; 'Von der Musikparade bis zum Hafenkonzert. Stabsmusikkorps der Volksmarine pflegt Liedgut und Traditionen der Arbeiterklasse', *Neues Deutschland*, 1 Feb. 1979; 'Dokumente zur Dorfgeschichte', *Neues Deutschland*, 30 March 1979; 'Töpfertradition wird gepflegt', *Neues Deutschland*, 3 Aug. 1979; 'Folklorefeste in Thüringen', *Neues Deutschland*, 23 Aug. 1979.
21. T. Bennett, *The Birth of the Museum* (London, 1995), p.126.
22. Ibid.
23. M. Crang, 'Spacing Time, Telling Times and Narrating the Past', *Time and Society*, 3, 1 (1994), 32.
24. Ibid.
25. Autorenkollektiv, *Kultur-Politisches Wörterbuch* (Berlin, 1978), p.501; I. Köhler (1981) *Sportgeschichte. Der Weg zu olympischen Medaillen* (Berlin, 1981), p.11; *Neues Deutschland*, 20/21 Nov. 1976; *Neues Deutschland*, 19 Jan. 1977.
26. S. Frenzl, 'Aus der Kenntnis der Vergangenheit das Verständnis für Gegenwart und Zukunft gewinnen', *Körpererziehung*, 29, 7 (1979), 314; *Neues Deutschland*, 23 March 1979.
27. *Neues Deutschland*, 13 Feb. 1979.
28. M. Thieß, 'Traditionspflege im Kinder- und Jugendsport', *Theorie und Praxis der Körperkultur*, 28, 7 (1979), 556.
29. Autorenkollektiv, 'Körperkultur und Sport in der entwickelten sozialistischen Gesellschaft der DDR', *Theorie und Praxis der Körperkultur*, 27 (1978), 29–41; Autorenkollektiv, *Lehrerausbildung Sport. Klassen 1 bis 4* (Berlin, 1983), p.60; S. Forbrig, 'Mehr Aufmerksamkeit der Traditionspflege im Sportunterricht und im außerunterrichtlichen Sport', *Theorie und Praxis der Körperkultur*, 21, 8 (1972), 682; H. Schwidtmann, 'Standpunkte und Gedanken zum Beitrag von Körperkultur und Sport für die Herausbildung allseitig entwickelter Persönlichkeiten und ihre kommunistische Erziehung', *Theorie und Praxis der Körperkultur*, 27, 7 (1978), 486; Thieß, 'Traditionspflege im Kinder- und Jugendsport', 556.
30. M. Harmel, 'Traditionen der Kinder- und Jugendspartakiden der DDR – Mittel zur effektiven kommunistischen Erziehung', *Theorie und Praxis der Körperkultur*, 32, 4 (1983), 254; A. Weiß, 'Traditionspflege im Sportunterricht', *Theorie und Praxis der Körperkultur*, 27, 7 (1978), 512; Bundesarchiv Abteilungen Potsdam (BAP) File: Z-12 10 332: Sekretariats- und Präsidiumsvorlagen VII Turn- und Sporttag, 18-20.05.1984, Diskussionsbeitrag, Rainer Henschke, pp.149–50. For a further discussion of the dual traditions in German worker sports history, see A. Krüger, 'The German way of Worker Sport', in A. Krüger and J. Riordan (eds.), *The Story of Worker Sports* (Champaign, 1996), pp.1–26 and G. Wonneberger, 'Arbeitersport in

der DDR. Zur Realisierung der Ziele und Träume deutscher Arbeitersportler im ersten deutschen Arbeiter- und Bauernstaat', in A. Krüger and J. Riordan (eds.), *Der internationale Arbeitersport* (Cologne, 1985), pp.14–34.

31. Forbrig, 'Zur erzieherischen Nutzung progressiver Traditionen', p.89.
32. *Neues Deutschland*, 4 Dec. 1971.
33. Autorenkollektiv, *Lehrplan Sport. Klassen 1–4* (Berlin, 1989), p.5; W. Schröder, 'Traditionspflege in Schnepfenthal', *Theorie und Praxis der Körperkultur*, 25, 4 (1976), 263; Weiß, 'Traditionspflege im Sportunterricht', 512; BAP: Z-12 10 332: Diskussionsbeitrag, Rainer Henschke, pp.149–50.
34. Although there is a common assumption that elite national sport was the most important means of inculcating a national identity into the citizens, this was not entirely accurate. Indeed, contemporary East German successes in international sport were thought to be limited in their ability to raise *long-term* national consciousness, because athletes and athletic success were decontextualised and, as a result, less politicized. In this context, public attention would tend to concentrate on individual results and performances, rather than on social structures or political concerns. National and international sport were, therefore, not thought to be *ideal* communicators of political ideology because a decline in an athlete's performance could weaken any identification not only with that particular athlete, but with what they represented both politically and nationally. A commitment to sports history and to the internal significance of sport provided citizens with a more secure and long-lasting means of identifying with the nation. As such, officials regarded historical consciousness as the most effective measure of the public's commitment to the nation and the state. For further discussion on this see Günter Nachtigall 'Sporttraditionen in der Familie und ihre Bedeutung für die allseitige Entwicklung der sozialistischen Persönlichkeit', *Theorie und Praxis der Körperkultur*, 20, 4 (1971), 326; Erich Krauß, 'Anforderungen an die Geschichtspropaganda und Traditionspflege im DTSB der DDR', *Theorie und Praxis der Körperkultur*, 30, 12 (1981), 894.
35. Schröder, 'Historisches Erbe, Traditionen und Traditionspflege', 30.
36. W. Schröder, 'Erbeaneignung und Traditionen im DTSB der DDR', *Theorie und Praxis der Körperkultur*, 28, 7 (1979), 547–8.
37. Schröder, 'Erbeaneignung und Traditionen im DTSB der DDR', 548; BAP: Z-12 10 206: VI. Turn- und Sporttag 1978, Diskussionsbeitrag: Manfred Ewald, p.61.
38. Schröder, 'Erbeaneignung und Traditionen im DTSB der DDR', p.548; BAP: Z-12 10 206: VI. Turn- und Sporttag 1978, Diskussionsbeitrag: Manfred Ewald, p.61.
39. W. Schröder, 'Traditionspflege in Schnepfenthal', *Theorie und Praxis der Körperkultur*, 25, 4 (1976), 263.
40. Schröder, 'Traditionspflege in Schnepfenthal', 268.
41. W. Schröder, M. Thieß and W. Riebel, *Wir pflegen Traditionen* (Berlin, 1985).
42. Riesenberger, *Geschichte und Geschichtsunterricht in der DDR*, p.52.
43. Kuhrt and von Löwis, *Griff nach der deutschen Geschichte*, p.237.
44. Ibid., p.225.
45. Weiß, 'Traditionspflege im Sportunterricht', 512.
46. BAP: Z-12 10 206: VI. Turn- und Sporttag 1978, Diskussionsbeitrag Manfred Ewald, p.60.
47. *Neues Deutschland*, 15 Jan. 1972.
48. *Neues Deutschland*, 17/18 Feb. 1979; SAPM: FDJ-A 8443: 'Die Führung der Bewegung zur Aneignung der revolutionären Traditionen der Arbeiterklasse', p.4.
49. BAP: Z-12 8 996: 8. Tagung des Bundesvorstandes des DTSB vom 29.03.1973, 'Zum Beschluß über die weitere Entwicklung des Leistungssports in der DDR', p.6; BAP: Z-12 9 638: 13. Tagung des Bundesvorstandes des DTSB am 14.03.1978, Referat: Manfred Ewald, p.27.
50. BAP: Z-12 8 996: 8. Tagung des Bundesvorstandes des DTSB vom 29.03.1973, 'Zum Beschluß über die weitere Entwicklung des Leistungssports in der DDR', p.6; BAP: Z-12 7 580: Entwurf: Entschließung des V. Turn- und Sporttages des DTSB 1974, p.10.
51. BAP: Z-12 9 638: 13. Tagung des des Bundesvorstandes des DTSB am 14.03.1978, Referat: Manfred Ewald, p.27; BAP: Z-12 7 580: Entwurf: Entschließung des V. Turn- und Sporttages des DTSB 1974, p.10.
52. Forbrig, 'Mehr Aufmerksamkeit der Traditionspflege', 682.
53. S. Forbrig, 'Sporthistorische Traditionspflege', *Körpererziehung*, 35, 2 (1985), 240.

54. H. Simon, 'Arbeitersport und Tradition', *Theorie und Praxis der Körperkultur*, 25, 1 (1976), 815.
55. BAP: Z–12 7063/7064/7065: 23. Tagung des Präsidiums am 14.06.1972, Konzeption über Inhalt und Ablauf der zentralen Werner-Seelenbinder-Ehrung im Bezirk Frankfurt/Oder, p.1.
56. *Neues Deutschland*, 21 Sept. 1972.
57. Autorenkollektiv, 'Körperkultur und Sport in der entwickelten sozialistischen Gesellschaft', pp.38–40; Schröder, 'Zum Problem der Traditionen', 549; BAP: Z-12 10 32: Diskussionsbeitrag, Rainer Henschke, p.150.
58. BAP: Z-12 9 732: 5. Tagung des Bundesvorstandes des DTSB der DDR am 29.09.1979, p.24.
59. Autorenkollektiv, 'Körperkultur und Sport in der entwickelten sozialistischen Gesellschaft', 38–40; Erbach, 'Traditionspflege – fester Bestandteil sozialistischer Körperkultur', p.745.
60. W. Mattausch, 'Zur Funktion des künftigen Sportmuseums der DDR', *Theorie und Praxis der Körperkultur*, 36, 2 (1987), 129–30.
61. BAP: Z-12 10 206: 9. Tagung des Bundesvorstandes des DTSB am 18.06.1981, Diskussionsbeitrag, Manfred Ewald, p.91; S. Frenzel, 'Aus der Vergangenheit das Verständnis für Gegenwart und Zukunft gewinnen', *Körpererziehung*, 35 (6) (1985), p.315; Witt, *Sportler feiern, Sportlerfeiern* (Berlin, n.d.), pp.155–8; Schröder, Thieß and Riebel, *Wir pflegen Traditionen*, p.27; *Neues Deutschland*, 12 Aug. 1971; *Neues Deutschland*, 10 June 1972; *Neues Deutschland*, 7 Jan. 1973; *Neues Deutschland*, 3 Nov. 1978; *Neues Deutschland*, 3 Jan. 1979; *Neues Deutschland*, 10 Jan. 1979.
62. *Neues Deutschland*, 10 June 1972.
63. Witt, *Sportler feiern, Sportlerfeiern*, p.156.
64. *Neues Deutschland*, 29/30 May 1976; *Neues Deutschland*, 26 Aug. 1977; *Neues Deutschland*, 20/21 May 1978.

Sport and the Scottish Office in the Twentieth Century: The Control of a Social Problem

CALLUM G. BROWN

One of the major characteristics of sport in twentieth-century Britain has been the increasing role of the state in promoting and regulating the people's games. Our understanding tends to focus on two critical periods. First, historians have identified sport in the 1930s as an element in government's legislation for enhancing the quality of life, based on ideas of democratised access to leisure and recreation; in this period, the Physical Training and Recreation Act 1937, the Street Playgrounds Act 1938 and the Access to Mountains Act 1939 are located alongside the Holidays with Pay Act 1938.[1] Second, in the mid-1960s, the Labour government's appointment of the first Minister for Sport and the establishment of the Sports Council are taken as marking the political recognition of the significance of sport as an element in wider social policy, leading quickly to the increased incorporation of sport into government's handling of international diplomacy.[2] Where we are less well informed is in the evolution and methods of public policy resulting from these acts and other powers, and the roles played by the civil service and by sports quangos. Given both the paucity of detailed policy contained in legislation, and the intermittent nature of politicians' interest in sport until at least the later 1960s, there is a need to explore the way in which sports policy developed, the background and agendas of key sports administrators, and the nature of the interaction between sports organisations and state agencies.

This is the first of two essays which explore these issues in relation to Scotland. As a region of the United Kingdom with its own integrated government ministry, it provides a useful case study of the evolution of state policy on sport. Led politically by a Secretary of State and junior ministers, the Scottish Office was technically free from England, Wales and Northern Ireland to develop its own policies in sport and associated areas (ranging from policing and gambling through to education and community policy). The Scottish case highlights how sports policy was critically mediated by social issues of morality, crime, popular culture and gender – issues which took priority with government. This study explores how sport was regarded by government from the late Victorian period as a 'problem' because of its association with 'rough culture' – with gambling, drink, crowd misbehaviour and endangerment, and – a specifically Scottish issue – with religious sectarianism. The second essay, by contrast, discusses how sport emerged between the late 1930s and the early 1970s as a positive element in social policy, centred especially around the provision of facilities in industrial working-class communities and the widening of opportunities – and types of sport – for women.

Responsibility for sport was split between two of the five departments into which the Scottish Office was divided for most of the century: the Scottish Home and Health Department (the SHHD, which incorporated the Scottish equivalent of the Home Office and Department of Health) and the Scottish Education Department (the SED, the equivalent of the Department of Education). The SHHD assumed responsibility for 'policing' matters like spectator behaviour, crowd safety, licensing of sports grounds and sectarianism, whilst the SED dealt with sports development (including most funding). The role of the SED falls mainly within the next article, but it is important to note here that within the Education Department sport was assigned to those in its 'inspectorate' who co-ordinated youth and community policy. In this way, the government's approach to sport was conceived and administered in two opposing ways: control of a 'problem' and promotion of a 'social policy'.

This twin-track approach originated in perceptions drawn from the enduring legacy of Victorian ideology which placed sport beside moral issues in religion and popular culture. From the rise of Enlightenment reason and evangelical religion, sport – especially its communal and 'team' forms – was perceived as both irrational and in conflict with puritan introspection,[3] and by the mid-nineteenth century moral sensibilities were hyper-sensitised to sport as a cause of Sabbath-breaking, drink and violence. Despite evidence of social mixing in sports organisations of the 1850–80 period,[4] sport in Victorian Scotland created a powerful discourse on the 'rough' character and 'otherness' of the contact games played by the male working class. The early industrial sporting heritage of Scottish men based on rough pursuits of small-town 'baa games', horse-race meets, cock-fighting pits and prize knuckle-fighting changed in the 1860s, 1870s and 1880s as the working classes experienced their own sports revolution which perpetuated in soccer and other games the association with gambling, drink, petty crime and periodic crowd trouble.[5] When the urban middle classes started to develop a vigorous sports culture between 1870 and 1914, it was firmly separated in social perception from working-class sports: it was spatially segregated, overwhelmingly in the new suburbs which sprang up in the principal cities of Edinburgh, Glasgow and Dundee, and was located on rivers, roads, curling ponds, croquet lawns, tennis courts and golf courses, as well as in the private and 'superior' state schools (usually called 'high schools') on whose rugby and hockey pitches the games ethic flourished.[6] With key roles played by the church, the private school and the private sports club, Scottish bourgeois sport was by 1900 an essential element in the social fabric of suburban society, collectively conferring identity and a newly-athletic 'respectability' to the middle classes as well as the aspirant upper-working class.[7]

This divergence in image between plebeian and bourgeois, city and suburb, was critical to the context in which state policy on sport emerged in the twentieth century. A key element in suburban sports society was the opening it provided to women. Neil Tranter has convincingly demonstrated that 'separate spheres' hardly existed for male and female middle-class sports in central Scotland in the last 40 years of the nineteenth century, with widespread women's involvement in both sporting activity and club administration.[8] Women participated in this sports culture whether they played or not: curling, croquet, tennis and cycling were co-educational, but women's presence at other events allowed female virtues to de-brutalise the perception of middle-class sporting pursuits. Domestic ideology was physically drawn out of the home into the new recreational spaces of the late Victorian middle classes, in the process making sport a respectable family, elevating and partially feminised pastime.[9]

Two sporting worlds emerged, each representing a different set of social sensibilities. The middle-class sporting world was dominated by rugby, golf, croquet and curling, and its sensibilities were amateur participation, being 'clubable', 'old-school' loyalty, respectability and graduated gender association. By contrast, the working-class sporting world was dominated by soccer, boxing, quoits, billiards and bagatelle, and its sensibilities were fervent spectator loyalty, an almost exclusive masculinity, localism, widespread religious sectarianism, drink, gambling and the culture of the violent 'hard man'.[10] Whatever the social 'realities' of class segregation in Scottish sport, it was this social construction of sport upon which the state was to create its policy.

It was the second sporting 'world' of the urban working-class male that drew the Scottish Office very reluctantly into not so much sport itself as sports-related 'rough culture'. Moral politics dominated Scotland between the 1880s and the early 1930s. The teetotal movement was very powerful, achieving the granting of local prohibition in 1913 (leading from 1920 to popular plebiscites which sent many towns and villages 'dry'). The anti-gambling lobby was also a power to be reckoned with, especially in the 1920s. Both of these pressure groups were sustained by the churches, especially the presbyterian and evangelical denominations which from the 1840s and 1850s had made a great impact on puritanising popular culture. The Free Church had taken the lead in getting legislation which closed Scotland's public houses on the Sabbath in 1853, and in 1854 had successfully stopped the annual horse-race meeting at Stirling because of the drinking, gambling and petty crime.[11] Despite the growth of mass 'rough' sports in the late nineteenth century, lobbying by the pressure groups continued after 1900 unabated, targeting urban working-class sport as the instigator of social evils. The Scottish Office – once invited by such pressure groups – became an increasingly enthusiastic warrior for the rational recreation causes of post-Victorian puritanism.

In essence, the Scottish Office became drawn into using legislation to define 'permissible' and respectable sports pastimes by criminalising 'unrespectable' sports or behaviour arising from them.[12] Informal participant sport and some indoor sports were particularly targeted – notably, between 1905 and 1939, billiard and bagatelle rooms. These were neither seen as legitimate sporting activities, nor as places to which children and alcohol should be admitted, and were widely condemned by teachers, police and civic leaders.[13] In 1910–14, and again in the mid 1920s, more than 20 Scottish burghs obtained Scottish Office approval to make any place providing these games subject to bylaw enforcement.[14] In 1937 a survey found that between 21 per cent and 60 per cent of school children in West Lothian towns visited billiard rooms more than three times a week – in some schools making it more popular than playing football or going to the cinema.[15] Further restrictions on sport among children followed – including children playing sports in public playgrounds and, separately, playing football in the street. When adults committed the latter offence, it was still being prosecuted; in Stirling in 1950, some 2.3 per cent of convictions before Stirling Police Court were for playing football in the street, resulting in fines of ten shillings or seven days in gaol.[16]

But by far and away the biggest area of Scottish Office business in relation to regulation of sport – or indeed any cultural activity – during this century was gambling. Until 1874, gambling law was more lax in Scotland than in England and Wales, allowing ready-money betting to grow and making Glasgow the specialist centre for postal betting for English punters. But in 1874 the Betting Houses Act of 1853 was extended north of the border, and from 1892 Scottish gambling law started to become sterner than in England. From that year betting in streets or open places became illegal in every Scottish burgh (excluding Edinburgh, Glasgow, Aberdeen, Dundee and Greenock which had their own measures), followed in 1903 by the criminalisation of bookmaking ('inducing or enabling' betting) in streets and common stairs – both measures ahead of the British-wide Street Betting Act of 1906.[17] Off-course horse-race betting was the primary target of these measures, but three other forms of gambling helped to swell the burgeoning of popular betting in Scotland: slot machines of chance (which evolved into fruit machines), the football pools, and *pari mutuel* betting (the totalisator or tote) which sprang up with the birth of circuit-greyhound racing in 1926. As a result of pressure from churches, moral campaigners and the police, the Scottish Office became from the First World War panic-stricken over the growth of gambling. In 1917 it rushed through a Scotland-only act to ban 'automatic' gaming machines (the predecessors of one-arm bandits) which were being dumped in Scotland, inadvertently criminalising even non-chance amusement games;[18] this was followed by intense police activity against the fruit machine which arrived in Scotland in 1929 (and which, chief constables asserted, were being installed by 'a ring of foreigners, Italians' in ice-cream and grocers' shops).[19] Street betting, primarily on horse racing and the new-fangled football coupons, attracted renewed vigilance in the mid 1920s from moral reformers (especially in the powerful United Free Church), forcing the passage of the Betting (Juvenile Messenger)(Scotland) Act of 1928 which made it illegal to procure a child under 16 years to carry a betting slip or verbal bet.

Though not every form of illegal gambling was connected to sport, it was those forms that did have this connection which caused the greatest concern. As well as horse-racing betting, the football pools grew rapidly in Scotland in the 1920s. Like fruit machines, the pools were suspected of being controlled by Italians – with one Scottish Office informant claiming that Switzerland was their operating base. Pools betting in Scotland was initially built on top of ordinary horse-race betting, was conducted mostly by street bookies, and, according to police intelligence, during the First World War became a highly organised and capitalised business. The Chief Constable of Glasgow alerted the Scottish Office in December 1916 to around 16 main betting offices and 19 letter-drop offices in the business quarter of central Glasgow being used for the receipt of postal betting, chiefly on football matches. Fixed-odds bets were increasingly being placed by telephone during the 1910s and 1920s, with six or more phones in some bookies' offices.[20] In 1930 Edinburgh recorded 266 betting offences, whilst Glasgow recorded 2,759, or exactly two-thirds of the Scottish total.[21] However, football pools – so popular in Scotland that it was known as 'the Scotch coupon' – was effectively legalised by an appeal case in 1930 when a Glasgow pools operator was cleared of conducting a gambling business and 'gaming house' in Woodlands Terrace by successfully arguing that in pools betting the gamblers were betting against each other and not against the bookmaker.[22]

The tote was initially connected to greyhound racing which spread from Manchester in 1926 to Scotland where, by December 1932, there were 22 tracks in operation (four in Glasgow with the others mostly in satellite industrial towns) with another six scheduled to open.[23] Tote betting dominated greyhound racing from the start, giving concern not only because of its popularity at the tracks but because it had led to the opening of private 'Tote Clubs'. Thirty-seven of these clubs opened in Scotland in their first year, 1932, offering continuous betting on horses and greyhounds. When the Paisley Tote Club was raided by the police in that year, it claimed to be a social club 'to encourage social intercourse and rational recreation'; however, the police reported the place as being devoid of newspapers or games (excluding one pair of boxing gloves and one dominoes set), and counted 284 persons on the premises.[24]

The 1920s and early 1930s saw a very dramatic growth in gambling, and seemingly endless new ways of placing bets. Under pressure from the churches and anti-gambling organisations, the Scottish Office gave secret evidence to the 1932 Royal Commission on Gambling in which it recommended new legislation on all aspects of the 'social evil'.[25] A secret SHHD survey in 1933 showed very divided opinions among Scotland's chief constables – some desiring greater enforcement of existing laws on gambling, some favoured new laws, and others favoured legalisation. P.J. Sillitoe, Chief Constable of Glasgow, wrote: 'The bettors [*sic*] of the middle class would, I think, welcome the recommendation [to legalise postal betting], removing as it does the illegality and consequent furtiveness of their transactions.'[26] In the event, the SHHD's wish to establish a legislative onslaught did not prevail; the Betting and Lotteries Act 1934 legalised the tote on licensed racecourse and greyhound tracks, but banned it elsewhere. With the football pools fully legalised and already big-business, the 1934 Act effectively started the process of liberalisation of the gambling law, and led by the late 1940s to bookies operating virtually openly in betting 'shops' in Glasgow, Edinburgh and other Scottish towns.[27] Full legalisation of off-course betting in 1961 was merely the confirmation of an accepted defeat by the state in Scotland as in Britain as a whole in its 'war' against gambling.

Gambling prejudiced the state in Scotland against working-class sport. Between 1890 and 1920 betting became intimately connected with every major form of competitive working-class sport – indoors or outdoors. From billiards to football, quoits to greyhound racing, betting by participants or spectators characterised sporting recreation in urban Scotland. With every attempt at suppression came new forms. When the police in the shipbuilding town of Govan started to enforce the new ban on street betting in May 1904, quoiting in back closes became 'a blind' for gambling whereby betting adjacent to a sporting event was legal; in one court case the police alleged that the bets at a quoits game behind a tenement were actually being placed on horses. 'If there had been no betting,' the court was told, 'there would have been no quoiting.'[28]

The Scottish Office and the police connived in the fiction that legislation and suppression of gambling might work, but Scottish Office inaction (and its files) indicate that though off-course betting remained illegal until 1961, the police and the SHHD regarded the 1934 Act as intimating the effective concession of defeat to a burgeoning popular pastime. However, there was no immediate moral 'turn' in how working-class sport was perceived. Mass spectator sport was underpinned by possibly an even wider public participation in sports-based gambling, drawing in many – middle-class men and working-class women especially – who were otherwise neither participants nor steady spectators of sports. Whilst the Scottish Office was willing to give up the unwinnable pursuit of gambling, working-class sport was left tarnished as the cause of crime and in itself a major social 'problem'.

This 'problem' was defined in Scotland by football. Its reputation as a male-dominated and machismo sport, accompanied by drinking, gambling and vast crowds which were susceptible to periodic misbehaviour, drove the Scottish Office's approach to all working-class sport. Its Home and Health Department, like the Home Office in England and Wales, came to be involved in sporting matters primarily through football, and specifically through the issues of crowd misbehaviour and crowd safety. What happened in both England and Scotland was the neglect of the second issue on the false and prejudiced assumption that it was only a product of the first.

From 1899 until 1971 the SHHD believed that the football crowd was ungovernable. Football was an element in a culture of drink-sodden men from industrial occupations releasing considerable communal energy on a Saturday afternoon in foul-mouthed abuse and occasional violence. Religious sectarianism exacerbated the fierceness of spectator loyalty in the eyes of the Scottish Office. From the 1890s, Protestant Rangers and Catholic Celtic in Glasgow was copied, though never matched, by similar religious alignments between Hearts and Hibernian in Edinburgh and (less strongly) between Dundee FC and Dundee Hibernian (after 1923 United) clubs in that city.[29] Protestant hatred of Catholics was by no means confined to the working classes. In the 1920s the leadership of the main presbyterian churches exhibited open and profound hostility to both the Roman Catholic Church in Scotland and Irish Catholics,[30] whilst in the 1930s working-class anti-Catholic political parties emerged in Edinburgh and Glasgow attracting as much as a third of the vote at local elections.[31] For the Scottish Office, the bigotry of orange and green has been a perennial problem in the twentieth century, and one which it hoped would go away by ignoring it.

Bigoted, rough and violent, football crowds were untameable. This Scottish Office attitude emerged from its first interest in sport – the riot at Greenock on Saturday, 8 April 1899 when supporters of neighbouring Port Glasgow Athletic invaded the pitch at Cappielow during a cup game against the home side, Morton.[32] The riot itself was clearly a serious affair, as the Chief Constable of Greenock makes clear in his report to Sir Colin Scott Moncrieff, Under Secretary of State for Scotland. Not only had Port Glasgow Athletic FC supporters openly told police constables on duty at the start of the match that they intended to invade the pitch and have the cup tie abandoned if their team was losing, but the police – 1 inspector, 2 sergeants, 19 foot constables and 2 mounted constables – were unable to prevent the pitch invasion by some 2,000 supporters. When after serious rioting the two mounted police managed to push the crowd off the pitch, a supply line of stones was created from nearby Oswald Street by the Port Glasgow fans, leading to some police injuries. In the weeks that followed, 36 men and boys were arrested for offences relating to the pitch invasion.

The Scottish Office interest in this case was aroused with the arrest nine days after the match of Bailie James McLaughlin, a magistrate of the separate burgh of Port Glasgow, when he tried to obstruct the police in the arrest of a suspected football rioter. John Angus, the Chief Constable of Greenock, made a variety of allegations to the Scottish Office concerning McLaughlin's influence over the Port Glasgow Police. Angus wrote: 'From then till now the Port Glasgow Police have been at his mercy.'[33] A Greenock detective described McLaughlin as 'an Irishman and a leader of the rough Roman Catholic class in Port Glasgow to which I understand most of the men arrested belong'. The identification of football disturbance with Irish Catholics ran throughout the treatment of both the Chief Constable and the Scottish Office. The Greenock police chief defended his decision not to chase the rioters on the grounds that 'when I reflected that in Port Glasgow to one of the roughest working class populations in Scotland with a large male element in proportion to the female, there is only on day duty an Inspector, a sergeant and 4 constables, I came to the conclusion that the course I had contemplated might lead to a serious disturbance in Port Glasgow with which the local force would not be able to cope, and I dispersed the crowd and sent my men home for rest.'[34] In all, 36 alleged rioters were arrested, a large number of them at what was described as 'an Irish wake' in Port Glasgow. A follow-up inquiry by the Renfrewshire Football Association was relieved to hear from the match referee that all the missiles thrown by Port Glasgow fans at the game were aimed at the police and not at Morton players or himself. The Secretary of State, Lord Balfour, was happy that Bailie McLaughlin was to be prosecuted, and of the police action at the football match considered that 'so far as one can judge the police officers [seem] to have acted with pluck, and a good deal of self control'.

Neil Tranter has convincingly shown that the riot 'was the result of bitter and long-standing division caused by differences [between the supporters of the two sides] in class, ethnicity and religion'. The disturbance, he continued, was fostered by 'a strong sense of working-class deprivation and hostility to the established forces of law and order and by the sharpness of the distinction between the worlds of "rough" lower working-class culture, on the one hand, and 'respectable working-class and middle-class culture on the other',[35] It also shows, as Tranter further suggests, that there was a public perception that such disorder was an extension of the sport itself – of the violent play by the players – and, furthermore, that there was also premeditation by leading 'rough' supporters who would give signals when to commence disorder. Most obviously, though, the chief constable and detectives of the Greenock police deployed the words which would register with the Scottish Office and its political governors: 'rough', 'Irish Catholic' and 'working-class'. This was a discourse which relegated football to a different league from not just middle-class sport but from civilised society at large. It was the sport of urban heathens.

Most revealingly, at no point in this case, or indeed in any other case for another 50 years, did the Scottish Office or the Secretary of State express any serious interest in the wider issues of crowd behaviour or safety at football matches or other sporting events. Football was by the 1900s attracting up to 100,000 people to watch the big matches, and crowd misbehaviour and crowd safety incidents were common; most spectacular among the latter was the collapse of terracing at Ibrox Stadium in 1902 during a Scotland v. England international when 25 people were killed and 500 injured.[36] Yet between the Cappielow riot of 1899 and the late 1940s, it appears that not a single Scottish Office file was opened on the issue of crowd behaviour or safety.[37] This was contrasted with the state's concern with other forms of spectator events. Regulation of music hall, cinemas and dance halls gathered pace from 1878, showing especial concern for crowd capacities, fire exits and avoidance of crushing, and local authorities in Scotland as elsewhere in

Britain had been given special powers of inspection in all such venues.[38] Yet, no such special powers were forthcoming for sports grounds in Britain until 1975. To understand why, it is best to look at the circumstances in which the SHHD and the Home Office tackled the issue between the 1940s and 1960s.

The Home Office and the Scottish Office were shaken by the disaster at Burnden Park, Bolton in March 1946, in which 33 people died in a terracing crush. In England this gave rise to the Home Office's Hughes Report which recommended licensing and inspection of sports grounds.[39] In Scotland, the Scottish Office sought to parallel the Home Office, but found that it had no information base from which to start. It had absolutely no data at all on Scottish sports venues: not on their sizes, capacities or even their locations. In collecting what information it could, it transpired that most senior football clubs in Scotland had no fixed maximum crowd limits, and were able to offer the SHHD in most cases only the record crowd numbers. Not even the Scottish Football Association (SFA) had details on crowd capacities. Moreover, a trawl by Scottish Office lawyers found that, apart from general sewerage and building controls, the only specific law affecting sports grounds was a bylaw of 1903, possibly included in general legislation after the Ibrox disaster of 1902, which gave burgh surveyors rather generalised powers to specify access and exit points, and the safe construction of stands or enclosed terraces.[40]

The Burnden Park disaster gave rise to a Home Office conference on licensing and regulation of sports grounds in England and Wales, and a similar conference was called by the Home and Health Department at St. Andrews House in Edinburgh in November 1947. This was attended by 15 sports organisations, half of them at their own request. Despite some disagreement over details, there was a consensus in favour of legislating for sports-ground safety and licensing, and the SHHD was sanguine about it being obtained. But seven months later, in July 1948, the Scottish Office and the Home Office reached the conclusion that though licensing of sports grounds was desirable, it was not a legislative priority. Instead, a voluntary 'Memorandum of Measures to be Taken for the Safety of the Public at Sports Grounds' was drawn up jointly by the Scottish Office and the Home Office, recommending in a voluntary code that there should be local-authority inspection of all grounds with more than 10,000 spectators, agreed safety limits, and, for grounds with over 25,000 spectator limits, there should also be internal telephone systems and mechanical recording of spectator numbers at the turnstiles. This was a document with no sanctions, issued by the SFA, for instance, to senior football clubs in Scotland without enforcement. It resulted in no follow-up monitoring of enforcement or effect, and seems to have had little or no impact; certainly, neither the Scottish Office nor, it would seem, local authorities paid any attention to its enforcement.[41] As a result, the Scottish Office sports conference followed the example of its English counterpart in coming to naught.

However the issue did not go away. In June 1953 the Scottish Police Superintendants' Council wrote to the Scottish Office saying that 'we think the time has arrived when there should be regulations governing the conduct of spectators and the lay-out of grounds, etc., on the same lines as that provided for in the Cinematograph Acts and Regulations'.[42] This was followed a few months later, on 19 September, by a half-time riot at an Old Firm match at Ibrox in Glasgow when Celtic fans became incensed at the police tearing down a green and white streamer-banner whilst orange flags at the Rangers end were left untouched. In the disturbances twelve people were hurt and eight arrested. As the *Glasgow Herald* reporter put it, 'the impression had been given that discrimination has been shown by the police'.[43] This resulted in October 1953 in the Glasgow Magistrates Committee asking the Secretary of State for Scotland to introduce a licensing system to end disturbances at 'needle matches' in the city. The Secretary of State James Stuart and SHHD officials resisted this overture very strongly, and persisted in doing so through the next eight years of seemingly constant concern with crowd control and safety in Scottish senior football. Indeed, the policy position adopted in response to this first overture from Glasgow Corporation in early October 1953 defined the Scottish Office approach for nearly 20 years. The file minute records:

> I fail to see how licensing [of sports grounds] would have the result of preventing a repetition of the disorder that occurred at Ibrox Stadium on the 19th September. Simply to regulate the number of persons admitted to the ground would not prevent the throwing of bottles, etc. by the unruly element. It would restrict the attendance and so the number of those who might be injured as a result of the bottle throwing or in the stampede that would probably ensure would be reduced but only comparatively so since in any event there would a very large number of spectators.

A second minute added the next day, on 2 October, completed the policy, recommending the SFA to have the 'courage' to close grounds for a period after trouble as apparently the Football Association did in England:

> There is in fact very little disorder at matches in England, and I have no doubt that the action taken by the Football Association has brought about this happy result. I understand that the Rangers and Celtic are strongly represented on the Scottish Football Association and this may have a bearing on consideration of these cases of disorder.[44]

However, three days after that minute the Secretary of State was informed by his civil servants that there was 'pretty strong public feeling' about the Ibrox incident, and that he should after all meet and 'listen sympathetically' to the Glasgow magistrates. At this juncture, the SHHD increased its pressure upon the SFA which, as a result, issued a Memorandum in November which quoted article 114 of its constitution. This placed the onus for crowd control upon the clubs, specifically the home clubs. The SFA memorandum went on:

> The chief offenders [in crowd disturbances in Scotland] have been alleged supporters of the Celtic Club. Since 1935 Celtic FC have been ordered to post warning bills on their ground on six occasions. In 1941 their ground was closed for one month. In 1946, they were fined £50. On several occasions they have been instructed to insert warning notices and appeals for good behaviour in their club programmes.[45]

Eight days later the Secretary of State met a delegation from the SFA, and he asked them to use article 114 to close grounds after crowd disturbances. At the same time, the SHHD instructed all Scottish Chief Constables to report football rowdyism anywhere in Scotland to procurators fiscal, noting: 'It seems clear that rowdyism at football matches may occur not only in Glasgow itself but on any ground on which the Celtic Football Club is playing.'[46] Celtic were further pinpointed by Scottish Office inquiries with the SFA regarding the flying of the Eire flag at Celtic Park, which had been banned in 1952 but rescinded shortly after.

In this way, the issue of crowd control at sports became an object of studied inaction by the SHHD. It regarded all aspects of spectator sports to be matters for the governing bodies, and was ready to agree with the

SFA that problems were largely due to Celtic supporters. Its inaction persisted during and after a period of intense concern about crowd (and player) misbehaviour at senior football matches between 1958 and 1961, when incidents of crowd disturbances and safety at, or travelling to and from, twelve football matches were reported in detail to the Scottish Office.[47] The Rangers v. Motherwell match on 1 March 1961 is typical of how the issue was tackled. This flood-lit mid-week Scottish Cup tie at Ibrox was attended by 85,385 people, but some arrived late, not aware that it was a 7.15 p.m. kick-off. The latecomers rushed to get in, resulting in an enclosure barrier giving way in passage 6, with one boy suffering a fractured pelvis. The gates were closed, enraging 500 fans locked outside, and a further 500 who were already in the ground were allowed to leave at half time because of an uncleared crush below that passage. The Chief Constable's report made out that the game was nothing exceptional. There were, he reported to the town clerk of Glasgow, only two sudden deaths, two 15-year-old boys injured in crushes, and a 64-year-old man injured falling off a lavatory wall; in addition, six boys and one female fainted. The report is couched in terms that this death and injury toll was quite passable, if not normal. Apart from recommending a reduction in capacity for flood-lit matches from 90,000 to 80,000, this police report left both Glasgow Corporation and the Scottish Office with the impression that the match was a satisfactorily policed and regulated event.[48]

This was typical. Until 1967 the Scottish Office was involved in a general washing of hands and passing of the buck in relation to both crowd safety and behaviour. It neither felt that it had any role to play, nor was it willing to empower local authorities to license sports grounds. Nor was the latter merely a snub to Glasgow Corporation. Dundee Corporation took the matter so seriously that it considered promoting a private act of parliament to give it licensing powers at Tannadice (Dundee United FC) and Dens Park (Dundee FC). When again rejecting a request for licensing of grounds in 1958, the Scottish Office minute informed the Secretary of State:

> It does not appear that the general safety of the large crowds who attend these matches is endangered. But the possibility of serious danger is always there. When bottles are thrown there is a scramble to get away from the area and there are clearly circumstances in which serious accidents may happen.

The Scottish office acknowledged that such crowd endangerment or bad behaviour would not be tolerated in cinemas or dance halls, but felt that there were no methods of crowd control in sports grounds: 'There is nothing comparable at football matches, and it is difficult to invent anything.' Ticketing was considered unworkable, and the SHHD concluded – without any real evidence – that though legislation failed to get off the ground in 1947, the Burnden Park disaster had 'probably influenced clubs themselves to check on safety precautions'. In the end, the SHHD view was this:

> Would licensing cure rowdyism? One imagines there is no parallel in English football to Rangers-Celtic feeling. Similarly, there is no parallel to the effect on football finances of closing either Rangers ground or the Celtic ground or both: there are many lucrative grounds in England, and probably only these two in Scotland.[49]

Nothing changed until the late 1960s when a new impetus for concern at crowd safety and behaviour came from south of the border. In 1968 Britain's first Minister for Sport, Denis Howell, instigated the setting up of a Working Party on Crowd Behaviour at Football Matches, chaired by Sir John Lang, a retired civil servant and vice-chairman of the Sports Council. Among its 12 members there was one representative from each of the Scottish Football Association and the Scottish Football League, plus an Assistant Chief Constable of Glasgow and an official at the SHHD.[50] The Working Party took evidence from a variety of sources, including match reports from FA referees, and special evidence on a Newcastle v. Glasgow Rangers Fairs Cup tie which resulted in crowd disturbance. Its report of April 1969 indicated the level of inaction of the previous 20 years by re-stating the need to implement the recommendation for licensing of grounds contained in the Hughes Report following the Burnden Park disaster of 1946. As a second-level recommendation, it felt that though the suggested safety controls in the Home Office and Scottish Office Memorandum on Crowd Safety of 1947 'have generally been found to work satisfactorily', they should be repeated and updated.[51] Among new measures to be considered were the installation of closed circuit television (first used at West Ham's Upton Park in March 1969), the installation of perimeter fencing, walls or moats to prevent pitch invasions, increased seating of spectators, and the increased granting of liquor licenses to sports grounds. This last recommendation proved extremely troublesome to the SHHD, whose representative on the Working Party opposed it to the point of considering a Minority Report; he wrote in a file minute that it would be inconceivable for Rangers and Celtic fans to share a bar at Ibrox and Hampden, where the presence of alcohol for sale would inflame 100,000 supporters.[52] As a result of the Report, the SFA agreed to reissue the 1947 memorandum, recommending – but not requiring – annual ground inspection of senior clubs 'by a qualified person' with a certificate to be forwarded to the Association.[53] With some other mild recommendations to do with size of exits and the strengthening of crush barriers, the Working Party Report passed the responsibility for all of these issues back to the governing bodies of soccer.

In this way, despite the increased level of state interest in sport by the late 1960s, there was studied inaction over crowd safety and crowd behaviour, and confusion of the two issues. The low level of commitment by government to improve the quality of the spectator environment was matched by a lack of self-regulation by the football authorities. One of the most stark features of the period between the Hughes Report of 1946 and the Lang Report of 1969 is the absence of any real attempt to collect information about, and to set technical standards, of spectator behaviour and sports-ground design – whether in England or in Scotland. A further striking aspect is that though the Lang Working Party included two representatives from the Sports Council, issues of crowd safety and behaviour at sports events were considered to be the prerogative of the Home Office and the SHHD, whilst all other sport-related issues were for the sports quangos. This was causing irritation in certain quarters by the mid-1960s. By then sports quangos had established links with professional football, but they were hampered legislatively in what could be accomplished. This was one cause of May Brown, the general secretary of the Scottish Council of Physical Recreation, remarking in her evidence to the Labour government's inquiry into football in 1966: 'one point that has to be faced is that, in the eyes of many adults in authority, the game of soccer is not as socially acceptable as rugby'.[54]

As a consequence, government regarded football until as late as the 1970s as a commercial game of the working classes with little 'rational' social benefit. It was a 'policing' issue, a 'problem', one for the Scottish Home and Health Department (along with its other police and judicial responsibilities), and not one for either the Scottish Education Department or the sports-promoting quangos set up in post-war Scotland. Even the second Ibrox disaster of 1971 produced little urgency. In 1975, 90 years after music halls were first regulated and almost 70 years after cinema and dance-hall regulation started, safety certification of sports grounds was enacted which, reinforced by further legislation in 1987,[55] heralded the radical transformation of nearly all major spectator-sports venues in the 1990s. With such massive crowds and such immense and dangerous passions, sport was the last arena of industrial popular culture into which the state stepped to protect the ordinary spectator. Ignorance and prejudice, combined with a feeling that the football crowd was 'ungovernable', kept the state out. Yet, as the second article will go on to show, an alternative, or rather an *additional*, perception of sport had already emerged by the 1940s in Scottish Office thinking: that sport could and should be properly organised, regulated and promoted for the betterment of society at large.

NOTES

1. S.J. Jones, *Workers at Play: A Social and Economic History of Leisure 1918–1939* (London, 1986), pp.87–104; J. Walvin, *Leisure and Society 1830–1950* (London, 1978), pp.128–60; G. Cross, *Time and Money: The Making of Consumer Culture* (London and New York, 1993), pp.114–53.
2. R. Holt, *Sport and the British: A Modern History* (Oxford, 1989), pp.344–6; M. Polley, *Moving the Goalposts: A History of Sport and Society since 1945* (London and New York, 1998), pp.12–34.
3. D. Brailsford, 'Religion and Sport in Eighteenth-century England: "For the Encouragement of Piety and Virtue and for the Preventing or Punishing of Vice, Profaneness and Immorality"', *British Journal of Sports History*, 1 (1984), 166–83, at 167–8.
4. N.L. Tranter, 'The Social and Occupational Structure of Organised Sport in Central Scotland during the Nineteenth Century', *International Journal of the History of Sport*, 4 (1987).
5. W.H. Fraser, 'Developments in Leisure', in W.H. Fraser and R.J. Morris, *People and Society in Scotland vol II 1830–1914* (Edinburgh, 1990).
6. J. Lowerson, 'Sport and the Victorian Sunday: The Beginnings of Middle-class Apostasy', *British Journal of Sports History*, 1 (1984), 202–20, at 208; J.A. Mangan and C. Loughland, 'Fashion and Fealty: The Glaswegian Bourgeoisie, Middle-class Schools and the Games Ethic in the Victorian and Edwardian Eras', *International Journal of the History of Sport*, 5 (1988), 133–5.
7. For the similar English context, see J. Lowerson, *Sport and the English Middle Classes 1870–1914* (Manchester, 1993).
8. N.L. Tranter, 'Organized Sport and the Middle-class Woman in Nineteenth-century Scotland', *International Journal of the History of Sport*, 6 (1989).
9. N. Tranter, *Sport, Economy and Society in Britain 1750–1914* (Cambridge, 1998), pp.78–93.
10. R Holt, 'Football and the Urban Way of Life in Nineteenth-century Britain', in J.A. Mangan (ed.), *Pleasure, Profit and Proselytism: British Culture and Sport at Home and Abroad 1700–1914* (London, 1988).
11. G. Sloan, *Stirling Races* (Stirling, 1986), pp.20–7; C.G. Brown, *Religion and Society in Scotland*

since 1707 (Edinburgh, 1997), p.99.

12. A fuller account of the broader struggle for rational recreation appears in C.G. Brown, 'Popular Culture: The Continuing Struggle for Rational Recreation', in T.M. Devine and R. Finlay (eds.), *Scotland in the Twentieth Century* (Edinburgh, 1996).

13. S[cottish] R[ecord] O[ffice], DD5/1247 Billiard and Bagatelle Rooms.

14. SRO, DD5/1049 Bylaws – Public billiard and Bagatelle Rooms. See also the many files on burghs adopting these powers at DD5/1247–1894.

15. H.K. Clarkson, *A Survey of the Leisure Time of West Lothian School Children* (Edinburgh, 1938), pp.11–13.

16. SRO, DD5/1196, Stirling Children's Playgrounds 1924; S[tirling] A[rchive] S[ervices], SB2/1/1, Police Court Stirling, Ledger of Fines Imposed 1950–67.

17. Burgh Police (Scotland) Act, 1892, s. 393; Street Betting Act, 1906; Burgh Police (Scotland) (Amendment) Act, 1903, s. 51.

18. SRO, HH1/1841, Mechanical Games in Use at Fairgrounds; HH1/1843, Automatic Gaming Machines; HH1/1848, Royal Commission on Betting.

19. SRO, HH1/1843.

20. SRO, HH1/1838, Betting Offices in Glasgow.

21. Data from pamphlet by Scottish National League Against Betting and Gambling, in SRO, HH1/1848.

22. SRO, HH1/1847, Betting etc: 'The Scotch Coupon'.

23. Statistics calculated from data in SRO, HH1/1849.

24. *Royal Commission on Lotteries and Betting, Interim Report, 1933*, Cmnd 4234, 21–2.

25. *Royal Commission on Lotteries and Betting, Minutes of Evidence, Fourteenth Day, 1932.*

26. SRO, HH1/1849, Royal Commission on Betting.

27. By the late 1940s, bookies were operating openly in shop premises with grills, television sets and properly printed betting slips, and invited newspapers to print photographs of them. J. Prendergast, *'Edge Up': Memoirs of a Glasgow Street Bookmaker* (Glasgow, 1992), pp.212–42; *Edinburgh Evening News*, 28 Jan. 1955.

28. *Clydebank and Renfrew Press*, 28 April 1905.

29. See B. Murray, *The Old Firm: Sectarianism, Sport and Society in Scotland* (Edinburgh, 1984), and B. Murray, *The Old Firm in the New Age* (Edinburgh, 1998).

30. C.G. Brown, *Religion and Society*, pp.191–6.

31. T. Gallagher, *Glasgow: The Uneasy Peace* (Manchester, 1987), and T. Gallagher, *Edinburgh Divided* (Edinburgh, 1987).

32. SRO, HH55/297, Riot at Greenock Football Ground, 1899. N.L. Tranter, 'The Cappielow Riot and the Composition and Behaviour of Soccer Crowds in Late Victorian Scotland', *International Journal of the History of Sport*, 12 (1995), 125–40.

33. SRO, HH55/297, letter from John Angus to Sir Colin Scott Moncreiff, 20 April 1899.

34. Ibid. A civil servant, not allowing his minister to be fooled, wrote in the margin of this passage 'Population 12,000, sexes nearly equal'.

35. Tranter, 133–4.

36. T. Mason, *Association Football and English Society 1863–1915* (Brighton, 1980), pp.154–7.

37. Only issues of tackling 'controlleable crime', such as pick-pockets at horse races in 1902, were squarely faced. SRO, HH55/299 Lanark Races – Crime.

38. Metropolis Management and Buildings Acts Amendment Act 1878, s. 11–13; Cinematograph Act 1909, s.1; Celluloid and Cinematograph Film Act 1922, s. 1; safety licensing of dance halls in Scottish burghs was initiated under the Burgh Police (Scotland) Act 1903, s. 80.

39. *Enquiry into the Disaster at the Bolton Wanderers' Football Ground on the 9th March 1946. Report by R. Moelwyn Hughes KC*, Cmnd 6846, June 1946.

40. The byelaw was section 31 of the Burgh Police (Scotland) Act, 1903. SRO, HH55/726, Safety Measures at Football Grounds 1947–48. A Home Office Committee of 1924 had recommended no government interference, instead leaving ground regulation to the governing bodies in sport.

41. SRO, HH55/839, Rowdyism at Football Matches, minute 1/10/1953; HH55/991/1, Working Party on Crowd Behaviour at Football Matches 1968–9.

42. 42 SRO, HH55/839, letter of June 1953.

43. *Glasgow Herald*, 21 Sept. 1953; *Scottish Daily Express*, 21 Sept. 1953.
44. SRO, HH55/839, minutes 1/10/1953, 2/10/1953, 5/10/1953.
45. Ibid., SFA Memorandum, 26th Nov. 1953.
46. Ibid., minute 8/12/1953.
47. The matches with crowd and player misbehaviour were: Celtic v. Rangers on 6 Sept. 1958, 1 Jan. 1959, Hibs v. Celtic on 15 March and 11 April 1961, Hibs v. Barcelona on 22 Feb. 1961, Berwick Rangers v. Rangers on 2nd Feb. 1960, Hamilton Accies v. Stirling Albion on 14 March 1961, Stranraer v. Cowdenbeath on 11 March 1961, Rangers v. Fiorentina on 20 May 1961, and Dundee v. Celtic on 4 Nov. 1961. It also had reports on crowd safety incidents at Palmerston Park, Dumfries on 16 March 1958, and Rangers v. Motherwell on 1 March 1961.
48. SRO, HH55,727, Report of J.A. Robertson, Glasgow Chief Constable, to Town Clerk of Glasgow, 6 March 1961.
49. SRO, HH55/839, minute 22/12/1958.
50. The full membership was 2 representatives from each of the FA and the Football League, one each from the SFA, the SFL, the Welsh FA, the FL Secretaries and Managers Association, the PFA (also representing the Scottish PFA), the Home Office and the SHHD, plus the Director of the Sports Council and three co-opted senior policemen.
51. Ministry of Housing and Local Government, *Report of the Working Party on Crowd Behaviour at Football Matches*, HMSO 1968.
52. SRO, HH55/991/1, Working Party on Crowd Behaviour at Football Matches 1968–9, minute by V.C. Stewart 4 Feb. 1969.
53. SRO, HH55/992, Working Party on of Crowd Behaviour at Football Matches, letter of W.P. Allan (Secy., S.F.A.) to V.C. Stewart 13 April 1970. The Memorandum was re-issued by the SFA in Aug. 1970.
54. SRO, ED27/466, Inquiry into Association Football, evidence of May Brown, S.C.P.R., 6 Dec. 1966.
55. Safety of Sports Grounds Act 1975, Safety of Places of Sport Act 1987.

Sport and the Scottish Office in the Twentieth Century: The Promotion of a Social and Gender Policy

CALLUM G. BROWN

The first part of this study has shown how one department of the Scottish Office, the Scottish Home and Health Department (SHHD), perceived working-class sport between 1900 and the 1970s as a social problem associated with gambling, drink, religious sectarianism and male violence, and how this view led it to ignore crowd-safety issues in football. The present essay presents a contrasting development. It examines the emergence from the late 1930s of sport as a policy for social and gender equality, a policy which took root in 1946 in another part of the Scottish Office, the Scottish Education Department (SED). With a focus on amateur participant games and activities, sport started to be perceived as not only separable from 'rough' sports culture but as an antidote to it.

The development of the state's policies towards the promotion of sport owed little to party politics. There were a number of reasons for this. In the first instance, sports administration was not overtly a matter for significant party-political or ministerial concern until 1964, when the first Minister for Sport, Dennis Howell, was appointed by the Labour Government; even then – as will be suggested later – government policy was in most respects a continuation of a strategy already in place among professional and volunteer sports administrators. Scottish Office ministers were less concerned with the substance of their Department's sports policy than with protecting it from interference or, worse, take-over by 'English' ministries and British-wide sports quangos (quasi-autonomous national government organisations). The prime concern –

to be crude about it – was to 'keep the English out', and in that regard
Scottish politicians were happy to let their civil servants and the sports
community in Scotland develop policy. This had started as early as 1937
when the two-year-old voluntary organisation, the Central Council of
Recreative Physical Training (CCRPT),[1] started to be grant-aided by the
Ministry of Education (initially through the shortlived National Fitness
Council created by the Physical Training and Recreation Act 1937) in
England and Wales and became *de facto* the sports quango for Britain.
But the Scottish Fitness Council also created under that Act refused the
CCRPT grant-aid in 1937 to operate in Scotland, making clear 'it was
not wanted' (even though it had Scottish member-organisations like the
Scottish Amateur Athletics Association).[2] A similar though much more
furious debacle occurred when Dennis Howell sought in 1965–66 to
create a British Sports Council. Nobody in Scotland, either in the sports
community or, it seems, in the Scottish Office, had been consulted, and
the result was a vigorous campaign to prevent the English-based
Advisory Sports Council from enveloping Scotland. Though Scotland
lost this battle, it won the war, for a separate Scottish Advisory Sports
Council was set up in 1968 which, in 1972, became the Scottish Sports
Council, autonomous from English ministerial control.[3]

More fundamental to the 'apolitical' perception of sports
development has been the widespread perception that sport should be
viewed as an adjunct to social policy, and more particularly to youth and
community policy. From the 1930s sport was viewed as something in
which the state should participate to further democratic access –
primarily to the working classes and to women – to counter the social
problems of slum areas and council-housing schemes, and the lack of
recreational opportunities for women.

To understand the mechanism by which these social policy objectives
of sport became established, it is important to consider the backgrounds
of the civil servants, salaried sports administrators and voluntary sports
organisers who devised and implemented government sports policy in
Scotland during the key phase between the passing of the Physical
Training and Recreation Act in 1937 and the creation of the Scottish
Sports Council in 1972. Scottish Office civil servants were brought up
on the amateurism of the games ethic – of 'playing the game for the
game's sake' – in Scottish universities, private and 'superior' state
schools. The lead liaison officer for sport, youth and community policy
in the Scottish Education Department between 1946 and 1975 was

George J. Brown HMI.[4] He held responsibility for promoting the spread and development of governing bodies for sports, advising on the grant-aiding of sports development schemes, and liasing between the Scottish Office and the sports quangos in Scotland. Born into a working-class family in Clydebank, he earned a place at Glasgow University in 1929 and at the same time started playing football with Queen's Park at Hampden, Scotland's only amateur senior football club, where in the 1930s he won Scottish Amateur Cup and League medals. Teacher-training and high teacher unemployment led Brown later in that decade to an appointment as warden of one of Scotland's first community centres in the depressed mining town of Blantyre in Lanarkshire. Playing as a forward for 'the Spiders', the 'men with educated feet',[5] exemplified Brown's vision of sport as a civilising pursuit, whilst promoting football and other games among the youngsters of Blantyre displayed his evangelical zeal to spread this sporting gospel to the less fortunate. When the SED established a community education inspectorate immediately after the war, it was men like George Brown who worked-up the state's policy on sport.

Amongst the salaried sports administrators, the key figure in Scotland was May Brown (no relation), the general secretary of the main sports quango, the Scottish Council of Physical Recreation (SCPR) from its foundation in 1953 until 1968. Her father was general secretary of the Scottish Liberal Federation, and she attended George Watson's Ladies College, one of Edinburgh's leading private girls' schools. From there she went on to Anstey College of Physical Education in Warwickshire where she described the inspirational principal as 'not typical of the physical education world' but 'elegant and a woman of the world – a keen Suffragist'.[6] In 1937 May Brown was appointed a trainer of youth leaders for the Edinburgh area of the Scottish Fitness Council, quickly being promoted to be one of the Council's two permanent staff for Scotland – the other being a retired army Colonel. In that capacity in the remaining years of the 1930s, she worked amongst the depressed mining communities in Fife, training redundant miners as youth sports leaders. On the outbreak of the Second World War, she was invited by the YWCA to become the organiser of the Glasgow Keep Fit Movement, and with the help of other women 'PT' teachers such as Winnie Taylor and Doris Robertson, she was undertaking what by the end of the war was called 'sports propaganda'. This included running demonstration classes in the Glasgow Lyric Theatre in keep fit, skipping, Scottish country dancing, ballroom and tap dancing. At the same time, in 1941, she was recruited by the BBC in Glasgow to broadcast 'Early Modern Exercises' which were networked across the Home Service in Britain throughout the war. By these means, May Brown became a popular and well-respected figure, and in 1944 she orchestrated a campaign which led Tom Johnston, the Secretary of State for Scotland, to create a Scottish section of England's renamed Central Council of Physical Recreation (CCPR) with her as secretary. In 1953 this section was reformed into the separate Scottish Office-funded Scottish Council of Physical Recreation with May Brown its general secretary until 1968.[7]

May Brown employed Winnie Taylor and Doris Robertson among her 'technical staff' at the SCPR. Such women were generally not university graduates, but were usually products of teacher-training physical-education establishments like Dunfermline College in Edinburgh and Jordanhill College in Glasgow. Some joined the SCPR as technical staff, running training courses for sports coaches, but others were either grant-funded coaches for sport governing bodies (like the Scottish Amateur Athletics Association) or for individual sports clubs. Winnie Taylor's specialism was athletics, and as well as working for the SCPR from 1953 until 1971, she was from 1954 to 1962 the founding president (and executive committee member thereafter) of the Scottish Women's Amateur Athletic Association (SWAAA) and a well-known figure in the athletics world, becoming in the later 1960s the chairman (*sic*) of the British Women's Amateur Athletic Council. Doris Robertson was a specialist in country dancing, lawn tennis and youth sports, whilst a third officer, Jock Kerr Hunter, was associated with angling, canoeing, golf, pony trekking, sailing and skiing. These sports development personnel became key figures in governing and organisational bodies of their respective sports, creating an intimacy between state and 'governing' sectors which ensured the fusion of sports-policy aims.

The women formed a dynamic elite of committed evangelicals for women's sports. May Brown and Winnie Taylor were both spinsters at a time when quangos were covered by civil service rules and the marriage bar still held sway. Women volunteer sports administrators, on the other hand, were often married, but both sets tended to be drawn from the same social world and held similar social sensibilities. Like May Brown they were usually products of Scottish private girls' schools where in the 1910 and 1920s they had been brought up on hockey and gymnastic classes and had often been exposed to middle-class women teachers of the post-suffrage, post-evangelical age who encouraged young girls to self-fulfilment in the good of society and, especially, of their sex. Single-sex development of women's sporting sphere became their passion. One such woman was Christina Graham[8] who attended James Gillespie's School for Girls in Edinburgh where she was taught by the model for Muriel Spark's character Miss Jean Brodie. During the war she drove a lorry for the ATS, afterwards working as a secretary in the Scottish Education Department. She resigned upon her marriage in 1952 to George Brown of the SED, and in 1956 joined the executive of the SWAAA, serving as secretary from 1958 until 1969 and vice-president and president between 1965 and 1975. For women like Christina Brown, sport was a symbolic freedom to be encouraged upon young women. Solidly middle class, sport was a liberating message to be taken to the working-class girl in her mid teens who was emerging from mixed-sex state school and facing the temptations of boys, drink, rock-and-roll and 'delinquency'. Women's place might still (perhaps reluctantly) be in the home, but sport – especially gender-segregated sport – offered a means for young working-class women to attain personal achievement and fulfilment through getting out of their housing scheme or city for Saturday sports meetings. Summer Saturday afternoons in the 1950s and 1960s were spent by women like Winnie Taylor and Christina Brown in organising athletics meetings at barren 'stadiums' with cinder tracks where, in their furcoats and 'Sunday hats', they presented prizes to thin, tracksuited young women from industrial towns. Sport was the new bourgeois mission to the working-class girl.

Middle-class respectability was a powerful feature of this social world. It was a world of athletics dinners and sponsors' evenings, committee meetings in central Edinburgh or Glasgow, and hours of addressing circulars to women's athletic clubs around Scotland. It was a small world centred in Edinburgh's late Victorian suburbs of dressed sandstone houses. Winnie Taylor was an SCPR employee and worked as honorary president of the SWAAA; Christina Brown was SWAAA secretary and represented her Association on the executive of the SCPR. In the 1950s and 1960s, two committee members of the SWAAA (including the secretary), two committee members of the (men's) SAAA (including its president and secretary), plus the SED sports liaison officer, all lived on a 100-yard stretch of the same street in Edinburgh's middle-class suburb of Morningside.[9] Sports administrators formed a tight suburban corps of the deeply committed.

Jennifer Hargreaves has noted the key role played by women in early sports quangos in England – notably Phyllis Coulson whose initiative founded the CCRPT in 1935, and who with other female members ensured that women's sporting needs were given a high profile.[10] In Scotland, the equivalent person was May Brown who from 1940 until 1968 was the pivotal figure in Scottish sports development, male and female. In addition to being the moving force behind the SCPR from 1953, she initiated other committees and organisations to provide the venue where a nexus of sports promoters could meet, exchange ideas, and develop strategy. At the SCPR, sports governing bodies and promotional organisations could be admitted as affiliated members (numbering over 80 by the end of the 1950s), and an executive committee was elected from key member bodies. It was here that the real work of sports development was done, and an agreed agenda was already in evidence by 1953. First and foremost on this agenda was agreement on the social-improving character of amateur participant sport, both competitive and non-competitive. Second, sport should be made accessible to the urban working classes of Scotland. Third, women's access to sport should be not only improved but women – and especially young working-class women – should be actively encouraged to take up sport in a way they had never done before. And fourth, the process of sports development should involve the adoption of 'best practice' throughout: the best coaching methods should be taught, common systems of training applied to all sports, and the best equipment and facilities should be provided. From these four basic objectives emerged modern state promotion of sport in Scotland.

Government sports promotion in Scotland started as an element of the social policy of the 1930s. From 1927 some 80 playing fields had been provided under the King George V Trust scheme and the National Playing Fields Association, but by the mid-1930s more active sports promotion was being urged by teachers as a means to solve social problems among school-leaving males from the working classes. The scale of youth unemployment was very great in Scottish industrial and mining areas during the inter-war years, and various government committees, notably that on Juvenile Delinquency, had been pressing since the early 1920s for a government policy of promoting social and community centres in such areas. The policy started to take shape in the mid-1930s in the new housing schemes as local councils, education authorities and charitable bodies co-ordinated pioneering projects of youth and community centres, generally located beside sports pitches, leading to enabling provisions in the Education (Scotland) Act of 1936 which were superseded by (and were probably the model for) the Physical Training and Recreation Act of 1937. Walter Elliot, Secretary of State for Scotland, announced in a radio broadcast that a quarter of a million pounds would be available over three years: 'We want to avoid any suggestion of compulsion about physical training and sport. We want our young folks to take healthy exercise and play games for the fun of the thing.'[11]

This connection with youth and community service set the agenda for sports policy. Those who pioneered the implementation of this strategy 'on the ground' in the two years before the Second World War – notably May Brown and George Brown – were rapidly recruited to civil-service employment to make it a national state policy. Sport was to be promoted by outreach 'propaganda'. Between 1947 and 1951, large-scale 'Festivals of Sport' promoting sports participation were mounted in summer schools at St. Andrews and in demonstration events in Glasgow's Kelvin Hall and Edinburgh's Waverley Market.[12] Participation in sport was to be encouraged through existing voluntary organisations (such as boys' clubs and girls' clubs, the Scouting movement and the Boys' Brigades) and in new organisations (notably local-authority youth clubs and community centres). Local authorities in Scotland started to set up youth and community services in the 1940s (the pioneers being Ayrshire and Lanarkshire in 1943–4), and they recruited both part-time and full-time youth leaders to this work. In 1946 a section of the SED was set up to co-ordinate government support for sports and community facilities, empowered by the Education (Scotland) Act of 1945 to establish state 'camps, holiday classes, playing fields, play centres, gymnasiums, swimming baths, and other establishments ... for recreation'.[13] Community centres were seen in the short term 'to provide for relaxation and relief from the fatigue and stress which war conditions have imposed'. The SED subscribed to a circular from the London Ministry of Education in 1944:

> Already it is clear that there is little tradition of leisure amongst large classes of those to whom it has come, and the increase of leisure confronts us with a new social problem. Experience has shown that men and women do not as a rule make the best use of their leisure if the only facilities available outside the home are

those provided by commercial enterprise ... we are of opinion that
the provision of communal facilities for the rational and enjoyable
use of leisure, wherever this may be needed, is a necessary part of
the country's educational system.[14]

In housing estates, the 'social vacuum' was to be filled by community
associations funded to build centres and to employ wardens who 'should
combine the qualities of a parson, teacher, salesman and administrator'.
An SED circular of 1946 on 'The Provision of Facilities for Recreation,
and Social and Physical Training', also identified housing schemes as the
new priority, but it stressed the shortcomings of developments in the
inter-war period. Building community centres at the same time as new
housing was of 'paramount importance if past mistakes which have led
to juvenile delinquency and other social weaknesses are to be avoided'.[15]

Explicit statements of the rationale for state support of sport came in
two government reports of 1960: the Albemarle Committee's report on
the Youth Service in England and Wales, and the Wolfenden
Committee's report on 'Sport and the Community'. Albemarle argued
that sports and physical activities were major leisure-time activities for
adolescent boys and girls, and 'because this interest is unrelated to
academic ability or manual skill, it cuts across the stratification of
society, the incidental effects of which we have deplored'. It went on:

> To many of the young their world is a humdrum affair: their lives
> are tram-lined by the streets and time-tabled by the running of
> buses and trains. The colourful and the unexpected do not happen
> unless they make it. They can do so by violence, destructiveness or
> deliberate breaches of accepted public behaviour. Or they can go
> out of the town to find it. Scouting and Guiding and kindred
> movements ... have shown the young a variety of approaches to the
> object of their search ... It is more doubtful if they can succeed in
> attracting the corner-boy and his girl, with all their wariness and
> suspicion of standards and demands and guidance.

The shortage of facilities and proper sports administration was
identified by the Albemarle Committee as the great obstacle. Even
public parks were not properly used for sports, as they memorably
stated: 'Parks committees often work jointly with cemetery committees,
and they become dedicated only too easily to the task of keeping people
off or under the grass.' 'Recreation,' it concluded, 'is as important in

promoting the physical, intellectual and moral development necessary to turn the teenager into the responsible adult citizen.'[16] Wolfenden reinforced such views, though largely within the games ethic of the English amateur sporting elites.[17] The SCPR endorsed both of these reports – not because they were especially innovative, but because they reiterated the policy of the sports quangos since 1937.[18] Indeed, neither report seem to have had much impact in Scotland where the SCPR and the SED continued to operate along existing policy tracks.

However, there were two major problems. The first of these was finance. Most Scottish funding under the 1937 Act went in the next 30 years in small grants (of under £3,000) to rural areas for village halls and not for sports-dedicated facilities, thus side-lining the needs of both inner-city slum areas and new housing schemes. In addition, the government-funded training course for youth leaders was in suspension between 1950 and 1960.[19] By 1958 there were 152 youth and community leaders in Scotland, but they were unevenly distributed: Lanarkshire with a population of 1.6 million had only 12 leaders, whilst the county of Ross and Cromarty with a population of 60,000 had eight.[20] In the 1950s, officials in the Scottish Office were involved in both inter- and intra-departmental fights over priorities, with housing officials arguing for special-case status for community centres in new housing schemes, the Home Department refusing local authorities borrowing consent for such centres, and the Education Department split between different inspectors with one official stating that he 'felt that there were more urgent things than community centres – for example, children's playgrounds'.[21] Though funding rose appreciably from 1958 (tripling in that year to £245,947), it was to remain relatively modest until the later 1960s.

A second problem was the bias against existing working-class 'rough' sports, evident in Wolfenden. Both May Brown at the SCPR and George Brown at the SED were sensible enough to realise the potential that lay in such sports – especially football – among young working-class males in Scotland. But before the 1970s the amateur sports lobby was so strong that it prevented the SCPR and the Scottish Office from developing extensive links with the world of professional soccer.[22] The SCPR took the bold step of accepting annual donations from the Scottish Football Association, and allowing the latter to use its Largs Centre for coaching courses. In the late 1960s the SCPR instigated a recommendation from the Chester Inquiry into Association Football that the Scottish football league be reorganised from two leagues into three (a move which came a decade later), and sought – unsuccessfully – permission to make grants to professional football clubs for facilities which would be used by the community.[23] May Brown could make little headway in integrating Scotland's national game into government sports policy. By 1968, when she retired, there were 636 further-education classes in sport in Scotland, but not one of these was for football.[24] Other sports also suffered to varying degrees from exclusion from the SCPR – including snooker and, for a time, the new martial arts sports; perhaps in retaliation, the SCPR also excluded hunting and archery. The games ethic still seemed to dominate, distinguishing 'acceptable' and 'rational' sports from the rest.

Yet, the SCPR philosophy was far from elitist. Its remit was to encourage participant amateur sports, the development of approved small and new sports, assist the foundation of sports regulatory bodies, fund and also conduct training courses for coaches, and establish national sports centres. Participation in physical recreation by all was its aim long before the 'sport for all' slogan was endorsed by the Labour Government of the mid-1960s. Evidence collected by the SCPR in Scotland and the CCPR in England and Wales seemed to show that participant sport was growing whilst spectator sport was declining; in Scottish senior football, for instance, league attendances fell by 33.5 per cent between seasons 1948/49 and 1965/66.[25] The SED supported and funded the SCPR in this work, and arranged funding (usually through local-authority loans) for the construction of sports facilities (usually pitches and tracks), dovetailing sports policy with its youth and community policies. As the SCPR said in 1957, 'Very few young people, and certainly not those who might be a problem to the community, will take part in an activity simply because it is good for them.' What it called 'the masses of the population' must be given guidance in how to spend their increased leisure time productively.[26]

The key to attracting and sustaining public participation in sport in the 1950s and 1960s was identified as coaching. The various coaching schemes of the SCPR were designed to spread skilled coaching through sports governing bodies, sports clubs, youth and community services of local authorities, the SCPR-promoted Scottish Sports Holidays Scheme for city dwellers, and the Scottish Industrial Sports Association. There was constant concern that sports should by coached by trained personnel, especially for new or smaller sports. In 1945 it created the National Outdoor Recreation Centre at Glenmore Lodge in the Cairngorms for mountain pursuits (including skiing), and then in 1959 the National Recreation Centre (mainly for track, field and pitch sports) at Inverclyde near Largs (and two years later the water sports centre nearby). Glenmore Lodge had symbolic importance. In Scotland throughout the twentieth century there has been a belief among Scottish ramblers, mountaineers and walkers – especially their representative organisations – that there is a 'right to roam' in the countryside resulting from the alleged absence of a law of trespass as in England and Wales. Because of the absence of definitive legislation or legal judgments, the veracity of this belief is still hotly debated in the late 1990s, but it led civil servants and ministers to exclude Scotland from the Access to Mountains Act of 1939 and the National Parks and Access to the Countryside Act of 1949.[27] Glenmore Lodge signalled the SCPR's commitment to the outdoor movement in Scotland, presaging its negotiation in the early 1960s with Scottish landowners which produced the first access policy for rambling and mountaineering in the form of the 'Countryside Amenities Club' (composed of the Nature Conservancy, the National Trust for Scotland, the Scottish Landowners' Federation, the Forestry Commission, the Hydro-Electric Board, the National Farmers Union, the Scottish Tourist Board and the Scottish Youth Hostels Association) which formed the basis for the subsequent development in the 1970s and 1980s of Scotland's countryside policy.[28]

The SCPR also gave emphasis to 'minor' sporting activities, introducing to Scotland pony-trekking and skiing courses in the 1950s and the sport of orienteering in 1962. It increased the standing of underdeveloped sports – including mountaineering, hill-walking, canoeing and, though a little more cautiously, judo, karate and other martial arts sports. Its work at Glenmore Lodge fostered skiing in Scotland virtually from scratch, leading to the development of Aviemore as a winter tourist resort. Not only did the SCPR and its predecessors set many sporting pursuits on the road to major status in Scotland between 1945 and 1972, but popular access to them owes much to its work. This was no more evident than in women's recreations.

The policy on women's sport that emerged between the 1937 Act and the formation of the Scottish Sport Council in 1972 had several elements to it. Its first and foremost policy was the publicising of sporting recreation – or what the SCPR called 'sports propaganda' aimed at women. May Brown's varied work between 1937 and 1945 created the model which was sustained in the 1950s and 1960s: local publicity campaigns with posters, leaflets, touring exhibitions, newspaper and radio publicity, and demonstrations – often by physical education students, using new types of equipment such as trampolines. This publicity work could only work, however, if there were organisations able to support the would-be sporting girl or woman, and in this task the key role was that of governing bodies for women's sport. Very few such bodies existed in Scotland in the early 1950s, and some were moribund. Most competitive sports were dominated by men, and existing governing bodies provided a very poor service to women's interests. There was a need to provide role models of the competitive sportswoman, especially for working-class women, and to show women as a 'serious' part of the sporting world.

The Scottish Women's Amateur Athletic Association (SWAAA) exemplified the strategy of the SCPR. Formed in 1954, its first President was Winnie Taylor who, as a member of the technical staff of the SCPR, ensured a close relationship between the two bodies. Athletics had a key role to play in expanding women's sport. It was widely regarded as the premier amateur sport, sharing with swimming the status of 'core' sports in the Empire Games and the premier status in the Olympics. Its ethos of individual performance within teams gave it the potential for appealing to women in a way few men's team sports were capable of doing. But the task was daunting. Until that point, the men's association, the SAAA, had held responsibility for women's sport, and it was with some lethargy that it surrendered it in the face of Winnie Taylor's hard work in establishing a presence in the committees and organisations of British athletics (including those related to the Empire and Olympic Games).[29] The earliest success of the SWAAA was in women's cross-country running, but it was track and field athletics which was the heart of its business. In 1955 it inaugurated its own championships and an 'east versus west' contest between Scotland's regions. It imposed itself upon existing male-dominated athletic clubs by using systems of issuing permits for women's events, authorised judges, recognition of athletic records, and prohibition of unregistered clubs and athletes. Executive committee members travelled with 'authority cards' round Scotland to existing sporting occasions with women's events – usually of a local and informal nature – to encourage affiliation to its rules. Many of these were highland games, the most machismo of athletic occasions symbolised by strength events like tossing the caber and throwing weights over bars. Women's events were 'curios' at most highland games where local women were often enrolled on the day to compete against part-time professionals for small cash prizes. Similar events took place in the Lowlands and the Borders; some were factory sports, such as at Babcock and Wilcox Engineering at Renfrew, the Singers Sewing Machine Sports Day in Clydebank, Collins the Publishers Sports in Glasgow, Edinburgh Inter Works Sports, and the sports days of Aberdeen Corporation and the Coal Industry Social Welfare Organisation; some were local games, such as the Stewarton Bonnet Guild sports and the ironically-named Braw Lads' games in Galashiels. All of these and many others became targets for the SWAAA mission, in which executive committee members turned up to sell the benefits of becoming an authorised meeting for amateur women's events.[30] It bullied and cajoled games' secretaries around the country to admit its judges, use its rules and recognise women's events as 'serious' sport. It encouraged the mounting of events over recognised distances and use of proper weights in shot-putt, discuss and javelin, the proper laying out of lanes, the use of trained timekeepers, and good practice in field sports – in one instance banning the use of the judge's finger to mark where the shot-putt had landed. It used its disciplinary powers with severity; athletes from the Vale of Leven Athletics Club were banned in 1956 from entry to SWAAA meetings because the club failed to affiliate, and Butlin's had their SWAAA permit withdrawn in 1960 on two counts when they allowed a professional woman athlete to compete with amateurs over a three-mile road walk – judged by the Association an 'excessive distance'.[31] The Association brought other organisations and promoters under its wing, including youth and community workers, the Scottish Industrial Sports Association and the Scottish Schoolgirls' Athletic Association.[32] In return for accreditation, the SWAAA held out the prizes of specialist coaching, recognition of records, and entry to its championships.

In trying to turn informal girls' sports into formal and recognised events, the SWAAA had not only to impose itself on existing organisations and games meetings. It found that large numbers of women entered for events at games and then withdrew or failed to turn up; it sought strenuously to combat this lack of serious application – especially among women police officers at the Edinburgh Police sports days.[33] It took its mission to all corners of the country. Women's athletics was particularly slow to develop in the Highlands and Islands where in 1962 the North of Scotland Amateur Athletic Association reported that there were only 20 women competitors, a mere six of whom travelled outwith their own town or village to race. The SWAAA wished 'to dispel the idea that it is not "ladylike" to take part in athletics – a feeling prevalent in the North', and it sent 'top-class woman athletes' from the south to compete in northern athletic meetings.[34] But such demonstration and representative teams cost money, and the Association was under constant pressure from athletes – most from working-class backgrounds – to pay travelling expenses.[35] Equally important for the Association was the maintenance of femininity, decorum and respectability amongst its athletes. The wearing of proper racing singlets, shorts (which the Association specified should be dark-coloured) and track-suits between events was a constant issue for the executive committee in the 1950s and 1960s in its combat against what it called 'untidiness'.[36] The executive committee held matronly attitudes towards its young charges; at the 1962 Empire Games at Perth, Australia, only 1 woman athlete (and 3 women swimmers) were selected for Scotland, and the SWAAA issued a protest when it discovered that no provision had been made for 'a Team Manager or chaperone'.[37] Yet at the same time, the Association was seeking to confront male prejudice against the sporting woman. At a national inter-sport conference organised at the National Sports Centre at Inverclyde in December 1958, a demonstration of training exercises by two female athletes was reported as being 'received with some surprise and interest by the male members at the conference'.[38] The SWAAA always sought the most appropriate occasions for publicity; in 1962 it agreed to organise a demonstration women's relay race during the half-time interval of the Celtic v. Real Madrid football match at Parkhead.[39] Women's athletics had to be put on the map by confronting male sports culture in its 'roughest' heartland.

The number of athletic meetings over which SWAAA held control rose from two in 1955 to 25 in 1971. From being responsible for a mere handful of women competitors, it had 390 registered athletes by 1967 and 1,027 by 1973.[40] This striking success was achieved mostly outwith the schools and mostly within the framework of existing male athletic clubs in working-class industrial cities and towns: clubs like Bellahouston Harriers, Broxburn, Clydebank Harriers, Greenock Rankin Park, Maryhill Harriers and Shotts. There was little romance in the surroundings of most club training grounds, and even the tracks used for the premier competitions in the 1950s and 1960s were insalubrious: White City (also a greyhound track) and Ibrox in Glasgow, Meadowbank (the old track beside the speedway circuit) in Edinburgh, Shotts and many other cinder tracks with poor and cramped changing rooms. Despite the environment, romance was part of the attraction of mixed-sex athletic clubs, and a considerable number of marriages emerged from the sport. However, the SWAAA adamantly stuck to women-only championship meetings – even in the 1950s when it had to call on the men's association to supply the judges. It was important for young women to gain their own confidence in the sport, and to be free of the distracting machismo of male athletes who could run faster or jump higher and longer.

Success for women's athletics also needed competitive quality. When the Association sought to assemble its first international team, for the Empire Games in Cardiff in 1958, it had to ask around the clubs for names of 'promising' women athletes – in the end sending eight athletes who did not perform especially well; one of them told the Association 'that Scottish athletes were just not good enough and that more serious training was necessary'.[41] The following year at the British Games in Surrey, the SWAAA team won two gold and one silver medals (in discus, javelin and shot-putt) but only five Scottish athletes made the 'British standard'; the team manager commented that 'to improve Scottish performances, an effort will require to be made to collect suitable people for training'.[42] By 1961 no female Scottish athlete had been selected to run for Britain, but in 1965 a Scottish woman first broke a world record – May Campbell in the Indoor 600 yards.[43] At the Commonwealth Games in Jamaica in 1966, six athletes were sent and four of them recorded fourth places, but it was at the highly televised 1970 Games in Edinburgh, when the SWAAA entered 21 athletes, that the Scottish people became aware of the status of Scottish female athletics.[44] With ticket sales of 235,000 (over half for athletics), women's sports were for the first time widely perceived to be 'serious'. Scottish women athletes won 2 gold and 1 bronze medals compared to the men's 2 gold, 2 silver and 1 bronze.[45] That success raised the attractiveness of the sport to young women, and the number of registered female athletes in Scotland doubled in two years, paving the way for internationally renowned Scottish track and field competitors of the later 1970s, 80s, and 90s.

The work of the SWAAA was a model development for the SCPR and the SED. But if athletics put women's amateur competitive sport on the map of Scottish recreation by the end of the 1960s the SCPR – like its English equivalent – interpreted sport for women in the widest sense. In the late 1950s it produced a widely selling booklet called *Housework with Ease* which combined messages of physical fitness, safety and domestic efficiency.[46] The encouragement of new sports for women was of equal importance to the SCPR. When it fostered new sports, women's sections were integrated immediately: in orienteering (which the SCPR introduced in 1962 when it set up an exhibition run at Dunkeld with invited athletes from Scandinavia),[47] and in pony-trekking, mountaineering, hillwalking and outward-bound activities. In the era of comprehensive slum-clearance in the 1950s and 1960s, great store was laid by the benefits of removing children from the unhealthy inner-city areas of Glasgow, Edinburgh and Dundee to the clean-air and majesty of the Highlands. The 'Girls in Industry' course of the Scottish Industrial Sports Association was grant-aided to take working girls to the SCPR mountain centre at Glenmore Lodge.[48] With the Scottish hills perceived as men's domain until the 1950s,[49] the SCPR used many publicity photographs of young women in waterproof clothing and rucksacks. It was a mission to give the working-class female a self-image which could combine femininity with attainable sporting activity.

There was another major conceptual (and funding) leap identified to promote women's and working-class sports. By the late 1950s the provision over three decades of playing fields was recognised as a limiting policy, and the SED, the SCPR and the SWAAA, amongst others, were formulating proposals for community-based multi-sports centres. With attractive changing rooms, washing and toilet facilities, and properly lit, secure and managed premises, sport would lose its association with dark, dank and grimy facilities and, if sited correctly, would offer working-class women their first effective neighbourhood access to physical recreation. A series of conferences on 'The Future of Sport' were organised by the SED (and chaired by George Brown) between 1959 and 1963, and these mobilised support from sports bodies, youth organisations, local authorities, education officials and town planners.[50] The idea dovetailed neatly with emerging perceptions of the social problems associated with mass rehousing underway in the late 1950s. The stumbling block was government finance. Scottish Office funding for sport rose from a meagre £14,757 in 1954–55 to £26,000 in 1961–62 and £44,200 in 1963–64 – all of it channelled through the SCPR.[51] In 1962 Edinburgh Town Council announced plans to fund and build Scotland's first multi-purpose sports centre at Meadowbank (to include swimming pool, athletics and cycling tracks, sports hall and restaurant),[52] but when this was abandoned in January 1964 the SWAAA took the lead in protesting, mounting a press and lobbying campaign which resulted ten months later – after the election of the Labour government – in another conference at which the Scottish Office offered to fully fund one prototype multi-sports centre somewhere in Scotland.[53] From the ten local authorities which entered bids, Glasgow Corporation won (undoubtedly reflecting the Labour Party's strength in the city), and though the SCPR initially wanted the centre placed in the newly-slum-cleared Gorbals, it was decided to place it at Bellahouston in the south-west of the city.[54] Formally opened by Bruce Millan MP in April 1968, Bellahouston became the model both for the design and the management of sports centres in Scotland. The SCPR contributed half of the management team, some of whom were sent to the United States for training, and within a year the centre had 6,000 individual members, was fully booked in the evenings and at weekends, and national guidelines were established for sports centres. Within two years sports centres were opened at Glenrothes and Meadowbank in Edinburgh under SCPR guidance, the Bell's Sport Centre opened in Perth and an athletics and cycling stadium in Grangemouth, and steps were taken to set up Scotland's first course in recreation management.[55] In this process, women's sports organisations played a very significant part, contributing to the consultation process for the design of each sports centre, undertaking site visits and ensuring the interests of women and women athletes were accommodated. With the Commonwealth Games of 1970 adding further to sporting facilities in Edinburgh (aided by £750,000 from the Scottish Office), and Scotland winning a record 25 medals, amateur competitive sports became endowed with a new aura of both attractive environments and competitive success.

Between the 1940s and the early 1970s, the work of sports quangos (led by the Scottish Council of Physical Recreation), the Scottish Office and sports governing bodies like the Scottish Women's Amateur Athletics Association transformed the sporting life of Scotland. Inequalities in social and gender access were tackled within a social-policy framework of slum-clearance and council-housing programmes. Much had been achieved by 1972 when the Scottish Sports Council superseded both the SCPR and the grant-awarding role of the SED. Between 1968 and 1973 the number of sports classes in further-education in Scotland rose from 636 to 2,155, and the range of sports covered increased from 14 (from angling to swimming) to 48 (aikido to yoga). The number of indoor sports centres rose from one in 1968 to 25 in 1973 and to 42 by 1975. Increased access bred competitive success; Scotland's medal tally in all sports in successive Empire-Commonwealth Games between 1950 and 1966 ranged between 9 and 14 (and between zero and three for women), but then in 1970 rose to 25 (and 5 for women).[56] Class and gender equality in sports participation also grew. A survey in 1985–86 among Scots aged 20–24 years showed that social-class was a diminishing factor in sporting activity, and that 77 per cent of women participated in organised sport compared to 91 per cent of men; in swimming more women took part than men.[57] By the late 1980s sports clubs and centres almost uniformly had trained sports coaches, and even 30 per cent of non-sports organisations for young people (like the Boys Brigade and youth clubs) used paid or voluntary specialist sports coaches.[58]

The evidence of this article suggests two modifications to current understanding of British sports history. First, we should not over-emphasise the significance of the 1964 and 1966 Labour Governments in the creation of a linkage between sport and the welfare state.[59] What the Scottish case shows is the key role of civil servants and volunteers in promoting wider access to sport as part of social-policy objectives. The Labour government's main contribution, certainly in Scotland, was funding. Total state spending on sport in Scotland tripled from £44,200 in 1963–64 to £122,000 the following year, and rose to £335,737 in 1969–70 (excluding the Commonwealth Games). The Labour Government's commitment to sport opened a floodgate of money to sports governing bodies, sports clubs and local authorities, and special funds started in 1967 to send Scottish sportsmen and women to overseas competition.[60] But whilst Labour contributed the money, the essence of sports policy had been in place amongst the civil servants for decades.

Secondly, the period between 1937 and 1972 was critical to gender equalisation in Scottish sport. Post-suffrage, pre-feminist middle-class activists carved out a policy of gender 'separatism' in both governing bodies and competition which created a rate of progress in women's sports that, if anything, seems to have slowed with gender-integration in the 1980s and 1990s.[61] The loss of these women to sports administration between 1968 and 1975 left a vacuum that the Scottish Sports Council filled with men: its council in 1975 had only one woman among 19 members, a male chief executive and male heads of departments.[62] But by then, amateur sports were rapidly becoming 'feminised space', rid of dirty changing rooms and shared toilets, with amateur sportsmen and women growing accustomed to superior facilities than professional sport.[63] Sport-for-women policies had democratised, legitimised and broadened amateur sport, removing sport from the context of 'rough' culture, and thereby culturally paving the way for the erosion of the amateur-professional divide in the later 1980s and 1990s.

NOTES

1. The CCRPT (from 1946 the Central Council for Physical Recreation) started in 1935 as a self-help group financed by the Ling Physical Education Association. In 1940 it was asked by the Ministry of Home Security to conduct training courses, in conjunction with the Football Association, for selected Civil Defence workers, and in 1946 created the first National Recreation Centre at Bispham Abbey near Marlow.
2. Central Council of Recreative Physical Training, *Annual Reports*, 1942–3, 1947. M. Brown, *Alive in the 1900s: With Reminiscences of the Scottish Council of Physical Recreation* (Edinburgh, 1979), p.17; H. Justin Evans, *Service to Sport: The Story of the CCPR, 1935–1972* (Pelham Books, 1974), p.136.
3. S[cottish] S[ports] C[ouncil] L[ibrary], Scottish Council of Physical Recreation, uncatalogued minutes of Executive Committee (hereafter SCPR mins.), 9 March and 8 December 1965, and 9 November 1966; M. Brown, *Alive in the 1900s*, pp.88–90. The author is grateful to the SSC for allowing access to the records of the SCPR.
4. The author's father.
5. R.A. Crampsey, *The Game for the Game's Sake: The History of Queen's Park Football Club 1867–1967* (Glasgow, 1967); F.H.C. Robertson (ed.), *The Men with Educated Feet: A Statistical History of Queen's Park* (Glasgow, 1984).
6. M. Brown, *Alive in the 1900s*, pp.4–5.
. 7. Ibid., pp.10–28; Evans, *Service to Sport*, p.136.; *SCPR, Annual Report*, 1967–8, p.3
8. The author's mother.
9. Comiston Drive.
10. J. Hargreaves, *Sporting Females: Critical Issues in the History and Sociology of Women's Sports* (London, 1994), pp.137–8.
11. S[cottish] R[ecord] O[ffice], ED14/328, Physical Training and Recreation Bill.
12. Evans, *Service to Sport*, p.137.
13. SRO, ED14/460, Education Scotland Bill.
14. *Ministry of Education, Community Centres* (1944), 3–4, 16.
15. *Scottish Education Department, Circular No. 5*, 8 Feb. 1946.
16. *Albemarle Committee Report on the Youth Service in England and Wales*, Feb. 1960, paras 55, 296, 211, 234, 351.
17. R. Holt, *Sport and the British: A Modern History* (Oxford, 1989), p.345.
18. SSCL, SCPR mins, 24 October 1960, 9 Feb. 1961.
19. SRO, ED27/372, Physical Training and Recreation; ED27/396 Alexander Committee on Adult Education, draft report, pp.12–13
20. Calculated from data in SRO, ED27/369.
21. SRO, ED27/372, note of meeting on 5 June 1958 between Housing, Home, and Education Departments.
22. SSCL, SCPR mins. 9 Nov. 1966.
23. SRO, ED27/466, Inquiry into Association Football, General Papers.
24. Calculated from data in *Scottish Sports Council, Second Report, 1973–5*, p.29.

25. Figures calculated from data in W. Winterbottom, 'The pattern of sport in the U.K.', ms speech to Conference at Crystal Palace National Recreation Centre, 9 July 1966, located in SSCL, SCPR mins. 9 Nov. 1966.
26. *SCPR Annual Report*, 1956–57, pp.4, 6.
27. SRO, HH1/1102–1105, Access to Mountains Bill.
28. SSCL, SCPR mins. 9 March 1965; *Countryside Commission for Scotland: Planning for Sport, Outdoor Recreation and Tourism*, two volumes (Edinburgh, n.d. c.1976).
29. Author's copy of Scottish Women's Amateur Athletic Association, minutes of executive committee (SWAAA mins.), 14 April 1955–20 Oct. 1971.
30. Ibid., 11 May 1957, 13 June 1959, 1 Oct. 1959, 21 May 1961,1 May 1968.
31. Ibid., 6 Oct. 1956, 21 May 1960.
32. Ibid., 6 Oct. 1956.
33. Ibid., 6 Oct. 1956, 9 Oct. 1958
34. Ibid., 23 March 1962.
35. Ibid., 5 Dec. 1958
36. Ibid., 8 Dec. 1956, 10 May 1958, 1 Oct. 1959, 25 May 1962.
37. Ibid., 19 Oct. 1962, 22 Feb. 1963
38. Ibid., 24 Jan 1959.
39. Ibid., 6 Sept. 1962.
40. Author's copy of SWAAA, minutes of AGM, 5 May 1967, 24 Nov. 1973.
41. SWAAA mins., 8 Dec. 1956, 26 Jan. 1957, 9 March 1957, 17 Sept. 1957, 15 June 1958, 24 Jan. 1959.
42. Ibid., 25 July 1959.
43. Ibid., 13 Jan. 1961, 9 April 1965.
44. Ibid., 26 Aug. 1966, 30 Sept. 1970.
45. W. Carmichael and M.M. Hood (eds.), *The Official History of the Ninth British Commonwealth Games* (Edinburgh, 1970), pp.194, 216, 376.
46. SSCL, SCPR mins. 3 Oct. 1962; Hargreaves, *Sporting Females*, p.138.
47. SSCL, SCPR mins. 3 Oct. 1962.
48. Ibid., 10 March 1959.
49. H. Taylor, *A Claim on the Countryside: A History of the British Outdoor Movement* (Edinburgh, 1997), esp.pp.234–8. The Ladies Scottish Climbing Club had been formed in 1908 creating a small hardcore of women mountaineers, but the sport retained a masculine image. I am grateful to Carol Osborne, University of Lancaster, for this information.
50. *SCPR Annual Reports*, 1962–63, p.6; 1965–66, p.23.
51. *SCPR Annual Reports*, 1955–1972.
52. SWAAA mins. 25 May 1962.
53. SSCL, SCPR mins. 29 Jan. 1964; SWAAA mins. 7 Feb. 1964, 17 April 1964.
54. SSCL, SCPR mins. 20 Feb. 1963, 29 Jan. 1964, 29 Oct. 1964, 9 March 1965.
55. Ibid., 28 May 1968, 10 Oct. 1968, 5 June 1969, 22 Sept. 1970; Glasgow Sports Centre Association, *Bellahouston Sports Centre: Notes and Comments for the Use of Designers of Future Sports Centres …* (Glasgow, 1970).
56. *Scottish Sports Council, Second Report*, pp.27, 29; *British Empire and Commonwealth Games Council for Scotland, Report 1963–1967*, pp.30–3; Carmichael and Hood (eds.), *Ninth British Commonwealth Games*, pp.216, 281.
57. *Scottish Sports Council, Participation in Sport by Young People* (Edinburgh, 1988), p.6.
58. *Scottish Sports Council, Survey of Youth Organisations* (Edinburgh, 1988), pp.8–10.
59. Holt, *Sport and the British*, p.345; Polley, *Moving the Goalposts*, pp.20–6.
60. *SCPR, Annual Reports*, 1963–71.
61. Cf. Hargreaves, *Sporting Females*, pp.198–208.
62. *Scottish Sports Council, Second Report*, pp.3, 35.
63. In 1973 the Scottish Office took its first interest in the re-development of professional soccer, starting with Hampden Park in Glasgow; *Scottish Sports Council, Second Report*, pp.24–5.

Sport in the Slavic World before Communism: Cultural Traditions and National Functions

WOJCIECH LIPOŃSKI

GENERAL HISTORICAL BACKGROUND

The Slavic tribes were probably the last of the Indo-Europeans to arrive in Europe. At the peak of their territorial expansion between the sixth and eighth centuries they occupied vast areas between the Don river in contemporary Russia and the Elbe river in Germany (the name 'Berlin' is of Slavic origin from the Slavic *berło* – 'ruler's sceptre'). To the South their settlements stretched as far as contemporary Macedonia in the Balkans. It was then that the original, non-Slavic Macedonians lost their original ancient language and acquired a Slavic one. Basically the Slavonic nations have remained in the territory they acquired some 1400 years ago except for parts of contemporary Eastern Germany where only small remnants of earlier Slavic Lusitians survive. They were politically subdued by German border grafs circa the eleventh and twelfth centuries but they are still able today to maintain some of their ethnic features, including their language, and live mostly in the region of Cottbus (Chociebuż). Today tourists are surprised by Slavic and German sign-posts and local newspapers in that part of modern Germany.

All the remaining Slavonic nations are divided into three main language and culture groups: Western (Poles, Czechs, Slovaks, Moravians); Eastern (Russian, Belorussians and Ukrainians), and Southern (Serbs, Croatians, Slovenians). Macedonians and some Asian nations of the former USSR speak Slavonic languages though they are not original Slavs. Bosnians are a combination of different races including some Turks. This has resulted in the Bosnian dialect of Serbian-Croatian.

Some early Slavonic nations, like Bulgaria, Moravia (today a part of the Czech Republic), Ukraine (which belonged in the Middle Ages to

Kiev, Russia, then Bohemia, Poland and finally Russia in different epochs), were regional or even pan-Europe political powers. Apart from Russia, all of them were eventually subdued.

Bulgaria is the oldest known Slavonic kingdom, established in the seventh century shortly after the Slavs arrived in the Balkan Peninsula. The first kingdom in central Europe was Moravia, established in the ninth century by King Svetopelk, but at the beginning of the tenth century it was destroyed by the Hungarians. Moravia became a bone of contention between Poland, Bohemia and Germany until in 1031 it was finally absorbed by powerful Czech kings. The Czech Kingdom, in turn, after several centuries of competing with Poland for control over Central/Eastern Europe was conquered by the German-speaking dynasties.

After the fall of Constantinople the Turks gradually conquered the Balkan Peninsula and all Balkan Slavonic countries became part of the huge Ottoman Empire. From the fifteenth to eighteenth centuries the Moscow Principality, soon Great Russia, gradually came to pre-eminence and in the course of time absorbed Belorussia and Ukraine (which were earlier joined with Lithuania or Poland). Poland maintained its powerful position until the end of the seventeenth century. In 1683 it was even able to defend Europe against the Ottoman Empire at the battle of Vienna. When Austria, and possibly the rest of Central Europe was saved by military action of the Polish king, John Sobieski the Third.[1]

Poland, however, after defending its own and European borders against the Turks for several centuries was so militarily exhausted by constant wars, not only with the Turks but also with the Russians and Swedes, that at the turn of the seventeenth century, it lost its political significance and after some decades of political and economic corrosion was partitioned in 1795 among Russia, Prussia and Austria. By the end of the eighteenth century all the Slavonic nations except Russia had been conquered.

Bulgaria was the first Slavic country to regain its independence when it was liberated from the Turks in 1875 with the decisive assistance of Russia. Continuing military and political conflicts with Turkey, however, greatly affected the country's economy before 1914 and indirectly slowed down the development of Bulgarian culture, including sport. The Czechs obtained substantial autonomy under the Hapsburg Empire at the end of the nineteenth century. This facilitated participation in international sports federations and the Olympics (the Czechs had a member of the IOC from the beginning of the modern Olympic Games). Full freedom, however, was regained by the Czechs together with the Slovaks only after the creation of Czechoslovakia in 1918. In the same year Poland was recreated after over 120 years of partition and a series of exhausting national uprisings. The Balkan Slavonic nations were combined into Yugoslavia in 1919. The Ukraine, after a short period of fighting for independence (1918–20), was forcibly united with the USSR although parts of Western Ukraine remained in Poland.

The Belorussians emerged as a separate ethnic group as a result of the integration of Old Russian culture with Polish and Lithuanian influences. Belorussia was for a long period dominated by the pagan Lithuanian Principality and then together with Lithuania at the end of the fourteenth century entered the political union of Lithuania and Poland under the Jagiellonian Dynasty. This union lasted until Poland lost its independence in 1795.[2] After the heavy Russification experienced in the nineteenth century, in 1919 Belorussia became a semi-independent republic ruled by a Revolutionary Council of the Soviet type, then became part of a combined Lithuanian-Belorussian Soviet Republic and finally in 1922 a separate Soviet Republic. However, even the Soviet Union regarded both Belorussia and Ukraine, as ethnically different enough to allow them in 1945 to separate, through rather fictitious representations in the United Nations.

Slavonic history of nineteenth and twentieth centuries, was, in short, a history of constant struggle for national identity and independence. It was not only a fight against oppressors but also against Western political self-interest. Many times the Western Powers traded the Slavonic peoples in order to promote their own well being: shamefully selling Bulgarian Roumelia immediately after its liberation to the Ottoman Empire (Treaty of Berlin 1878), trading Czechoslovakia to Hitler's regime (Munich, 1938), and at Yalta (1945) leaving all the Slavonic nations, except Yugoslavia, under Stalin's rule are merely some of the best known examples.

These brief remarks on the stormy history of the Slavonic nations proves adequately enough that conditions for developing their culture, including sport, were most difficult. What they achieved in these circumstances should be appreciated, as well as better known in Western Europe.

WESTERN EUROPEAN IGNORANCE OF SLAVONIC SPORTS

It was only a few years ago that thanks to the political changes initiated in Poland by the Solidarity Movement and later by Gorbachev's perestroika that all the main Slavonic nations, except some small remnants of the Lusatians in Germany, regained their full independence. For the first time ever all simultaneously have the chance to reveal and demonstrate their real political and cultural identities. Today the Slavonic nations (excluding the non-European part of Russia) occupy some 58.8 per cent of Europe and constitute 39.3 per cent of the European population.

Arguably, the Slav nations could expect reasonable consideration, therefore, in the Western history books but such expectations, as far as Western historiography is concerned, appear rather groundless. It seems obvious that those Slavonic nations which were for so long deprived of their sovereignty could not influence, or enlighten, Western historians due to the censorial or language limitations imposed by their political oppressors. Eastern Europe, as a result, was until recently considered at the European margin and projected through the eyes of those who oppressed it, mostly German or Russian historiographers and ethnographers, interested only in diminishing the ethnic and cultural originality of the subdued according to the imperial needs of their masters. The well-known limitations of the Communist period added further distortions to the history of Eastern Europe. All Western historiography written during the last 200 years, almost without exception, can be accused of 1) uncritical acceptance of Russian and German imperialistic perspectives; 2) ignoring the views of the oppressed. Fortunately tradition was recently broken by Norman Davies whose *Europe: A History* (1996) is the first Western history of that continent which objectively respects its Eastern part.[3]

The long neglect of Slavic Europe affected, of course, the history of sports and an ethnographical knowledge of Slavonic play and games. In all Western histories and encyclopaedias of sport, without exception, Slavonic tradition is either totally ignored or at best heavily under appreciated. The most recent example is the three-volume *Encyclopaedia of World Sport* edited by David Levinson and Karin Christensen (1996). There is not a single entry on any one Slavonic or East European folk sport or any reference to them within the other larger entries. Surprisingly, even Russian traditions, largely responsible for the Soviet

Union's unique sporting achievements for several decades, are treated with extraordinary incompetence. Some individual modern athletes are occasionally listed. That is all. At least in the entry 'Traditional Sports' some reference to the numerous Polish folk-sports, or Bohemian *hazena*, Bulgarian *pelivan* wrestling or Russian *sambo* might have been expected. There is not even a comment on *gorodki*, a national pastime in Russia. Meanwhile sports practised by marginal tribes of Australasia, Africa or South America receive better treatment.

The *Encyclopaedia* has 152 contributors – 137 British and American writers, 5 Germans, 4 Japanese, 3 Belgians, 2 Italians and 2 Norwegians, and single authors from Singapore, Switzerland, Denmark, Africa, Finland and Israel. There is not, however, a single contributor from any Slavonic or East European country. Even Russia, a nation with one of the richest medieval histories of folk games and pre-eminent in sport in the twentieth century (whether one likes it or not) is without a single author or entry adequately depicting its achievements.

No wonder then that there is nothing about Russian *narodnyie gulanya, kulatshnoie boi,* Polish folk sports like *rochwist, czoromaj, łapa, browar,* or *kwadrant*. Nothing about Bulgarian *djilyak, djangur, butanitsa,* or *pouplyak*. Most of these games were *once* described in English and other international languages, including Russian and German, not to mention the Slavic languages, but who among the Western ethnographers or sports historians has ever made use of such sources? *The Encyclopaedia of World Sport*, and its numerous predecessors (F.G. Menke, J.L. Pratt and J. Beneagh, J. Arlott, for example) are for Western readers and, of course, the compilers have every right to select for their publication whatever they wish. But there is every reason to ask what the title 'World Sports' actually stands for? World sport surely includes Belorussian, Bohemian, Bulgarian, Croatian, Lusitian, Polish, Russian, Serbian, Slovak, Slovenian and Ukrainian sports. Are they less important than Mongolian *buh*, or traditional African sports to which the editors devote almost five full pages? This treatment of the Slavonic world represents unjust and arbitrary selection. It means that English-speaking readers are deprived of valuable information. Any publication with such glaring omissions must appear to be an expression of conscious discrimination.

What follows below is an attempt to begin the education of Western historians of sport. The timescale covered is extensive and the records in short supply. Of necessity the information, therefore, is fragmentary, fractured and incomplete. Nevertheless it is intended as a stimulant, something to spur future scholarship on the Slavic nations and peoples and their culture in recognition of their importance to the cultural history of Europe. There is considerable scope for exploring the relationship, for example, between sport and gender, class and politics. In what follows, this relationship, especially in the case of class and gender, is often implicit rather than explicit. In the future it is hoped that the reverse will be increasingly the case.

THE ANCIENT ORIGINS OF SLAVONIC SPORT

Slavonic tribes appeared for the first time in ancient Greek and Latin sources as long ago as the fifth century BC. The Neures, who in all probability are the proto-Slavic tribe, were mentioned by Herodotos. Later, the Venedes, whose name is preserved in some Polish place names (the river Wda for instance), are listed by Pomponios Mela, Pliny the Elder, Strabon, Tacitus and Ptolomy.

It is not known, of course, what kind of sports they played over 2,000 years ago. Nonetheless the first Slavic tribes to appear in the Balkan Peninsula (the proto-Bulgarians), almost from the beginning, are described in the extant sources as practising various sports, including horse racing and wrestling. Clearly they brought with them their own traditions but at the same time they found in their newly conquered territory numerous sports venues built by the ancient Greeks and Romans.

Western scholars rarely appreciate how far Mediterranean influences reached into Eastern and Central Europe. Ancient towns and military garrisons were built by the Romans as far north as modern Budapest, where today tourists can still admire their grandeur. Calisia, mentioned in ancient Latin sources, was the first name of modern Kalisz, in the very middle of contemporary Poland, historically the oldest Polish town being over 1,800 years old. Calisia flourished thanks to the famous 'amber route' drawing Greek and then Roman traders to the Baltic Sea. Close to the Baltic there was another ancient town, Truso, described in the ninth century by Wulfstan the Sailor to Alfred the Great. In 1996, on the spot of ancient Truso (burnt and destroyed about the tenth or eleventh century by its jealous neighbours), remnants of a wooden paved route was discovered. Archaeologists were unanimous in considering certain features of this route to be Roman in influence. The route linking the Mediterranean and the Baltic seas was still used by Jewish and Arab traders in the tenth century, as is made clear by Ibrahim Ibn Jacob of Tortose who travelled to the kingdom of Poland at about the time of its Christianisation (965 or 966) and whose description was preserved in the famous El-Bakri's *Book of Routes and Kingdoms*.

It is not known whether the Ancients who reached the Baltic Sea brought with them any physical exercises. We do know, however, that stadiums were built by the ancient colonists in the area which later became the Southern Slavonic kingdoms and that their inhabitants had the opportunity to use them. The most conspicuous ancient stadium excavated on Slavonic territory is in modern Constantsa (ancient Tomi). The Bulgarian scholar Goranka Toncheva describes it as follows:

> It is situated between the slopes of two hills – Texim Tepe and Sahat Tepe. The seats of stone are arranged along the natural sloping ground and the hills, while the track for the competitors is on the lowest and level ground between the hills. The entire ensemble is laid out in the Corinthian style, as expressed in the frieze, architraves, cornices and other architectural details in its outlines. The building is decorated with many statues. The track is 177 metres long and 29 wide. The rows of seats are interrupted along their length by the distributing aisles of staircase and form separate radial sectors. The seats are made of white marble. The entire structure could seat 25,000 spectators.[4]

In Tomi the greatest Thracian Games were held at the beginning of the second century AD for the members of the so-called Pontic league. In another Bulgarian town, Varna, called in ancient times Odessos, archaeologists have found a monument erected to a certain Pumenios who won the Tomi Games.[5] Other Thracian *agones* of importance were the so-called Kendrissian Games held in honour of the god Apollo Kendrissos in Philippopolis (now Plovdiv). The principal event of these Games was wrestling, as reported by Ioannis of Antiochia about the year 235 AD. Moreover, these Games obviously survived the famous edict of Theodosius prohibiting the Games within the Roman Empire, because they are mentioned by Eugenius Scholasticus who wrote in about 450–457 that the Thracian ruler Marcianus won his title thanks to defeating his rival in a wrestling match. The Turkish occupation of this area began with the fall of Constantinople. Subsequent isolation from the rest of Europe, and the economic backwardness inherited by the Balkan peoples from their Muslim occupiers, has been responsible for the most complete ignorance of such historical evidence among Western sports historians.[6]

In the sixth century the Northern area of Thrace was conquered by then heathen proto-Bulgarians who were organised into the union known in Bulgarian historiography as Great Bulgaria or Kuberat Bulgaria. Before the Bulgarians were Christianised in 865 AD different forms of sport, combining pagan Slavic tradition and some Greek-Thracian elements found in the newly occupied territory, were practised. Despite numerous wars, the earliest rulers of the so-called First Bulgarian Empire were able to organise local Games. It was just one year after the Christianisation of the Bulgarians that Pope Nicholas I was asked if some earlier customs of the new Bulgarian converts could be continued. In point 33 of the Pope's answer we read that 'You tell us that it is your custom, when going into battle, to set aside certain days and hours and to engage in conjuration, games, singing, and some kinds of soothsaying, so you want us to teach you what to do on such occasions.'[7]

Upon the arrival of the Slavonic people in the Balkan Peninsula their wrestling, brought from the Asian Steppes, was confronted with classical Thracian wrestling which was soon assimilated by the newcomers. The resulting combination of the two styles had to be comparable with the classical Greek style continued at the Byzantine Court if the Bulgarians could fight on equal terms in Constantinople in 851 AD. It was then that one servant of the Bulgarian mission fought with an officer of the Imperial Guard and the later Emperor Basilius I of Macedon. The Byzantine writer Josephus Genesius has suggested that Boris, then the ruler of Bulgaria, sent his wrestler to Constantinople in order to prove the superiority of his people. Unfortunately, the first 'international match' ever staged by a Bulgarian athlete was not as successful as Boris had hoped. Basilius threw his opponent to the ground so violently that the Bulgarian wrestler almost died.[8] Incidentally, Christian proscription of later 'pagan games' was ineffective in both the Byzantine Empire and Bulgaria. In the ninth century the Bulgarian Presbyter Koźma complained that 'many people go more frequently to Games than to church'.[9] In the later so-called Second Bulgarian Kingdom wrestling continued and some medieval legends contain information about folk heroes of unusual strength. One of such heroes was Krali Marko who fought for his bride with Moussa Kesedzhiya:

Get down from the horse, and let us wrestle,
Whoever wins, the girl will be his bride.[10]

ASIAN LINKS AND MEDIEVAL DEVELOPMENTS

Bulgarian wrestling seems to possess characteristics typical of the peoples invading Europe from Asian steppes, beginning with the Huns and ending with the Tartars. These characteristics certainly initiated and preserved among the peoples of the Asian steppes, influenced non-Asian tribes, who in turn had direct contacts with the neighbouring European nations. Today it is possible to discriminate between 'Asian steppe' and 'classical Mediterranean' styles of ancient wrestling. For instance Greek *agones*, at least since Homeric times, were held for the 'honour of victory' and eventually for material prizes. Wrestling for solving 'life situations' was untypical in the Mediterranean world, and this is why fighting for martial status (usually for the bride), or to determine unresolved military arguments should be associated rather with non-Mediterranean styles. In Bulgarian wrestling both features exist. In medieval, pre-Ottoman wrestling the Bulgarians fought for 'life purposes' among their own people but 'for honour and prizes' at the Byzantine court. Another difference involved oiling the body for the fight. Bulgarians never used oil and this became the source of a serious confrontation with the Turks, who acquired the practice of Mediterranean 'oiled' wrestling (see below).

In the North, in Russia and on its border with Poland and Belorussia and Lithuania there are recorded matches exclusively for 'life purposes': for a bride or to settle economic, political or military conflicts. Mediterranean 'fights for honour' did appear here later, at the end of European Middle Ages but never became predominant. The oldest Polish sources cover the year 997 AD (though recorded much later). As the Polish medieval chronicler Jan Długosz described it, a wrestling match was staged after a long war between the Russian Prince Wladimir and the steppe tribes of Polovtsy and Pyietshingas of Turkish stock. Because no side was able to win the war, their commanders decided that victory will be granted to those, whose representative would win in a kind of wrestling involving elements of boxing. 'When it came to the struggle the Russian warrior threw his giant opponent to the ground and the army of the Pyetshingas fled.'[11]

Similar matches are mentioned several times in medieval Polish and

Old Russian chronicles. An extraordinary poetic description, however, characterises the match staged in 1306 between the delegate of the Khan of the Tartars of unknown name and a certain Boreyko, representative of the Lithuanian prince Gedymin (then ruler of not only Lithuania but also Samogitia and the great part of what is now Belorussia and Ukraine).

This match was commemorated in folk songs, which are known about but are not preserved. Fortunately in 1577, on the basis of one such unpreserved song, the Polish/Lithuanian chronicler and poet, Maciej Ossostevicius Stryjkowski, wrote a poem with the lengthy title *On the Impudent Mission Sent by Volgian Tsar and on Wrestling between the Samogitian Knight Boreyko and the Giant Tartar and on the Chodkiewicz Family of the Year 1306.*[12]

The purpose of the match is described precisely at the beginning of the poem:

> When Gedymin rested with his knights in Vilna,
> And enjoyed what he got from his war raids,
> From the Crimean the envoy of the Volga Tsar arrived
> Demanding contribution from the Russian State.
> For his Mongolian glory he brought one Tartar
> Who was bigger than the ancient Cyclops
> And said to Gedymin proudly at the table
> 'Show me who is equal in strength to my man,
> And if one will be found among your people
> My ruler will not demand any tribute from Russia
> But if our hero defeats your man
> You'll pay from Russia the normal tribute or be our slave.[13]

Surprisingly Stryjkowski described the subsequent 'steppe catch as can catch' as the classical form modelled on the Games described in Virgil's *Aeneid* (Book V – the match between Dares and Entellus), an unusual literary combination of Asian and Classical elements. Thanks to it, however, clear differences between Asian and Mediterranean traditions can be seen: in the *Aeneid*, according to 'classical sporting rules' the match ends when Dares suffers too much and the superiority of Entellus is sufficiently demonstrated. They do not fight 'for life' but for 'sporting honour'. In Asian wrestling, with an element of boxing, the fight lasted until one or the other lost his life. The purpose was political and the match took the place of war, so it required a visible sign of victory: a dead opponent. In the final part of the match we read that Boreyko caught his Tartar rival 'under his ribs', so strongly that

His fingers got stuck in the giant's body;
He threw him against the earth, so his foe's soul
Left the body flying to Pluto's kingdom.[14]

In some old Polish and Russian sources we find numerous references to 'Russian pugilism' later called in Russian *kulatshnoie boi*. Alexander Gwagninus, the Italian chronicler who lived in Poland and was even knighted for his services to the Polish king, described in his *Sarmatiae Europae Descriptio* fist fighting popular in the area of Russia close to Polish border:

Every year youngsters and even married men leave their towns and ... villages going ... to the vast fields in the Summer and to the frozen lakes or rivers in the Winter . There, according to their custom ... without any weapon they punch each other's heads with their fists ... and hit other parts of the body so strongly that some of them ... come back as half dead while others are killed ...'[15]

Russian literature is full of folk songs based on this popular pugilism. The best ballad of this kind, going back in time to Ivan the Terrible, was later used in Lermontov's poem *Song about Tsar Ivan Vasylyevitsh, the Young Courtier and Brave Merchant Kalashnikov*.[16] It is a romantic story of a young merchant Stiepan Paramonovitsh Kalashnikov and his beautiful wife Alyiona Dmitrievna. She was seduced and raped by Kirybyievitsh, an alluring courtier of Ivan the Terrible. Wishing to defend the honour of his wife, Kalashnikov, due to class regulations, could not challenge the *boyar* (Russian aristocrat) to a duel with swords. Only a 'fist-duel' (*kulatshnyi boi*) was possible. From other sources it is clear that the Russians usually fought with bare knuckles, but this case was an exception: boyar Kirybyievitsh, to emphasise his noble birth, 'combative gloves he puts on'. After a short exchange of diplomatically expressed accusations:

... silence divided them.
Soon the heroic fight began.

So, Kirybyievitsh took a swing
And hit Kalashnikov, the merchant,
Hit him in the middle of his breast
[...]
Breast of the young man just creaked
Stiepan Paramonovitsh his balance lost;
On his breast the copper cross had he –
Saint relics from Kiev inserted in it;
The cross into his breast was inclined,
And bloody dew from it was dropped
And Stiepan Paramonovitsh thought:
'What was destined that should be,
I must fight for the truth to the end'.
He composed himself and ready made,
Reassembled his powers again,
And hit his hostile opponent
From his shoulder, in the left temple.
[...]
The courtier staggered slightly
Then tossed he suddenly and fell dead,
Fallen he was upon the snow so cool.[17]

The story ended tragically for the winner. Ivan the Terrible, angry at losing his beloved courtier, asked Kalashnikov the reason for the fight. If he had given the Tsar the real reason, he could have been saved according to Russian custom. But all around would have been informed about the seduction of Kalashnikov's wife who would have had to live in shame to the end of her days. So the young merchant kept the secret to himself and gave no reason to the Tsar, who ordered his execution. Kalashnikov avenged his wife's honour but lost his life.

A number of other Old Russian and Old Polish games and competitions were influenced by the Asian peoples. This is especially true of archery. A brief look at the Mongolian short, deeply curved bow and the English long bow reveals their differences from a purely technological point of view. Equally interesting, however, are the cultural characteristics and customs associated with them.

In Poland Eastern archery was technologically superior but adapted to occidental rules of competition. This is quickly seen in the shooting at the cap or pile of caps, the Mongolian *sur kharvakh*. This sport entered Poland probably at the end of the fifteenth century together with other types of Asian archery, such as Mongolian *bay haran* – shooting from a galloping horse at goat skins or horse-tail ensigns, called in Polish respectively *strzelanie do buklaka* and *strzelanie do buńczuka*. All became popular in East Poland due to the frequent encounters with Tartars. In Polish literature, especially memoirs, but also in art there are masterpieces associated with those sports, such as the well-known painting *Shooting at the Horse-Tail Ensign* by Józef Brandt. Poland 'westernised' some of these sports, made them less wild and better regulated to an extent acceptable to other Europeans. This was done mostly by adding the chivalric morality typical of Western sports as in the competition between the Germans and the Poles held in the form of an early 'international match' in Rostock in 1651. The circumstances were as follows: a group of Polish nobility was travelling from Gdańsk to Lübeck by ship. Due to unfavourable winds they stopped for several days in Rostock. Here they were invited to take part in a local festival which included various sports events. According to the subsequent report entitled *Sea Navigation to Lübeck*, written about 1652 by Marcin Borzymowski[18] the Poles first took part in typically 'Western style' horse racing, arranged by the Germans and in return, suggested Eastern style *strzelanie do czapki* – shooting at the cap, obviously modelled on the Mongolian *sur kharvakh*. This Polish-German 'biathlon' was described in no less than 296 verses (87 verses devoted to shooting and 209 to several racing events).

After eating and drinking competitions at which neither Germans nor Poles were able to win, the two competing parties went through decorated streets, full of loud music to the field outside the town gate:

... And so, great crowds
And almost all the great families of the town,
Followed those who went out to the field,
To shoot at the cap to prove who was best.[19]

In the poem it is emphasised that the Germans were not acquainted with the oriental type of archery. One Polish archer, shooting last, won. The verse went:

He aimed well, and all spectators praised him
And though the Germans did not know

This style of shooting, they were delighted
because of what happened,
And looked at us with admiration.[20]

The most interesting moment arrived after the last horse race finished.
All returned to the town in a truly Western chivalric spirit:

After their horses were heavily heated,
They turned back to the town
Making merry jokes
Although some were unsatisfied
Because they lost during that competition;
But they made it not a serious matter
And covered their disappointments
With jokes and did so without hesitation
As if no one had anything against each other
And with joyous faces to the beautiful town
They neatly returned ... [21]

Russia absorbed more Asian sports than Poland, including some
brutal blood sports in which animals were victims. In Western Europe
so-called blood sports, such as bull and bear baiting, were gradually
prohibited during the seventeenth and the eighteenth centuries (with the
shameful exception of the Spanish *corrida*). In Asia the brutal treatment
of animals lasted longer, as in *Buzkashi*, the rough Asian game,
extremely popular in Afghanistan, Mongolia and bordering countries.
Buzkashi, in Mongolian 'blue wolf', is a game in which a group of
horsemen fight for an animal thrown into the wide ring, where it is
tormented by throwing spears and pulling off its legs or even head by
lasso (called in Mongolian *urga* and in the Slavic languages *arkan*).
Originally it was a wolf, a symbol of evil to be fought, but as this animal
became more and more rare and difficult to capture alive, in the course
of time sheep or calves were used instead. The purpose was to deprive
the unfortunate animal of its legs and finally its head, then to seize the
trunk quicker than the other competitors and offer the headless and
legless trunk covered in dirt and blood to, for example, one's bride.
There is no record of this sport entering Western Ukraine or Poland.
The last 'frontier' of the bloody sport was, and still probably is, Eastern
Ukraine inhabited by the Cossacks, an ethnic group composed in the

fifteenth to seventeenth centuries of peasants fleeing from serfdom in Russia and Eastern Poland with an admixture of those of Turkish blood. They became famous for some of their sports, especially *dzhigitovka* – gymnastic exercises executed on horseback at full speed. The Polish border of 'moral sensitivity' was plainly visible in another Old Russian sport named *palotshnyie boi* – 'club fighting' in which two opposing individuals or teams beat each other, mostly on the head with thick clubs. Deaths were commonplace. It never crossed the Polish border.

It was not only in the Ukraine and Poland that Western and Eastern principles of competition confronted each other. After 1456 in the Balkan Peninsula old Slavic folk games met Muslim tradition. Traditional Bulgarian wrestling, for instance, came into sharp conflict with the Turkish authorities who tried to impose certain characteristics alien to local Balkan custom. One of the most durable conflicts was associated with so-called dry wrestling. The Balkan tradition of wrestling excluded oiling the body before a match. The Turks recognised oiling as a symbol of 'Turkisation' and even prosecuted, though usually to no effect, those wrestlers who fought 'dry'. Thus paradoxically Asian Turks were all for Mediterranean and, in fact, Greek wrestling custom, while Bulgaria, a European outpost within the Ottoman Empire, defended a custom brought from the Asian steppes (even today in Mongolian wrestling [*buh*] bodies are not oiled). Nonetheless matches between representatives of both ethnic groups were frequent and considered a source of national pride by the Bulgarians deprived of other means of expressing their national identity. One of the best public and popular means to demonstrate anti-Ottoman feelings in Bulgaria, for centuries was 'to come out and publicly challenge Turkish wrestlers'.[22] The finest wrestlers in those Balkan countries under Turkish occupation were treated as national heroes. The most famous of them all was Kanatli Dimo, who won at the most important Muslim tournaments, including the famous Kirkapanar Wrestling Tournament. His prestige was strengthened by the fact that he did not submit to the pressure of the Turkish authorities and oil his body. The national poet of Bulgaria, Hristo Botev, in his youth a famous local famous wrestler, won tournaments in Zadunayevskaya.

Today wrestling is still a cause of sharp confrontation between modern Bulgarian and Turkish historians over the genesis of the sport. Turkish historians maintain that the Bulgarians learned wrestling from the Turks, while Bulgarian historians are convinced that the Muslim influence was of minimal importance. Another East–West confrontation is still celebrated in Croatia, once an important point on the route used by Crusaders travelling to the Holy Land. Through history Croatia was constantly on the border between European and Ottoman influences – mostly on the European side. It was in Croatia, that traditional Western type chivalric tournaments gained a long-lasting foothold and outlived even similar events in the West. One tournament, called in the local language *alka* (ring), over time resisted all political suppression. In 1715 its fading existence actually gained new vigour when it became a part of the celebrations commemorating the victory of the Croatian leader Ivan Filipović over the Turkish Pasha Mehmed of Bosnia.[23]

THE FALCON MOVEMENT AS A SLAVONIC RESPONSE TO THE EUROPEAN GYMNASTICS MOVEMENT

The Czechs were the only Slavonic people who did not experience direct Asian influence: the Mongolian incursions ended at Legnica in Poland in 1241 AD some 120 km from the present border with the Czech Republic, while the Turkish invasions were stopped in 1683 by Polish troops at Vienna, almost 250 km from Prague. The Czechs paid a high price for looking too much to the West. Indirectly it delayed the development of post-chivalric sports. At the end of the Middle Ages the ideas of the English Lollards and John Wycliff inspired John Huss, the great Czech Protestant who was burnt at the stake in 1415 after the famous, or rather infamous verdict of the Papal Inquisition Haeriticae Pravitatis. The Hussitic knights were among the most valiant in Europe. Jan Žižka won many European medieval tournaments and supported the Poles in their battles against the Teutonic Knights at Grunwald (Tanneberg) in 1410. Hussitism was bloodily suppressed in 1434 at the battle of Lipany. The Protestant spirit of the Bohemians survived, however, and some 200 years later it was again one of the main reasons for Catholic reaction and responsible for a series of religious wars in Central Europe. When the Thirty Years War ended with the famous battle at Bilá Hora (White Mountain, 1630) the Czech nobility and middle class were destroyed so completely that the whole nation was on the verge of biological and cultural extinction and for 250 years ceased to exist politically. It was an unimaginable tragedy for the whole nation, and also a clear break in the evolution of traditional chivalric sports into modern sports, so typical of the West. Bohemia, for its part, was easily suppressed by the German speaking Hapsburgs and the denationalisation of the Czechs was a real threat for several generations. No wonder then that Bohemia, subdued by the Austrian Hapsburg Empire, was the first Slavic country to staff a national movement to save its threatened cultural identity. The German nationalist Friedrich Ludwig Jahn and his *Turner* Movement inspired action. In 1862 the Czech historian Miroslav Tyrš and the merchant Jindřich Fuegner initiated the Sokol (Falcon) Movement, building up a covert national movement through organised and widespread gymnastic exercise. The first, though unsuccessful, attempt to follow the Czech example was made by the Poles, split as mentioned earlier into three sectors, each under different foreign occupiers. In 1862 the Polish press wrote with enthusiasm of the Czech initiative: 'The Czechs wrestle heavily with Germanism ... They do not lose hope, however, and they have the right weapon to stop the Germanic flood. Their youth have organised themselves into associations having as their purpose, bodies exercised according to the principles of the Germans.'[24] The first attempt to organise a gymnastic culture on Sokol lines was made by the Polish teacher Bonifacy Łazarewicz in the autumn of 1862 in Poznań. Unfortunately, in January 1863 the Polish national uprising in the Russian sector of partitioned Poland attracted young men from all parts of the divided country and thus the first Polish gymnastic association collapsed. The next possibility was used more effectively in 1867, when the liberal policy within the Hapsburg Empire allowed ethnic organisations in Polish Galicia. The Polish Sokol Association (Stowarzyszenie Gimnastyczne Sokół) was established first in 1867 in Lvov and than one year later in Cracow.

However, it was Slovenia that became the second Slavonic country to have a Falcon Association (i Slovenian Juzni Sokol). It was established by Dr Viktor Murnik in Lublana in 1863. In no time at all it had 13 so-called 'nests' and 2,000 members. In Croatia, a gymnastic movement was started in 1861 under conditions of limited autonomy gained somewhat earlier from the Hapsburg Monarchy. The first Falcon 'nest' was organised on the initiative of Dr Franjo Bučar, who had studied physical education at the Royal Institute of Gymnastics in Stockholm. In Serbia, under Turkish rule, a gymnastic movement was started by the Serbian Gymnastics and Martial Arts Association (Prvog Srpskog Društvo za Gimnastiku i Borenje) founded in 1857 by Steve Todorović. Falcon, in the Serbian language *Soko*, was created only in 1891, building on the foundations of the Belgrade Civic Gymnastics Association (founded 1882). For some years its rival was *Dušan Silny* (Strong by Spirit) founded in 1893. The two organisations merged in 1910. In Bulgaria, Falcon had various names. The first organisation modelled on the Czech Sokol was established in Plovdiv as Eagle (*Orel*). In Bourgas it was called Sea Eagle, in Haraskovo and Yambol it was simply Falcon while in Sliven its members named it Lion.

All the Slavic Falcons co-operated in international games and gatherings organised under the auspices of the Bohemian Falcon in 1891, 1895, 1901, 1907 and 1912. These events were comparable to the early Olympic Games. There were also some attempts to use Falcon to strengthen the pan-Slavic Movement, initiated by Russia. This movement might have had a chance if Russia had not attempted to use it to further its own imperial goals. In fact, the Russian pan-Slavic ideologists tried to use the ambition of eventual unity of all Slavonic countries to undermine the political structure of rival monarchies. When this tendency became apparent the most populous Falcon organisation, the Polish, resisted. As the ideology of national liberation associated with Falcons evolved, it made the Russian authorities afraid that the organisation might undermine the multinational structure of the Russian Empire. Thus a dubious policy of encouraging Falcon abroad and prohibiting its activity within Russia's own borders was maintained until 1917 (except for 1905–6 when Russia temporarily allowed Falcon on Russian soil). Without the complete support of the Polish Falcon and with the impossibility of organising Falcon in Russia, plans to use Falcon for pan-Slavic goals had minimal appeal and finally failed. Nevertheless the pan-Slavic aim among the Czech, and especially the Bulgarians, had strong backing from the Falcon Movement. The Bulgarian association was founded in fact under Russian rule during the provisional government of the Russian Army which liberated Bulgaria from Turkish occupation. No wonder then that the Bulgarians gave strong support to Russian ideas. It was in Slovakia and Bohemia that Russian and Ukrainian minorities created their Falcons under local law and Russian and Ukrainian gymnasts were especially active after 1918 when they supported other Czechoslovakian sports organisations, such as Vysokoškolský Sport.

Russia was not far behind the other Slavic states in the development of gymnastics and sport when not associated with the sometimes unwelcome Sokol ideology. The first teachers of modern gymnastics were invited to Russia in the 1820s (the Frenchman Grisse, and the Swede Maur de Paula). The first Gymnastic Society on Russian territory was organised by Germans employed in Petersburg and was called 'Palma' (1863). The Germans also established the oldest Gymnastics Society available to the pupils of Russian high schools, but because German language was obligatory only 10 Russian pupils participated (there was a total of about 300 members). An indigenous Russian Gymnastics Association (Russkoyie Gyimnastitsheskoyie Obshtshestvo) was established only in 1883.

BRITISH SPORT ENTERS THE SLAVONIC SCENE

British sporting influence was much earlier than either German or Swedish gymnastics, though it never played any role in national movements. In absorbing influences from Britain Russia went hand in hand with Poland. In both nations interest in British recreations and sports became evident at the end of the eighteenth century, much earlier than in the other Slavic countries. The English recreational garden in London, the Vauxhall Gardens, became a model for similar venues in both Warsaw and Petersburg. The name itself was 'slavicised'. The Polish Vaux-Hall ('Foksal') was created in Warsaw in 1783. Today Foksal Street is in the very centre of Warsaw, exactly where the first Vauxhall Garden was built. Russian Vauxhall ('Vokzal') was established in 1793 in the district of Petersburg called Moyka in the garden of the Naryszkin Family ('Vokzal v Naryshkinovom sadu').[25]

The British do not appreciate how their recreation and sports were received abroad beyond the Anglo-Saxon world. A history of British influences on the Slavonic countries would be a large book.[26] The British influence had a mixed reception. It was ridiculed in innumerable satires and even complete plays while at the same time glorified in painting and 'serious literature'. The English model of sport became a demonstration of national aspirations in those fields of public life where the traditional games of particular peoples were prohibited by political oppressors, who hoped that English influence would be an additional factor in the decline of ethnic culture which resisted Russian rule. In fact, English influences as a demonstration of free choice were used in some circles of the conquered society as a counterbalance to, and a denial of, the unwanted cultural and political influences of the oppressors.

Horse riding was the first pursuit to model itself on British practice.

Horsemanship, of course, was nothing new and was well developed in all Slavonic countries well before the appearance of a British influence. In Poland, for example, the first description of horse riding is contained in the medieval so-called *Polish Chronicle* by Vincent Kadłubek. It is also to be found in the work of the most famous Polish medieval chronicler Jan Dlugosz. He recounts how the Polish Council of the Elders decided that pretenders to the throne should compete for the position in a horse race. In the night one placed iron spikes on one side of the track and won the next day. The trick was discovered and the honest competitor, who lost, became King.[27] Horse riding was important factor in Polish national history. In Poland, tournaments were organised from at least 1142. Polish medieval chronicles are full of references to tournaments. The most famous achievement of a Polish knight at the joust was the victory of Zawisza Czarny (Zawisza the Black) over John of Aragonia, long considered by Western nations to be invincible (1415). Old Polish regulations for tournaments and duels are well preserved and could contribute substantially to the history of European sports rules and regulations.[28] In the sixth century the first Polish textbooks on the art of horse riding and breeding were published and even translated into Russian.[29] The heavy influence of Oriental culture (due to frequent wars with Tartars and Turks) was a central characteristic of Polish horse riding. These were reflected in the technique of riding and even more obviously in the harness, saddle and other elements of riding equipment including its adornments.

British-style horse racing entered Poland in 1777 when the Polish Count Kazimierz Rzewuski raced against the British envoy Wentworth. Subsequently political instability, loss of freedom and the Napoleonic wars proved scarcely favourable to the sport. Nevertheless in the Polish national epic poem *Pan Tadeusz*, the plot of which concerns the years 1811–12 , one of the main heroes, the young Count Horeszko, is dressed in British clothes and surrounded by a group of young Anglomaniacs called *Żokieje* – 'jockeys'. Some of the most popular British rural sports, like fox hunting, were cultivated in Poland. The first Polish Jockey Club was established in 1839 in Poznań, Western Poland (then under Prussian occupation) as a sporting division of the Association for Supporting Agriculture, Cattle and Horse Breeding, which was founded some months earlier. This Association became responsible for the organisation of the first regular British-style horse races in Poland. The association served as a cover for the military training of Polish youth necessary to prepare them for the future national uprising. When this was discovered by the Prussian police, the Club was suspended from 1846 to 1849, when a number of the Club's members participated in an anti-Prussian uprising. In 1862 the Club was disbanded.

In Warsaw the first horse racing on an annual basis was established two years after Poznań. However, Warsaw did not have a Jockey Club until about 1876. Before the end of 1850 similar organisations and regular horse racing were established in Cracow and Lvov and irregular events were features of some other minor towns. The emergence of British-type organisations was associated with a change of artistic styles, both in painting and literature. In Polish horse-painting exuberant motion, so characteristic of Oriental horse riding, was replaced by well-controlled behaviour and gestures, romantic Oriental clothing was replaced by the typically English red jacket and silk hat. The first Polish artist to paint English-style horses was Aleksander Orłowski at the beginning of the nineteenth century. This tradition was later continued by Juliusz Kossak, his son, Wojciech and grandson Jerzy, whose paintings are full of English red jackets. As early as 1850 strong criticism was directed against both horse racing and the English style of living associated with it. The first attack was launched by a playwright, Konstanty Gaszyński, in his comedy *Horse racing in Warsaw*, written in 1856 and produced in 1857. It is a story of a young aristocratic Anglophile who wastes his money on English horses and clothing. This leads him, of course, to bankruptcy. Fortunately, at the last moment before the total collapse of the whole family's estate, his grandfather, a Polish traditionalist, appears on the scene and saves his grandson. All ends well with the following verse statement:

My grandson after excesses of youthful boasting
After reflection returned to the ways of wisdom
And while the banker who arrested horses still us calls
From that unfortunate English buffoonery freed us all.

A similar plot can be found in a satirical novel published serially a few years later in 1861 in the *Illustrated Weekly*. The impoverished nobleman Windrover (in Polish Wietrzycki, i.e. which means 'blown by the wind' throws his money away), attempting to gain prestige among rich horse-breeders and aristocracy.

It is worth mentioning that attempts to gain prestige by buying an

English horse or indeed, a whole racing stable, are very frequent in Polish literature. In *The Doll* (*Lalka*) by Bolesław Prus, one of the best three or four Polish novels of the nineteenth century, the main hero, the merchant Wokulski attempts to marry Countess Isabella. To gain her love, he buys an English horse and publicly demonstrates his feelings towards her by having his jockey win a race for her. The author of the novel was, by the way, one of the most assiduous promoters of English culture in Poland, in all its aspects, not merely in sport. He was responsible for the famous Polish aphorism: 'Going West we see everything getting better and better. The French are better than the Germans and the English are better than the French. Beyond the English we meet nothing but the ocean.'

Nevertheless, despite the Anglophiles, Englishness was considered a danger to local traditions in all Slavonic countries. In 1859 in the Polish *Daily Gazette* we read:

> No one is able to understand or even read these crazy English words. If all these Anglomaniacs would kindly translate this vocabulary into Polish it would have some sense. Meanwhile we do not understand why they wear upon their hats inscriptions in English when all that can be named in Polish. All these inscriptions, not only on their hats but also in printed programmes of the race prove beyond any doubt that these people are childishly reckless, that they do not respect their own traditions and that they completely disregard any serious work and care for the welfare of their country.[30]

Anglomania was common in Russia. Ludwik Berghofer provided a characteristic picture of one Russian returning from England, in a book published in 1844 whose title was *Now Everything Should Be English*.[31]

It is impossible to list here all newspaper and literary articles devoted to criticising the British style of horse racing. Some decades later one of the strongest satirical poems appeared in the *Illustrated Weekly*; again, due to a play on Polish words it is almost impossible to translate effectively. The poem effectively describes 'English' snobs of Warsaw watching a race:

> One young man, looking nobly
> Displays fashion from overseas
> Like the British King Edward
> Tries to be an example of smartness and elegance.

[...]
Oh, my noble pseudo–Lords
Waiting at the finish line
He who wins – gains prestige,
He who loses – remains sad and lost.
[...]
All those full of sporting vigour
I would lead to their dreamed ends
If the race of stupidity would be started
All of you could easily win.[32]

When the word 'sport' appeared in Russian newspapers it was printed
not in Russian Cyrylic letters but in Latin, as in *The Zhurnal*
Konnozavodstva i Okhoty (Journal of Horse Racing and Okhota) where
the word was used probably for the first time in the Slavonic world in an
expression: *sport loshadyiey* ('horse sport').[33] The Russians tried to
substitute the word 'sport' with the Russian *okhota*, but as early as 1843
it was recognised that 'the English word *sport* cannot be translated into
any language ... In its basic meaning sport denotes all possible joys,
games, plays and pleasures but in contemporary language sport means
also horse races, hunting, and fishing.'[34] The Polish appearance of the
term 'sport' is a similar story, except that there was no need to print a
Latin word among Cyrillic lettering. The oldest written and published
appearance of the word can be found in Gaszyński's comedy *Horse*
Racing in Warsaw in the following context:

We have horse races at last,
Sport develops all around
And if the government will allow us
We will organise even the Jockey Club.[35]

The very first encyclopaedic entry on sport appeared in 1861 in
Orgelbrand's Encyclopaedia. The author of the entry was the Polish
Count Henryk L. Levestan, who provided the following definition of
sport: 'It is what in England is called an outdoor play or game such as
hunting, fishing or racing ... Sport enlarged its original sense of simple
play and became a kind of higher art and science, treated carefully and
absolutely necessary for the education of a complete gentleman.'[36]
    In Bohemia, English Association football was played regularly in the

middle of the 1890s. The very first match was played in Cracow in 1894. The oldest Cracow football club, Cracovia, had become so strong by 1908 that it invited the very first English player to Poland, William Benjamin Calder, who had played formerly for Fulham. Another player invited the same year was a certain Dawson (Christian name unpreserved): 'he was poor player but a very good umpire'.[37]

In 1911 the Polish club Wisla ('Vistla') played against Aberdeen FC, the first international match against representatives from the British Isles.[38] In Bulgaria, the first demonstration of a soccer match was arranged in 1900 by the Yunak sports organisation.

Lawn tennis was usually initiated by British diplomats or specialists employed for different purposes. This was true of Petersburg (1889) and Sophia (1896). Warsaw was then only a regional capital of a 'Russian' province, but it had a British Consulate, a station of the British Indian Telegraph and workers employed by William Lindley and his son (also William) who were for several decades responsible for building and then expanding Warsaw's water supply and sewerage system. Thanks to the employees of both institutions lawn tennis was introduced about 1886. In 1887 the Polish artist Stanislaw Reychan painted the British playing tennis with their Polish friends.

Croquet became popular in Poland after the *Illustrated Weekly* published a long series of illustrated articles in 1866 entitled 'Evenings upon the River Thames', in which English culture, literature and sport were enthusiastically popularised. Croquet (*krokiet* in Polish) was initially known in Poland as cricket because the author of the articles confused both sports. Cricket was not played in any Slavonic country, except Russia, where in 1860 foreigners established the St. Petersburg Cricket Club (with Lawn Tennis included later). It had as many as 116 members at its peak, including a handful of Russians. The official president of the club was Prince Vladimir of the Tsarist family.

Modern rowing arrived in Poland through German Rudder Clubs but it is well known that the German rowing organisations were primarily modelled on those from Oxford and Cambridge. The first Polish rowing club was established in Warsaw (1882). In Bulgaria the Rowing Gymnastic Society 'Lebed' ('Swan') was set up in 1899. Rowing was frequently combined with yachting. The oldest, and at the same time strongest, yachting club in the nineteenth-century Slavonic countries was organised in Russia. It was the Imperial Yacht Club established in 1846 and modelled on the British Royal Yacht Squadron.

Polo gained a foothold among the aristocracy at approximately the same time that Winston Churchill's passion for the sport was responsible for the injuries he sustained during his period as cavalry officer in India. Scouting was not considered a sport but nevertheless it was associated with the fitness of the young. In 1912 Andrzej Małkowski, a Polish enthusiast of scouting, went to one of the jamborees organised by Baden-Powell and authorised by him, brought scouting to Poland. In Bohemia scouting was introduced in 1912 also by the well-known sports organiser František Potlacha.

Not all modern sports in the Slavonic countries arrived by way of British influence. While Russia, Bohemia and Poland experienced direct British influence, the Balkan countries were acquainted with modern sport via Austria or France. Boxing, skating, athletics, rowing and even soccer were begun in Bulgaria thanks to Swiss gymnasts teaching physical education in Bulgarian high schools. These gymnasts were Georges de Régibusse, Louis Ayé and Emil Kupfer, who taught at Varna schools. Despite the unfavourable Southern climate, in some mountainous areas of Bulgaria skating and then skiing was introduced at the end of the nineteenth century. The first skis were made in 1903 by Peter Morozow, after reading about them in a Norwegian book. The first swimming school was organised in Russia in Petersburg in 1827 by French fencing instructor Grips (first name unknown). Russian officers began swimming instruction in Bulgaria in 1878. In 1900 in Sofia a complex of two swimming pools was built with one pool for men and another one for women. In Poland the first swimming pool was built in 1839 in Poznań on the initiative of the German Army stationed there. From the beginning because it was 'co-educational' the local press was full of complaints on the 'immoral behaviour of both sexes when bathing together'.

Cycling arrived in Bohemia, Poland and Russia from Germany and Austria. In this sport the sharpest fight for women's emancipation took place. It was reflected not only in press polemics but also in satirical poetry and serious novels. Cycling was introduced in Poland as early as 1868 and the first bicycle race in Warsaw was held in 1869. In Russia and Bohemia it became popular at about the same time or slightly earlier. In Bulgaria, on hearing about the popularity of bicycles in the West, Geno Arabadjiyata, who lived in Nova Zagora, tried to build one according to his own design. But the real story of Bulgarian biking began in 1883 when merchant Metodyi Hadjipetkov imported the first bicycles from Germany and France.

Whatever influences determined the introduction of a sport to particular countries, they were unavoidably associated with the English language. The Slavonic languages were not prepared for the invasion of different British sports. Lack of Polish, Russian and other linguistic equivalents for the new English terminology soon became apparent. The Polish language can serve as a model for noting the early influences of English following on the arrival of British sports. These influences covered not only equestrian terminology but soon also the language of tennis, rowing and Association football. Cycling was mainly an Austrian and German sport but surprisingly British bicycles were more widely appreciated than the products of Poland's closest neighbours. Bikes produced by the English Rover factory provided the name for the Polish word for bicycle. Today 'bicycle' in Polish is 'rower' after the English 'Rover'. This linguistic invasion caused a panic among the language purists. Before 1914 there was a strong campaign in Russian newspapers against English terminology entering 'our old language able to produce its original words'. There were some attempts to substitute word 'sport' with the Russian *okhota* ('hunting or any activity made for pleasure at one's will'). In Poland at least two public concourses were announced in the press to invent Polish equivalents for English sports terms. The biggest linguistic competition for readers was organised by the Polish monthly *Koło* (The Wheel). The results were only partly successful. In the last of these competitions 19 English words, such as 'sport' and 'training', were proposed for substitution. In the case of 'sport' all attempts failed. One of them was the Polish word *ochota*, similar to the Russian *okhota* meaning in Polish 'willingness to act'. But it did not cover all shades of 'sport'. More successful was word *zaprawa* suggested as a substitute for 'training'. It did not replace 'training' but in the course of time it started to mean 'basic training' and shared its language function with 'training' which, in turn, started to mean rather 'advanced forms of physical conditioning'. Some English loan-words obtained Polish substitutes under the pressure of the growing popularity of some sports, such as association football. Among the masses there was little concern for a knowledge of English or any English snobbery, and new Polish words for new sporting situations were created rather quickly. Thus, for instance, English 'corner' found its Polish equivalent in *rzut rożny* and 'goalkeeper' in *bramkarz*. But in the course of time, the frequent usage of sports terms in the mass media caused a phenomenon which can be described as 'wearing out' words, which had to be used many times in the same sports report in the press, radio, or somewhat later on television. Due to the frequency of sports events, such 'wearing out' is stronger than in other cultural areas where it is not known to such a degree. Due to this, mass-media men look for possibilities to enrich and differentiate the vocabulary at any price. This, in turn, after some years caused 'feed-back' appearance in Polish of even those English loan-words which initially had disappeared due to the pressure of Polish creativity. Today, for instance some English calques, such as the just mentioned *rzut rożny*, or *bramkarz* have coexisted with polonised English loan-word *golkiper* or *korner* written differently from the English originals, but pronounced almost the same way.

Eventually a modern basic sports vocabulary became part and parcel of all Slavonic languages. 'Sport' itself remained unchanged, except in the different shape of letters in languages where the Cyrillic alphabet is used (i.e. Russian, Belorussian, Ukrainian, Bulgarian and Serbian: спорт. English 'sportsman' was employed in almost the same form in most Slavonic tongues as 'sportsmen. There are slight differences in Belorussian *spartsmien* and Russian *sportsmien*, however. Such forms resembling the English plural but being the Slavonic singular denoted at the beginning all who practised sport. In due course, however, 'sportsman' started to mean a snob or amateur practising sport and carried a hint of irony. This was the result of a long-standing criticism of sport as a foreign cultural invader by local conservatives. Thanks to it other forms appeared: Serbian and Croatian *sportas*, Czech *sportovec*, Bulgarian *sportist* and Polish *sportowiec* meaning just 'athlete'. But when the first women entered the scene 'sportsman' was modified by the typical Slavonic ending *-ka*, denoting feminine gender. In this way Russian *sportsmienka*, Belorussian *spartsmienka*, Ukrainian and Czech *sportsmanka* or Polish *sportsmenka*, based on the English masculine form of the word, denotes in most Slavonic languages any woman practising sport. The only exception is the Serbo/Croatian language where *sportasica* denotes woman of sport. Also other derivatives of 'sport', especially adjectives equivalent to English 'sporting' or 'sports' kept the word root basically the same or not far from the original, while their endings differed substantially, like in Russian *sportivnyi*, Ukrainian *sportiwnii*, Belorussian *spartyny*, Serbo-Croatian *sportski*, Bulgarian *sportien*, Polish *sportowy*, Czechish *sportovni*. A similar story is associated with many other sports terms, like 'football' for instance: Russian, Belorussian, Ukrainian and Bulgarian *futbol* (pronounced in all these languages as 'futbow'), Polish *futbol*, Serbian *fudbal* and Croatian *futbal*. The situation was different in less popular sports, where Anglophilism was stronger and limited to a society of members more familiar with foreign languages. This guaranteed the more effective circulation of English terminology. Snobbery supported this attitude to a great degree. One of the most snobbish sports was tennis. The Serbian Nobel Prize winner Ivo Andrić recollected in one of his short stories that as a young man he demonstrated his occidentalism among his countrymen by having with him a tennis racquet even if he did not intend to play. According to Professor Jacek Fisiak in his 1964 work on English sports terms in Polish, 'out of 721 English loan-words in Polish, a large group of 131 are terms referring to [all] sports and games'.[39] Almost 30 years later, in 1992, I started an MA seminar on the influences of Britain and the United States on the history of Polish sport. Of 17 theses eight were devoted to English loan-words in Polish sports terminology. My students were able to gather almost 2,000 English loan-words in eight selected sports. Tennis had the most – 467 English loan-words.

In general, in the Slavonic countries, modern sports, based on the British or indeed any other cultural model, have been important to national aspirations during the era of foreign domination or on independence. When Polish cyclists commemorated the 25th anniversary of their activities in 1912 the press commentaries were clear: 'In a society deprived by fate of any possibility to conduct its cultural work in a normal, economically based way, with the help of its own taxes and legal system, every institution becomes the substitutive centre of the effort to ensure a national culture and that includes business establishments as well as sports and clubs.'[40]

DECLINE OF FOLK GAMES

The appearance of modern sport was responsible for the gradual elimination and virtual extinction of traditional sports. In Bulgaria even the traditional sport of wrestling was neglected. Old style wrestling maintained its position there until the 1890s. Then a new style, called 'French' (in fact Classical) was introduced to Bulgaria by athletes and instructors from Germany, France and Croatia. In towns the new style gradually displaced folk-wrestling, which did not guarantee international contacts, very important for the best wrestlers who wanted to go abroad and be 'international athletes'. Political isolation, for long enforced by the Turks, was no longer a barrier. So gradually the best Bulgarian athletes left their village spectators behind and adapted to new way of fighting. Among the first successful modern wrestlers was Alexander Dobrich, winner of several international matches in Budapest and Hamburg. The first world champion from Bulgaria was Nikola Petrov, who won his title in Paris at Cirque d'Hiver in 1900. It was here that also representatives of other long-suppressed nations tried to find international recognition not only for themselves but also for their unhappy countrymen. An awareness of performing and winning for their countries was especially strong among them. Poland, although not independent until 1918, had two World Champions in wrestling before 1914: Władysław Pytlasiński in 1904 and Zbyszko Cyganiewicz in 1906 (he regained the title in 1921 and 1922). When Pytlasiński won his first championship, officially for Russia of which he was citizen, but in the minds of Poles for Poland, one of the newspapers wrote: 'After the recent success of Pytlasiński we have more courage to show ourselves to the world.'[41]

The poverty of the Bulgarian, Serbian or Polish village kept folk sports alive longer than in the town. But industrialisation which started to soak up peasant populations, in conjunction with other phenomena of modern civilisation experienced in the West several decades earlier, began at the turn of the nineteenth century its destructive work on folk culture, dancing, music and, of course, folk games. Ethnographers and the more aware physical educationists sounded the alarm. Eugeniusz Piasecki, originally a university professor of medicine, and in the 1920s the great reformer of the Polish physical education system, co-operated voluntarily for several decades with ethnographers in saving folk sports and play. He wrote:

We are nation of beautiful and rich traditions in all areas of culture. We have, however, little inclination to research such traditions, and certainly little interest in nursing those elements which can be accommodated to contemporary life. One of the most striking examples of blameworthy indifference pertaining to the treasures of native civilisation is our attitude toward Old Polish play and folk-games. Among many Western nations many serious scientific works were published on this matter and ancient games, pastimes and songs were made part of national education. Not in our country.[42]

From the early 1900s Piacecki was able to gather dozens of old folk games. He described them in many articles and in a series of books. In 1928 Piacecki announced in Polish newspapers a large-scale questionnaire research project. Over 2,800 individuals filled in questionnaires in response, not only from ethnic Polish areas but also from those parts of the Ukraine and Belorussia then within Polish borders. Of these nearly 3,000 questionnaires most provided information on the same kind of games or play, but nonetheless Piasecki was able to preserve several hundred original folk activities.

Unfortunately, it has not helped much to save those activities from extinction. Some of them entered Polish school textbooks for physical education, but none of them achieved any status in modern Polish national sport. A similar situation was apparent in the nations of newly created Yugoslavia where interest in 'imported' sports appeared stronger than love of their own traditions. To be sure, some 'village sports' were still continued, but not one of them was as popular of some Western sports, such as British, French or Italian ball games (cricket, golf, boules, boccia) which were initially disregarded and even prohibited by official royal or church edicts but gained in the course of time their status of national pastime.

The attitude towards folk sports is closely associated with the question of national originality in inventing new sports. In this respect Slavonic countries do not lead the world, though some sports 'invented' on the basis of folk games have proved that something could be done. In 1935 the Polish sports instructor W. Robakowski, watched a game of volleyball played with a net worn into holes. On the basis of this observation he invented *pierścieniówka* (ringball). Its idea was to play the ball, of volleyball size, through (not over) the net in which three holes framed by metal rings had been made.[43] Regrettably, the Second World War put a stop to the potential development of ringball.

The Czechs were more fortunate when on the basis of some folk games combined with Western style rules Václav Karas and Antonín Krištof created *hazena*, a kind of handball played in a court divided into three parts (with playing allowed only in one's own sector). It had a golden age in the 1920s and 1930s when it was quite popular not only in Czechoslovakia but also in France, Poland, Switzerland, Yugoslavia and Hungary. World Championships were held. It is still played in both Bohemia and Slovakia and enjoys a certain degree of popularity in some Balkan countries including Serbia. In the Czech Republic local *hazena* leagues still exist, as well as the annual match between Bohemia and Moravia (once separate medieval kingdoms, later absorbed by the Czechs but still having some sense of separate ethnic identity).[44] The temporary popularity of *hazena*, called in Polish *jordanka*, can be measured by the fact, that when in 1937 the first Polish texbook on the sport was published it contained 64 additional pages of advertisements: the sport was important enough to attract such commercial interest.[45]

Russia before 1914 also experienced a slow decline of folk games and sports but after the 1917 October Revolution the state provided for folk sports – official support to a degree never seen in other Slavic countries. What happened to Russian folk games will be discussed in the sequel to this chapter concerning sport in Slavonic countries of the Communist era.

In Poland, in 1959 Włodzimierz Strzyżewski, another sports enthusiast (a former national fencer) attempted to popularise *ringo*, an activity similar to that earlier *ring-tennis* invented in the 1920 by the German N. Schneider (a rubber ring was thrown over the net for points as in volleyball or table-tennis). Polish *ringo* gained some popularity as a recreational sport but hardly attained the status of a national sport.[46]

BETWEEN THE WARS (1918–39)

The period after the First World War did not result in a stable Europe but surprisingly it was a time of remarkable stabilisation for European sport. Slavic Europe gained a number of benefits from this. Sports structures were well established in most Slavonic countries but with varying degrees of completeness. Bulgaria gained its freedom in 1875, Serbia in 1878 but other Slavonic nations were liberated from foreign domination as late as 1918. Poland was freed, Slovakia united with Bohemia, Croatia and Slovenia united with Serbia first as the Kingdom of three nations and then after 1929 as Yugoslavia. Russia, after the bloody October Revolution in 1917 changed its political system and divorced itself from Western sports developments. Ukraine and Belorussia finally entered the Soviet Union.

The first action for these newly liberated nations was to attempt to overcome the weaknesses and backwardness left by their oppressors. These were especially obvious in the Balkan countries which the Turks had left in considerable economic underdevelopment and extreme poverty. Such conditions were strongly reflected in the plight of sport.

As long as liberation was a national goal, sport could count on common support as a means of creating a strong nation ready for military action. When freedom was achieved sport was considered as an issue of lesser importance. Of course, the under-appreciation of sport was different in different countries: in Czechoslovakia, for example, support was at a level only slightly lower than in Western countries.[47]

The Czechoslovakian system of physical education was based on a system created by Augustin Otčenášek. It stressed not only gymnastics but sports, such as athletics, swimming and skating. This was the opposite of the Polish system of education, which was against competitive sport to the extent that students of high schools were not allowed to be members of sports clubs and participate in public competitions. This in turn caused massive participation by students in different sports clubs under pseudonyms. In Poland school physical education was the responsibility of the Ministry of Religious Denominations and Public Enlightenment. In 1929 the State Office for Physical Education and Military Training (Państwowy Urzad Wychowania Fizycznego i Przysposobienia Wojskowego, PUWFiPW) was established. Before 1939 there was no special law passed by the Polish Parliament concerning physical education though its necessity was emphasised in general Parliamentary bills concerning public affairs, especially education. All current legal questions were solved on the basis of governmental and ministerial directives. These were frequently suggested and evaluated before application by the State Scientific Council for Physical Education, established in 1927. On its suggestion, for instance, in 1931 a special National Badge for Sport (Polska Odznaka Sportowa, POS) was introduced, which could be won by anyone who was able to pass a series of certain physical tests or achieve results confirmed by participation in prescribed sports and tourist events.

In Bulgaria after 1894 the authorities introduced a number of laws concerning physical education. In 1924 for the first time the Law on Education provided for the establishment of the office of State Head Inspector of PE. In 1925 the Office of Physical Education was established and after 1926 its work was included for the first time in the state budget. In 1931 Bulgaria adopted the quite progressive *Law on Physical Education of Bulgarian Youth*, but as one Bulgarian historian has commented, 'the law was passed but it was never applied'.[48] The weakest point in the Bulgarian pre-1939 system of physical education was the preparation of physical education teachers. Some courses were initiated in the middle of the 1930s and some attempts at creating a Physical Education Division at the University of Sofia, but when in 1934 the posts of several District Inspectors of Physical Education were established almost all candidates for those posts appeared to be trained in Germany, Italy and Hungary. The first real academic school of physical education was established in Bulgaria only in 1949 under Communist rule. In contrast academic physical education departments worked well from the 1920s on at several universities in Czechoslovakia and Poland. The first courses for instructors of physical education were initiated at the Charles University, Prague, in 1891. Almost from the beginning these courses were open to women. The section for men was initially headed by Jan Laciný, for women by Jos Klenka and then Professor Provaznikova. After 1906 courses directed by Dr Janošik gradually acquired the standing of a full department, in which in 1925 as many as 149 students were taught (including 63 women).[49]

Similar physical education programmes were introduced after 1923 at another Bohemian University in Brno (There were 63 students, including 10 women in 1925), headed by physiologist Edward Babák, and after 1927 at the University of J. Komensky in Slovakian Bratislava (preceded by less systematic courses in 1921). Germans living in Czechoslovakia organised separate academic courses of physical education in Prague (1891, directed by the anatomist and orthopaedist Edward Pietrzikowsky). The most distinguished pioneer and organiser of academic physical education and sport in Czechoslovakia was Dr František Potlacha. He was especially active in establishing Physical education departments and sports clubs at academic schools not specialising in teaching physical education. The main purpose of such bodies was, of course, the provision of exercise for students, but students could, on a voluntary basis, obtain methodological knowledge and prepare for work as physical education and sport instructors, at the lower level. The most active institutions providing students with sports instruction were surprisingly the Mining Engineering College in the small town of Príbrami and the German Polytechnic in Brno.[50] Thus German organisations in Czechoslovakia accelerated positive changes, and somewhat later, especially in the 1930s became a political threat due to their pro-Nazi orientation.[51]

One of the most important agencies in the development of sport and physical education at Czechoslovakian universities was Vysokoškolsky Sport (Academic Sport), better known as VS, the very apple of

Potlacha's eye. This organisation, characterised by an unusual spirit of devotion, alone produced thousands of volunteers, who took modern sport to the most remote areas of Czechoslovakia. Potlacha and his organisation was obviously inspired by Anglo–Saxon sport, and was rather against non-competitive health gymnastics, which were predominant in all Czechoslovakian schools. Throughout continental Europe, including the Slavonic countries, gymnastics was then considered a non-sport and something incomparably 'higher' than sport in both moral and health respects. There were many published works on the superiority of gymnastics over 'immoral, barbarian, non scientific sport'. But Potlacha was aware, that despite all arguments for gymnastics and other 'calculated exercises' they could not match spontaneous, exciting sports competitions. He called the existing gymnastic system 'simply dullness for our students'.[52] No wonder then that he was accused both by those who criticised his stress on competitive sports instead of 'healthy exercises' and by those who accused VS of lagging far behind British universities. He wrote in irritation: 'some suppose that the first task of VS is to promote records and ... winnings ..., while others ... are anxious about results achieved by us and recall Oxford and Cambridge, forgetting that the situation of the English at their rich colleges and universities cannot be compared with ours.'[53]

In conjunction with Potlacha's efforts at the University of Komensky Academic YMCA (Akademická YMKA) was established in 1922. The YMCA was also very active in Poland after 1919 and up to 1939 and then again after 1945 until it was prohibited by the Communists in 1949. Surprisingly, however, the earliest YMCA agency in the Slavonic countries was established in Russia. It was the Society for the Moral and Physical Development of Youth, 'Majak', which become an official member of the YMCA in 1900.[54]

In Poland physical education as an academic study was introduced in 1890s at the Jagiellonian University as an irregular course. The first Polish Department of Hygiene and Physical Education was established within the Division of Medicine at the University of Poznań in 1919. Its main organiser and chairman was Eugeniusz Piasecki, professor of medicine and Poland's most distinguished scholar in physical education. He was also a Delegate to the Hygiene Section of the League of Nations in Geneva. In this capacity he visited European countries and produced his well-known *La science de l'éducation physique dans les différents pays de l'Europe*. On the basis of this document a big international conference was held in Copenhagen in 1930 after which a physical education section was established at the League of Nations (within the Hygiene Division). Piasecki was the founder and long-time editor of the most important Polish academic journal on physical education, *Wychowanie Fizyczne*.

In 1921, also in Poznań, the Military School of Gymnastics and Sport was established thanks to another pioneer, Colonel Walerian Sikorski. In 1927 it was moved to Warsaw and strengthened the rather weak Warsaw Institute of Physical Education which had been established a little earlier. This merger was the beginning of the State Institute of Physical Education in Warsaw (1929), later renamed the Central Institute of Physical Education. By 1939 it had produced several hundred high-quality teachers. This was still insufficient. By the Second World War Poznań, Warsaw and Cracow had produced between them some 1,500 professional physical educationists, while the Military School of Gymnastics and Sport before merging with the Warsaw Institute of Physical Education had produced 660 officers as instructors and coaches.[55]

Nevertheless, due to a lack of physical education teachers in primary schools, other teachers had to assume responsibility for the subject. By the middle of 1930s some 200 'crash' physical education courses were organised for several thousand primary school teachers. In the course of time various universities and educational institutions arranged systematic courses in such towns as Lublin, Łuck, Grodno, Katowice, Brześć, Przemyśl and Lvov. The number of instructors, so-called 'leaders', while not fully qualified but educated at these places for teaching physical education at the lower level, was quite imposing: 1930 – 3,500, 1931 – 4,400, 1932 – 13,750, 1933 – 14,600.[56] In Poland, incidentally, the Akademicki Związek Sportowy (Academic Sports Association) had a role similar to the Czechoslovakian Vysokoškolsky Sport in Czechoslovakia.[57]

Competitive sport in general reflected the level of general development of each country and its level of physical education. By 1923 when the Bulgarian National Sports Federation was established, all the Slavonic countries had similar unions co-ordinating (sometimes only attempting to co-ordinate) the development of sport. National Olympic Committees were established first in Czechoslovakia (1896), later recognised as the Czechoslovakian Olympic Committee, in Poland and Yugoslavia in 1918 (both recognised by the IOC in 1919); in Bulgaria in 1923 (IOC recognition 1924). While in Czechoslovakia and Poland

National Olympic Committees generally were secondary to state authorities, in Bulgaria it was the NOC that took the initiative and seems to have been a most active and successful sports body. On its initiative in 1931 the first Balkan Games were organised in Sofia (preceded by the Pan-Balkan Games in Track and Field in 1929). Nonetheless even the Bulgarian NOC was unable to overcome the sporting backwardness of the country and the competitive performance of the Bulgarians was extremely poor at all the Olympic Games up to 1952. The Bulgarians participated in the first Olympics in Athens in 1896, then failed to compete in the Games of 1900–1920 'due to a number of reasons, including a struggle for internal power ... low technical standards and performances in the Olympic sports, lack of interest by the state in promoting sports and the resultant poor finances ..., lack of a National Olympic Committee ... and finally the negative chauvinistic attitude to the Olympic Games by the bourgeoisie which happened to see in them Greek interference and influence.'[58]

From 1924 to 1936 Bulgaria did not win a single Olympic medal nor even a single final point! The performance of the other Slavonic countries was incomparably better. Poland could not compete in the Olympics between 1896 and 1912 because the divided country could not establish a National Olympic Committee. In 1920 a scratch Polish team withdrew from the games due to the Soviet invasion and Poland was represented only by a flag delegation. The first full Polish participation at the Olympic Games in 1924 brought two medals, silver in team cycling and bronze in equestrian sports. A Serbian team appeared at the Games in 1912, as Yugoslavian in 1920 and the first two medals were won in 1924. The Czechs had the best early Olympic performance. They participated in the Games from 1900 and won their first medal in the same year (František Janda, silver for the discus). Russia, as it is well known, did not participate in the Olympic Games from 1920 to 1948. At the 1900 Olympic tournament, the Czechs also won a silver in team gymnastics competition while bronze was taken by the Yugoslavs. The results of the Slavonic nations at the Olympic Games 1896–1936 are given in the table opposite.

Poland, Yugoslavia and Czechoslovakia held a series of tripartite international events including athletic and soccer matches. In 1922 the first athletic match was won easily by the Czechoslovakians with Yugoslavia second and Poland third. In 1926 Poland improved significantly and beat Yugoslavia in Warsaw and then in 1927 in Zagreb

Country	Gold	Silver	Bronze
Czechoslovakia	7	1	12
Poland	3	6	11
Russia (up to 1912 only)	1	4	2
Yugoslavia	2	1	–
Bulgaria	–	–	–

won so comprehensively (872/3: 421/3 and 96: 46 respectively) that the Yugoslavs abandoned the event. Czechoslovakia was a more difficult rival and of seven matches staged before 1939 (Greece replaced Yugoslavia) the Czechs won 2 and the Poles 5, but three of them were won by the Poles by a single point (1928 – 79:78; 1932 – 76.5: 75.5; 1932 – 79.5: 78.5!

Bulgaria did not take part in these 'Slavonic Matches'. It had organised the first Balkan Games in 1929 but the relatively poor standard of Bulgarian athletics did not permit competition with far stronger Northern neighbours.

The poor athletic standard of the Bulgarians was due to the fact that 'The number of sports clubs which provided for the practice of athletics increased very slowly and with many difficulties, because the sports involved required relatively expensive facilities and installations ... it was as late as 1940 that the first drained track was built in Bulgaria.'[59]

Yugoslavia, unable to compete successfully with other Slavonic countries in athletics, did much better in other sports such as water polo, and above all soccer. It was in soccer that Yugoslavia became the first Slavonic participant in the first World Cup Championships in (1930). The Yugoslavian team found itself among the four best teams in the world, losing in the semi-final to Uruguay, the eventual champions. During the 2nd Championships in Italy the Czechoslovakians, appearing for the first time, came second, losing to Italy in the final. Poland and Czechoslovakia played in the 3rd Championships in France in (1938) and Czechoslovakia reached the quarter-finals. During the whole inter-war period the Czechoslovaks had indisputably the best soccer team. It was in soccer that the national ambitions of particular countries were best demonstrated in, for example, the so-called Slavonic Tournament held as early as 1928 on the occasion of the tenth anniversary of Czechoslovakian independence. Between 1922 and 1938 Poland played Yugoslavia 11 times while Czechoslovakia played Poland eight times. These matches indicate the strength of the relationship between the Slavonic countries. Sports contacts were seen as an expression of Slavonic identity unfavourable political circumstances. During this period the Czechoslovakian and Polish governments clashed continually over some border areas, and in 1939 the Polish Army invaded the small territory of Zaolzie. All-Slavonic tournaments and matches, incidentally, regardless of the type of sport, were of a good standard involving as they did teams which had experience of world or European championships in different sports.

The Olympic competitions in literature and art (1912–48) may be considered an indication of cultural achievements over and above sport itself. Only three Slavonic countries gained medals or distinctions:

Country	Gold	Silver	Bronze	Honorary mentions
Poland	3	2	3	11
Czechoslovakia	1	–	2	2
Yugoslavia	–	–	–	2
Russia (only in 1912)	–	–	–	–
Bulgaria	–	–	–	–

While Poland took pride of place among the Slavonic countries in art competitions, it was 5th overall after such 'sports art powers' as Germany, France, Italy and USA but before Austria, Great Britain, Belgium, Denmark, Switzerland and Finland.[60] Gold medals were won by the Poles in literature, sculpture and music. The Czechoslovakians won their only gold in music. Two teams of architects from Yugoslavia, one Serbian and one Croatian, won 2 honorary mentions in 1948 for stadiums in Belgrade and Zagreb respectively. Bulgaria did not win anything.

DURING THE SECOND WORLD WAR

Between 1939 and 1945 the progress of Slavonic sport rapidly slowed down or stopped entirely but not to the same degree in all Slavonic countries, which declared themselves for one side or the other. This determined to a substantial degree the impact of the war: nations openly supporting the Nazis, survived the war without being too seriously affected: their losses were counted in scores or, at worst, hundreds of thousands of people, certainly not one million per nation. Those who openly opposed the Germans, like Poland and after 1941 the USSR were hurt to an incomparably higher degree. Poland lost nearly 1/5th of its population (about 6 million people, including over 3 million of its Jewish citizens). The war losses of the Soviet Union were slightly over 20 million. After the war these facts were important in determining many areas of national life, including physical education and sports in Slavonic countries.

The Second World War itself inevitably, but not equally, had a devastating impact on the Slavonic countries and on their cultures. Czechoslovakia was the first victim, shamefully sacrificed by the Western Powers for an illusory peace in Munich (1938). The Nazis created in the Western part of former Czechoslovakia the so-called Czech-Moravian Protectorate, with illusory autonomy, sufficient however for practising their own physical education in the schools and some sports activities though severely limited by war conditions. While a substantial number of Slovaks supported Germany as the guarantor of their limited but separate statehood, the Czechs' attitude towards Germany can be described as 'silent resistance'. There was an underground movement. Reinhardt Heydrich, for example, was assassinated. In response, as is well known, the Germans killed all men of the village Lidice which was completely burned. However tragic this was, it by no means compared with the complete annihilation of 817 Polish and over 2,000 Russian villages and small towns (in Poland, for instance, the whole region of so-called Zamojszczyzna, equal in size to a large English county, was almost completely levelled with dozens of villages burned and inhabitants killed; only some children 'racially fit' were saved and sent to German 'adoption houses').

Bulgaria was the only independent state created before 1939 which openly and voluntarily supported Germany. Physical education and sport were continued there until about 1943. In the first phase of the war Bulgaria was even able to develop some sports venues, like the first fully equipped stadium for athletics (1940). Shooting had especially strong support and some new venues were built. After the invasion of Yugoslavia, Croatia declared itself on the Berlin-Rome-Tokyo Axis' side, first under the Italians (1939) and then under the Germans (1943). Sport shrank to friendly soccer matches with Italian and German soldiers while in the remaining republics (Serbia, Slovenia and Macedonia) the partisans virtually prohibited sport except for 'morale-building' competitions in the guerrillas' camps.

After Russia, the worst affected country was Poland. The Slavonic people generally were the second came in the Nazi plans to annihilate *Untermenschen* – just behind the Jews. Only those Slavs who were supporters of the Germans had a chance of survival. The Ukrainians, for instance, were promised a state similar to Slovakia or Croatia and this is why a number of Ukrainian troops under Stefan Bandera supported Germany. Almost all the Slavonic people, including those Russians who opposed the USSR under a General Vlasow, provided troops for the German side. The only nation not to do so was Poland. But the price was heavy and included the virtual extermination of any cultural life, including education (except for primary classes and lower vocational courses). Sport was on the list of strictly prohibited civic activities. Such regulations were quite frequently ignored. Underground sports, a 'Polish war speciality', is a phenomenon probably unknown in similar size in any other European country during Nazi occupation. There were national and regional 'underground' championships in some sports, selected on the basis of simplicity in organisation (skating, selected athletics events and above all soccer). In 1941, in Kalisz German troops surrounded players and spectators at one soccer match and sent them to concentration camps as 'organisers of action directed against the 3rd Reich'. Wrestlers and weightlifters who organised in Warsaw secret gymnasium for exercising and competitions were more lucky: they were not discovered.[61]

A number of famous Polish athletes who participated in the underground movement or illegal sports activities were arrested and killed. This happened to Janusz Kusociński winner of the 10,000 metres at the 1932 Olympic Games in Los Angeles. The best Polish all-round skier Bronislaw Czech was offered the position of coach to the junior German national squad. He refused, was arrested and died in Auschwitz. The list goes on.

Sport might seem in these circumstances a foolish waste of precious energy but in occupied Poland it was a demonstration of vitality and defiance – a refusal to bow to circumstances. It was also matter of psychological health, an important element of maintaining life as near to normality as possible. In POW's camps and concentration camps this attitude found especially dramatic expression. Sport was allowed by the Germans in most of the POW camps in both World Wars. In fact, in the Great War Polish prisoners learned handball from the Germans in Szczypiorno village and this is why this sport is even now called in Polish *szczypiorniak*, most probably the only sport which gained its name in such circumstances. Sport as practised by the POWs is frequently mentioned in memoirs written by former prisoners of different nations, like New Zealander John Borrie, who was at Lamsdorf (*Despite Captivity. A Doctor's Life as Prisoner of War*, 1975). The British officer Patrick R. Reid described sports activities in the prison's camp in the notorious Castle of Colditz, where some 80 Polish officers were kept: 'here we played something resembling soccer – the hazards were the trees amongst which the game surged backwards and forwards. Our ball games amused the Jerries'.[62] There was also boxing, volleyball and stool-ball. As Reid wrote, sport was 'a manifestation of our suppressed desire for freedom. While the game was in action we were free. The surrounding walls were no longer a prison, but the confines of the game we played, and there were no constraining rules to curtail our freedom of action. I always felt much better after a game. Followed by a cold bath it put me on top of the world.'[63] Exactly the same feelings and almost the same words can be found in the memoirs of Polish soldiers, who organised sports competition in Stalag II at Nuremberg and especially those officers who organised at Dobiegniewo (Woldenberg) the great sporting festival called 'The Olympic Games' to commemorate the Olympic Year of 1944.[64]

Incomparably more moving were, however, attempts to organise sport in extermination and concentration camps, such as Auschwitz where mass murders were commonplace. Some sports were organised at the order of the German Commando in order to mimic 'normal life' for the Red Cross inspections, or just for the amusement of SS-men. Two leading Polish boxers were imprisoned in Auschwitz: Antoni Czortek and Zygmunt Malecki. They were accompanied by the Italian professional Eufratti and the German Walter, who was sent there for his unfavourable opinions of the Führer. Some fights were arranged between them in order to amuse the Auschwitz Kommando. 'We fought seriously,' recollected Małecki, 'because the Jerries did not allow mild and make-belief boxing. I personally saw cases when those competitors ... who did not beat each other seriously enough were baited by dogs. Refusal to fight meant the gas-chamber.'[65]

However, prisoners themselves organised their unofficial secret sport just to keep their sanity. There are a series of personal memoirs in Polish describing sports competitions in Auschwitz and Mauthausen. The system operated in such a way that some SS-men were bribed and the selected groups of prisoners, usually former athletes, were excluded from heavy work and fed additional meals obtained by a 'food tax' on other prisoners. There is a substantial number of short-stories, novels and even some films on the topic. The most famous sports story is the Polish short novel by Józef Hen titled *The Boxer and Death* (*Bokser i śmieć*, 1954). It is part fact and part fiction about a Polish boxer, who was selected as a sparring partner by the commander of a German concentration camp who dreamt of a sporting career after the war and wants to preserve his technique and stamina. (This story was used by Czech film-director Peter Solan in his movie *Boxer a smrt* (1963), and is an example of inter-slavic cultural co-operation.) The story was recently included in an anthology of the world's best boxing literature published in Germany in 1997, *Ring frei*.

From the purely moral point of view, the most moving Polish literary piece on sport in concentration camp is the short-story by one of the most distinguished Polish writers, Tadeusz Borowski, a former prisoner of Auschwitz, who played in the officially sanctioned football match as goalkeeper. Here is the most sensitive moment of his short story:

> The ball went out of play and reached the barbed wire of the fence. I followed it. When I picked it up I looked up at the rail-road ramp. The train had just arrived. From cattle-cars people started to get out and moved towards the wood ... I returned with my ball and sent it back into the playing field. It passed from one player to another and with a curved flight came back to my goal. I knocked it to the corner. Again I went to pick it up. But when I picked it up and looked up at the ramp, the ramp was empty ... Between the two corners of the pitch behind my back some three thousand people were gassed.[66]

Polish officers and soldiers imprisoned by the Soviets after the Red Army invaded Poland on 17 September 1939 had little opportunity for sport. In the POW Camps of Katyń, Ostashkovo, Myednoyie and Kozyielsk over 20,000 Polish officers and rank-and-file were killed by the inglorious NKVD by one shot in the back of the head or neck. This included a high percentage of sportsmen, doctors, coaches and athletes who were in the Polish Army or Police as reserve officers. Over 80 physical education and sports officials, presidents and vice presidents of different associations, including the Polish Olympic Committee, editors of sports newspapers and journals were murdered at Katyń and other

places of the USSR. This substantially weakened the Polish sports elite
after the war. The tragic situation of Polish wartime sport is best
reflected in at least four well-known volumes of poetry. The best of them
is titled *Olympic Odes* (*Ody olimpijskie*, 1948); it received an honorary
mention at the last Olympic Poetry Competition in London in 1948. Of
course, sport was practised in POW and concentration camps by many
people, not only the Slavonic peoples. Only in Poland, however, was
sport reflected in the memoirs, poetry and prose of its most
distinguished athletes and writers.

All Slavonic countries without exception, of course, came under
Communist rule after the Second World War. All, except Yugoslavia,
which had its own totalitarian system, found themselves in the Soviet
sphere of influence. The Communist system of sport and physical
education in Slavonic countries after 1945 is, however, separate story
which will be discussed elsewhere.

As mentioned at the start of this study, of necessity, this has been a
somewhat fractured, disconnected and incomplete survey of pre-
Communist sport in the Slavonic world. The intention is to stimulate
interest among historians, sociologists and anthropologists of *both*
Western and Eastern Europe in this neglected but important dimension
of the cultural life of the Slavonic peoples and to ensure that in the post-
millennium period this neglect characteristic of the past will be a thing
of the past and that with sustained, careful, thorough attention to what
records remain, the sport of the Slavonic world, folk and modern, will
eventually be recorded, analysed and understood as completely as it is in
Eastern Europe.

NOTES
1. To whom even the English poets dedicated their hastily written poems:
    Great Champion of the Cross
    Whose glorious name
    Entered forever
    Christian books of fame.
2. Ethnic consciousness of Belorussians was not strong until in the nineteenth century. Russia
    sought to turn them against the Lithuanians and Poles (all nations absorbed then by Russian
    Empire) in an attempt to undermine the former unity of those nations. They were so close that
    they even produced common historic personalities almost ethnically indistinguishable. For
    instance, Tadeusz Kościuszko, one of the most internationally revered fighters for Polish (and
    American) independence, was born a Belorussian, as well as Stanisław Moniuszko, composer
    and founder of the Polish national opera, or Adam Mickiewicz, Polish national poet of mixed
    Polish-Lithuanian and Belorussian origins.
3. Unlike numerous 'specialists' in Polish history who have neither touched Polish soil nor know
    the Polish language, Davies studied Polish history in Poland, has superb command of Polish,

and after studying original Polish sources wrote the famous *God's Playground. A History of Poland* (1982) and then *Heart of Europe* (1984). But even after Davies' publication the traditional ignorance of Eastern Europe and all Slavonic countries is continued in such works like, for instance, *An Intellectual History of Modern Europe* by Marvin Perry (Cambridge Massachusetts: Houghton Mifflin, 1993). For Perry, intellectual history of Europe is exclusively history of Western Europe though in the title he speaks of the entire continent.

4. G. Toncheva, *Sports and Games in Our Lands in Ancient Times*, in A. Solakov (ed.), *Physical Culture and Sport in Bulgaria Through the Centuries* (Sofia 1983), p.20.

5. Ibid. p.18.

6. When during my lecture at the 1994 Session of the International Olympic Academy in Ancient Olympia I informed my audience about Bulgaria's ancient stadiums, Professor Nikolaos Yalouris, then director of the Greek National Archaelogical Museum and Excavations in Olympia, could not believe it. 'How could it happen, that such excavations remained unknown to us, here in Greece'? Fortunately enough Mrs Nadiezhda Lekarska, representative of the Bulgarian Olympic Committee, confirmed the information which the Western part of the audience doubted. Moreover, Professor John Lucas, lecturing during the same session, while supporting me informed the astonished audience that during his visit to nearby Albania he discovered high in the mountains a Greek-style stadium not recorded in any archaelogical source. Albania, as is well known, was closed to Western visitors before 1990. I am convinced that in the future there will be further revelations. As a matter of fact ancient Bulgarian stadiums and other information on their ancient sports were described fully in a 240-page book in English (*Physical Culture and Sport in Bulgaria through the Centuries*, ed. A. Solakov, Sofia Press, 1984). In no Western book on sports history have I found a single quotation from it. The Bulgarians did everything they could to inform their foreign colleagues about such discoveries in international languages. The book is available from a number of international libraries world-wide. Some years ago they would send it free of charge to any scholar demanding it (I obtained my copy this way), so there is no justification for Western ignorance of such and similar facts.

7. Quot. after M. Damyanov, *Horseback Riding in the Bulgarian Lands*, in Solakov, *Physical Culture and Sport in Bulgaria*, p.39.

8. All above information after R. Petrov, *Emergence and Development of Wrestling in Bulgaria*, in Solakov, *Physical Culture and Sport in Bulgaria*, p.33.

9. Ibid.

10. Ibid.

11. A. Przeździecki (ed.), *Mistrza Wincentego zwanego Kadłubkiem biskupa krakowskiego Kronika Polska* (Polish Chronicle of Master Vincent Called Kadłubek, Bishop of Cracow) (Kraków, 1862), pp.53–53; J. Długosz, *Dziejów Polski ksiąg dwanaście* (History of Poland in Twelve Books), vol.1 (Kraków, 1867), pp.136.

12. This poem is written and titled in Polish (with some letters missing or unclear, taken in the parethesis): *O Poselstwie hardym Cara zawolskiego i o zapasach żmodzkiego szlachcica Bore[j]ka z Tatarzynem O[l]brzymem i o familii Chodkiewiczow roku 1306*. It has 134 lines and is a part of a larger versed chronicle which remained in manuscript until 1968 when I discovered it in the Library of the Warsaw University (nr rkps 85 poz. 4). The part concerning the fight of Boreyko with Tartar was printed for the very first time in my anthology *Zapomniani piewcy sportu* (Forgotten Poets of Sport) (Warsaw, 1970) , pp.99–102. There is a lot confusion in this poem, because Stryjkowski mixes Polish, Samogitian, Russian and Mongolian names and traditions. He calls, for instance, Khan of Tartars 'Tsar of Volga Area'; a delegation of that ruler arrives from the Crimean Peninsula whereas Crimean Khanat was established some 100 years later and the Tartar Khans certainly could not use the Russian title 'Tsar': In addition Gedymin is called ruler of Russia because Lithuania was then a possession of what is now Belorussia.

13. Ibid., p.99; all translations from non-English sources in this article are mine unless otherwise indicated.

14. Ibid., p.102.

15. Quot. after Polish version of Gwagninus' work titled in Polish *Kronika sarmacyi europskiej*, 1603 and later published several times. I used the Warsaw edition of 1768, pp.415. Gwagnin also described Russian troops of archers on skis and it was in his book that a famous picture of such

troops appeared, many times reproduced in Western sources, but never properly explained. Similar troops were organissd in Poland under King Stefan Batory at the end of the sixteenth century, with a view to fighting the Russians on equal terms.

16. M.J. Lermontov, *Piesnia pro Caria Ivana Wasylievitsha, mowodovo opritshnika i udawogo kuptsa Kalashnikova*, in *Poemy* (Moscow, 1959), pp.415–32.

17. Ibid., pp.428–9.

18. Borzymowski's poetic report, originally entitled in Polish *Morska nawigacya do Lubeka*, remained in manuscript until 1938 when the full text was edited by R. Pollak. The 'sporting fragments' were extracted and published in my anthology *Zapomniani piewcy sportu* (Forgotten Poets of Sport), pp.103–11; all following quotations are from that anthology; see also W. Lipoński, 'Polnisch-deutsch fair-play-Vergangenheit', 'Olympisches Feuer. Offizielles Organ des Nationalen Olympischen Komitees für Deutschland', 1997, nr 5.

19. Lipoński, *Forgotten Poets of Sport*, p.103.

20 Ibid.

21 Ibid., p.111.

22. Quot. after R. Petrov, p.35.

23. Alka Tournament, where tilting at the ring is the main event is until today held yearly at the road linking Croatian towns Sinje and Split. I was personally assured of it by Dr Rudolf Vouk, Deputy Minister of Ministry of Education and Sport in Croatia, during the International Conference on Sport and Olympic Education in Kalavryta, Greece, Sept. 1997.

24. *Tygodnik Poznański* (Polish weekly of Poznań region in Western Poland), 4 (1862).

25. See: I. Grys, 'Antecedencje rosyjskiego sportu w osiemanstowiecznej tradycji plebejskiej i dworskiej' (Antecedents of the Russian Sport in Eighteenth-century Plebeian and Court Traditions), 'Wychowanie Fizyczne i Sport' (Polish academic periodical), 1, 3 (1986), 123; W. Lipoński, '*Echoes of Britain*', *Polish Perspectives* (Polish periodical in English), 10 (1975).

26. In fact about 1983 I gathered materials for this book inspired by English sports activist Don Anthony who promised to help publish it in England, but later he withdrew from the project for reasons never explained. These materials were lost during three house-moves, but original sources in Polish and Russian archives and libraries are still available and the whole idea to show British sports influences in Poland and Russia, and also in other Slavonic countries, can be revived at some future date.

27. *Polish Chronicle of Master Vincent*, pp.65–7.

28. These are for instance *Artykuły gonienia do pierścienia* (Articles on ring tilting) prepared by Royal Marshall Andrzej Opaliński of Bnin for a great chivalric tournament in 1578. Also preserved are individual agreements between so-called 'God Judgment Duels' when an outraged knight fought his opponent to the death or to 'first blood'. This can be exemplified by *Czeduła czyli zapis na Sądy Boże między Mikołajem Turskim a Mikołajem Smolikowskim* (Agreement or Written Regulations Concerning God's Judgment Duel Between Nicholas Turski and Nicholas Smolikowski, 1511). Both documents were edited by K. W. Wóycicki from manuscripts in *Obrazy starodawne* (Ancient Descriptions) (Warsaw, 1843), pp.21–24 and 6–8 respectively.

29. For instance, the best-known Old Polish treaty on horsemanship: *Hippika to jest o koniach księgi* (Horsemanship or books on mounts, 1603). In 1647, on the order of an unknown Russian aristocrat, it was translated into Old Russian and published in Cracow as *Hippika ili nauka o koniach*. There is a lot of information about this book, but no single example was preserved in Poland. Perhaps a search in Russian libraries would be more successful.

30. *Gazeta Codzienna* (Daily Gazette), 247 (1859).

31. L.Berghofer, *O konnozavodstvyie voobshtshe i pryieyimushtshyiestvyienno v Rosyi* (About Horse Racing in General but First of All in Russia) (Moscow, 1845), p.34; quot. after I. Grys, p.137.

32. Anonymous satirical poem titled *Wyścigi* (Horse Races), *Tygodnik Illustrowan*, 19' (The Illustrated Weekly) (1909).

33. *Zhurnal Konnozavodstva i Okhoty* (Journal of Horse Racing and Okhota, 1843), IV, quot. after I. Grys, 'Obce wpływy w dziewiêtnastowiecznym sporcie rosyjskim' (Foreign Influences in Nineteenth-century Russian Sport), *Wychowanie Fizyczne i Sport*, 1 (1989), 136.

34. *Syievyiernayia Ptshela* (Northern Bee), 1850; quot after I. Grys, 136.

35. K. Gaszyński, *Wyœcigi konne w Warszawie* (Warsaw 1857), p.1.

36. *Encyklopedyja Powszechna Orgelbranda*, Vol.23 (Warsaw, 1866), p.902.
37. J. Kukulski, *Pierwsze mecze, pierwsze bramki* (First Matches, First Goals) (Kraków 1988), pp.51–2.
38. Ibid., p.113.
39. J. Fisiak, 'English Sports Terms in Modern Polish', *English Studies*, XLV (1964), 230–6.
40. *Świat* ('The World', Polish weekly), 2 (1912).
41. *Kolarz-Wioślarz-Łyżwiarz* (Cyclist, Rower, Skater, Polish sports monthly), 3 (1899); see also P. Godlewski, *Sport żapaśniczy w Polsce w latach 1890–1939* (Polish Wrestling in the Years 1890–1939) (Poznań, 1994).
42. E. Piasecki, *Wychowanie fizyczne* (Physical Education) (1928), special announcement.
43. W. Robakowski, *Pierścieniówka* (Warsaw, 1935).
44. See J. Trousil, 'Česka hazena', in E. Bosák *et al.*, *Strueny poehled vývoje sportivních odvitví v Československu* (Prague, 1969). I would like to express my deep thanks to Dr. Vlastimil Štekr of the Dept. of Physical Education at the University of Olomouc for sending me recent information on *hazena*.
45. See: S. Szmid-Berżyńska and W. Kwast, *Hazena (Jordanka)* (Warsaw, 1937).
46. See W. Strzyżewski, *Ringo: Sport for You* (Warsaw, 1991).
47. M. Waic, 'Československá Školni Télesna Výchova v obdobi hospodáøské krize 1929–1934' (Czechoslovakian Physical Education During the Economic Crisis 1929–1934), *Teorie a Praxe Tilesne Výchovy* (Theory and Practice of Physical Education), 1 (1989).
48. N. Petrova, 'Nature and Functions of Physical Education, in Solakov, *Physical Culture and Sport in Bulgaria*, p.68.
49. All information and data on F. Potlacha, *Kniha o tělesné výhově na vys. školách v ČSR* (*Book on Physical Education in Higher Schools in Czechoslovakian Republic*), Prague 1925, passim.
50. Ibid.
51. See V. Olivova, *Nazizm and the German Physical Training Movement in Czechoslovakia*, in A.M. Olsen (ed.), *Sport and Politics 1918–1939/40* (Oslo, 1986), pp.171–70.
52. 'Naprostou nutnost pro naše studentsvo', Potlacha, p.12).
53. Ibid.
54. See P.T. Żebrowski, '*Symbol of Symmetrical Development: The Reception of the YMCA in Poland*', *International Journal of the History of Sport*, 1 (May 1991), 96–110; E. Kałamacka, 'Polska YMCA a olimpizm' (Polish YMCA and Olympism), in J. Lipiec (ed.), *Logos i etos polskiego olimpizmu* (Logos and Ethos of Polish Olympism) (Kraków, 1994), pp.529–34. YMCA was re-established in Poland again at the end of the Communist rule in 1988. For the YMCA in Russia see I. Grys, 'Obce wpływy w dziewiêtnastowiecznym sporcie rosyjskim', p.143.
55. All above data after J.Gaj and K. Hądzelek, *Dzieje kultury fizycznej w Polsce* (History of Physical Education in Poland) (Poznań, 1997), p.99.
56. Ibid.
57. See an exhaustive work by R. Wryk on that association, *Akademicki Związek Sportowy 1908–1939* (Poznań, 1990); and anthology of memoirs on Polish academic sport also under editorship of R. Wryk, *Akademicki Związek Sportowy 1908–1983. Wspomnienia i pamiętniki* (Academic Sports Association 1908–1983. Memoirs and Diaries) (Poznań, 1985).
58. A. Solakov, 'Bulgaria in the Olympic Movement and in the Olympic Games prior to the Revolution of September 4, 1944', in Solakov, *Physical Culture and Sport in Bulgaria*, p.122.
59. V. Tsonkov, *Track and Field*, in Solakov, p.97.
60. For a full list of artists and writers awarded in the Olympic Literature and Art Competitions 1912–1948, see S. Favre, *Civilta, Arte, Sport* (Citta di Castello, 1969), pp.482–93. Places of particular countries result from my own counting: 5 points for gold, 3 for silver, 2 for bronze and 1 for honorary distinction. In the period 1912–48 in all Olympic Art and Literature Competitions 211 artists from 28 countries were awarded while nearly 1,300 competed.
61. See P. Godlewski, pp.152–3.
62. P.R. Reid, *Colditz* (1952), p.99.
63. Ibid.
64. For a basic bibliography of Polish works on sport under Nazi occupation, see W. Lipoński, 'Still an Unknown European tradition: Polish Sport in the European Cultural Heritage', *International Journal of the History of Sport*, 13, 2 (August 1996), 39, note 24.

65. Z. Małecki, 'Sport in Auschwitz', *Kurier Sportowy* (Sports Courier), 16 Aug. 1945.
66. T. Borowski. *Ludzie którzy szli* (The People Who Passed By), in *Wybór opowiadań* (Selected short stories) (Warsaw, 1959), p.156.

Epilogue

J.A. MANGAN

Mirrors are kind; mirrors are cruel. This consideration of European sport as a mirror in which nations, classes and the sexes see themselves illustrates benign and malign political authority, class conviction and gender assertion. The images in the mirror will grow larger. Cultures are caught in the reflected image of sport in society – and this is a condition that will grow as the so-called Third World becomes as enamoured as the First World now is, with sport as identity, catharsis, and realisation. Glass, of course, is brittle and mirrors crack. Flaws cause damage. Modern sport has many flaws reflected in the wider culture; among them corrosive commercialism, addictive drug abuse, crude racial intolerance, ugly national xenophobia.

The image of sport in tomorrow's metaphorical mirror in Europe and elsewhere, is as dark as it is bright.

Notes on Contributors

Callum Brown is Senior Lecturer in History at the University of Strathclyde, Glasgow.

Adrian Harvey teaches Victorian history and literature at the Workers' Education Association.

Wojciech Lipoński is a professor at Adam Mickiewicz University, Poznań.

Tara Magdalinski is a lecturer in the Faculty of Arts and Executive director of the Youth Studies Research Unit at Sunshine Coast University College, Queensland, Australia.

J.A. Mangan is a professor in the Faculty of Education, Strathclyde University and Director of its International Research Centre for Sport, Socialisation and Society.

Alethea Melling lectures in social history at the University of Central Lancashire, St Martin's University College, and Lancaster University.

Gertrud Pfister is Professor of Sport History and Sociology at the Free University, Berlin.

Teresa Ziółkowska is Professor of Physical Education, Physical Education Academy, Poznań.

Abstracts

Women and Football – A Contradiction? The Beginnings of Women's Football in Four European Countries
Gertrud Pfister, Kari Fasting, Sheila Scraton and Benilde Vázquez

This essay discusses how football spread as a male domain to various countries in Europe prior to the Second War War. It seeks to discover how women managed to infiltrate this masculine terrain, the arguments put forward to hinder them, and the differences and similarities between the development of women's football in these countries.

Cultural Differentiation, Shared Aspiration: The Entente Cordiale of International Ladies' Football, 1920–45
Alethea Melling

'The Entente Cordiale of ladies' football' is a term used by Raymonde Wolfs, a veteran of the French team, to describe the lasting relationship between women's football teams from Lancashire and France from 1920 to 1945. This essay examines the relationship which developed out of and extended beyond the patriarchal infrastructures of the First World War. It views the experience of both the Lancashire and Parisian players within the wider European socio-political context and the ever shifting set of values regarding the gender roles of women.

A Contribution to the History of Jewish Sport and Education in Poland: The City of Poznań, 1904–39
Teresa Ziólkowska

This study discusses the activities of the Jewish Gymnastic Society (Posener Turnerbund) in the Polish city of Poznań. The organisation was established in 1904 to promote gymnastics, swimming and tourism, at a time when Poznań was under German occupation. The role of Jewish gymnasts is examined in this unique ethnic environment.

English Elementary Education Revisited and Revised: Drill and Athleticism in Tandem
J.A. Mangan and Colm Hickey

By the First World War, physical education in English elementary schools had undergone a radical transformation. This essay shows how drill, originally introduced into the school timetable as military drill and intended as a means of instilling discipline, was assimilated in the early twentieth century into a physical education programme reflecting a holistic view of education, embracing the philosophy and practice of the upper middle-class ideology of athleticism.

Football's Missing Link: The Real Story of the Evolution of Modern Football
Adrian Harvey

Harvey contends that until the 1860s codified football in the public schools had little or no impact on popular culture. Indeed, between 1830 and 1860 a substantial football culture existed in Britain outside the public schools. This consisted of large numbers of teams, playing games that were regulated by rules and often administered by referees. This essay considers the impact of the most sophisticated component of this culture, Sheffield, and the relative contribution of the public schools and their popular counterparts to the emergent Football Association. The author concludes that public school intervention was not necessary for the appearance of codified football in Victorian Britain.

'Touched Pitch and Been Shockingly Defiled': Football, Class, Social Darwinism and Decadence in England, 1880–1914
R.W. Lewis

Despite the rapid growth of professional football in the second half of the nineteenth century, the middle and upper classes resented this working-class infiltration and refused to surrender control of the game without a struggle. This essay investigates the ideological opposition to professional football in the late Victorian/early Edwardian period in the context of an intellectual climate embracing imperialism, Social Darwinism, economic individualism, class bias and athleticism.

Organised Memories: The Construction of Sporting Traditions in the German Democratic Republic
Tara Magdalinski

This study explores the ways in which meanings about national identity were generated by the state in the German Democratic Republic. It shows how the process of identity formation was crucial to the success of the socialist regime and involved creating a culture of political and social legitimation at a time of national social disorientation.

Sport and the Scottish Office in the Twentieth Century: The Control of a Social Problem
Callum G. Brown

The growth of state interest in sport is explored through this first of two case studies of Scotland. The Scottish Office became drawn initially into sport over the 'social evils' of gambling, drink and spectator misbehaviour. Between the 1890s and the 1960s it took over the mantle of the post-Victorian defender of 'respectability', and used legislation in attempts to 'reform' working-class male popular culture, driven by discourses on 'acceptable' and 'unacceptable' sports. As a result, crowd safety and crowd misbehaviour at football matches were conflated, leading to almost complete absence of protection for the sports spectator until the mid-1970s.

Sport and the Scottish Office in the Twentieth Century: The Promotion of a Social and Gender Policy
Callum G. Brown

This study examines the Scottish Office's development of an ideology of promoting amateur sports as antidotes to industrial 'rough' culture. From the mid-1930s until the early 1970s, a handful of closely networked sports administrators in the civil service and governing bodies brought an evangelical zeal to encouraging 'sport for all' through the incorporation of informal works and community sports within national governing bodies, the development of national and community sports centres, and the emphasis placed on encouraging working-class women to participate in sport. The result was increased access to and feminisation of working-class sports venues.

Sport in the Slavic World before Communism: Cultural Traditions and National Functions
Wojciech Lipoński

The Slavonic countries constitute 39.3 per cent of the European population and occupy as much as 58.8 per cent of European territory. The contribution of these countries to the historical development of sport is significant but has been overlooked by Western historians and researchers. The author proves this neglect by providing new evidence and sources ignored by Western historians.

Select Bibliography

Women and Football – A Contradiction? The Beginnings of Women's Football in Four European Countries
Gertrud Pfister, Kari Fasting, Sheila Scraton and Benilde Vázquez

J. Hargreaves, *Sporting Females Critical Issues in the History and Sociology of Women's Sport* (London, 1994).

S. Lopez, *Women on the Ball – a guide to women's football* (London, 1997).

M. Goksøyr, '"We are the best in the world! We have beaten England!" Norwegian football's function as carrier of nationalism', in G. Pfister, T. Niewerth and G. Steins (eds.), *Spiele der Welt im Spannungsfeld von Tradition und Moderne* (St. Augustin, 1996), pp.367–74.

G. von der Lippe, 'Women's Sports in Norway in the 1930s: Conflict between two different body cultures', *Stadion*, 19/20 (1993/1994), 178–87.

G. Pfister, 'Sport auf dem grünen Rasen. Fussball und Leichtathletik' in G. Pfister and G. Steins (eds.), *Von Ritterturnier zum Stadtmarathon, Sport in Berlin* (Berlin, 1987), pp.68–96.

G. Pfister and G. von der Lippe, 'Women's Participation in Sports and the Olympic Games in Germany and Norway – A Sociohistorical Analysis', *Journal of Comparative Physical Education and Sport*, XVI, 2 (1994), 30–41.

R-K. Torkildsen, 'Norsk Kvinnefotball. En historisk undersckelse om norsk kvinnefotballs utwikling', Master's thesis (Hogskolen Levanger, 1993).

D.J. Williamson, *Belles of the Ball* (Devon, 1991).

Cultural Differentiation, Shared Aspiration: The Entente Cordiale of International Ladies' Football, 1920–45
Alethea Melling

P. Bell, *Britain and France 1900–1940* (London, 1996).

J. Williams and S. Wagg (eds.), *British Football and Social Change* (Leicester, 1991).

J. Hargreaves, *Sporting Females* (London, 1994).

R. Holt, *Sport and Society in Modern France* (Oxford, 1981).

S. Lopez, *Women on the Ball* (London, 1997).

G. Newsham, *In a League of Their Own!* (London, 1997).

D. Williamson, *Belles of the Ball* (Devon, 1991).

G. Pfister, 'Die Konstruktion von Weiblichkeit und Mannlichkeit im Sport – Ein Vergleich der Entwicklung des Frauen-Fussballs in Deutschland, England und Frankreich', from the proceedings of an ISCPES congress (1998), edited by Ken Hardman.

A Contribution to the History of Jewish Sport and Education in Poland: The City of Poznań, 1904–39
Teresa Ziólkowska

Zbigniew Dworecki, *Poznań i Poznaniacy w latach Drugiej Rzeczypospolitej 1918–1939* (Poznań, 1994).

Zdzislaw Grot and Jerzy Gaj, *Zarys kultury fizycznej w Wielkopolsce* (Poznań, 1973).

Andrzej Kwilecki, *Szachy w Poznaniu 1839–1988* (Poznań, 1990).

Grzegorz Młodzikowski, *Genealogia społeczna i klasowe funkcje sportu w latach 1860–1928* (Warsaw, 1970).

English Elementary Education Revisited and Revised: Drill and Athleticism in Tandem
J.A. Mangan and Colm Hickey

S. Humphries, 'Hurrah for England: Schooling and the Working Class in Bristol 1870–1914', *Southern History*, 1 (1979).

S. Maclure, *One Hundred Years of London Education 1870–1970* (London, 1970).

David Rubenstein 'Socialization and the London School Board 1870–1904: aims, methods and public opinion', in P. McCann (ed.), *Popular Education and Socialization in the Nineteenth Century* (London, 1977).

P.C. McIntosh, *P.E. in England since 1800* (2nd ed.) (London, 1968).

P.C. McIntosh, 'Games and Gymnastics for Two Nations in One', in P.C. McIntosh (ed.), *Landmarks in the History of Physical Education* (London, 1981).

Alan Penn, *Targeting the Schools. Militarism, Drill and the Elementary School 1879–1914* (London, forthcoming).

J.A. Mangan, 'Imitating their Betters and Dissociating from their Inferiors: Grammar Schools and the Games Ethic in the Late Nineteenth and Early Twentieth Centuries', *Proceedings of the 1982 Annual Conference of the History of Education Society of Great Britain* (Leicester, 1983).

J.A. Mangan, *Athleticism in the Victorian and Edwardian Public School. The Emergence and Consolidation of an Educational Ideology* (Cambridge, 1981) and (Falmer, 1986).

J.A. Mangan, 'Sport in Society: The Nordic World and Other Worlds', in Henrik Meinander and J.A. Mangan (eds.), *The Nordic World: Sport and Society* (London, 1998).

J.A. Mangan and Colm Hickey, 'A Pioneer of the Proletariat: The Proselytiser Herbert Milnes and the Games Cult in New Zealand', in J.A. Mangan and John Nauright (eds.), *The Australasian World: Sport in Antipodean Society* (forthcoming).

C.F. Hickey, 'Athleticism and the London Training Colleges', Ph.D. thesis, IRCSSS, University of Strathclyde, forthcoming.

Football's Missing Link: The Real Story of the Evolution of Modern Football
Adrian Harvey

Hugh Cunningham, *Leisure in the Industrial Revolution 1780–1880* (London, 1980).

A. Fabian and G. Green (eds.), *Association Football*, vol.1 (London, 1960).

Richard Holt, *Sport and the British: A Modern History* (Oxford, 1989).

J.P. Magouin, *History of Football* (Bochum-Langendreer, 1938).

Tony Mason, *Association Football and British Society 1863–1915* (London, 1980).

P.M. Young, *A History of British Football* (London, 1968).

'Touched Pitch and Been Shockingly Defiled': Football, Class, Social Darwinism and Decadence in England, 1880–1914
R.W. Lewis

J.A. Mangan, *The Games Ethic and Imperialism: Aspects of the Diffusion of an Ideal* (Harmondsworth, 1986).

J.A. Mangan, *Athleticism in the Victorian and Edwardian Public School* (Cambridge, 1981).

J.A. Mangan and J. Walvin (eds.), *Manliness and Morality: Middle Class Masculinity in Britain and America, 1800–1940* (Manchester, 1987).

E. Dunning, P. Murphy and J. Williams, *The Roots of Football Hooliganism* (London, 1988).

R.W. Lewis, 'Football Hooliganism in England before 1914: A Critique of the Dunning Thesis', *International Journal of the History of Sport*, 13, 3 (December 1996), 310–39.

J.A. Mangan, 'Images of Manliness and Competing Ways of Living in late Victorian and Edwardian Britain', *British Journal of Sports History*, 3, 3 (December 1986), 265–87.

G. Jones, *Social Darwinism and English Thought: the Interaction between Biological and Social Theory* (Brighton, 1980).

Organised Memories: The Construction of Sporting Traditions in the German Democratic Republic
Tara Magdalinski

Jens Hacker and Horst Rögner-Francke (eds.), *Die DDR und die Tradition* (Heidelberg, 1981).

Günter Heydemann, *Geschichtswissenschaft im geteilten Deutschland* (Frankfurt/Main, 1980).

Eberhard Kuhrt and Henning von Löwis, *Griff nach der deutschen Geschichte, Erbeaneignung und Traditionspflege in der DDR* (Paderborn, 1988).

Christel Lane, *The Rites of Rulers: Ritual in Industrial Society – the Soviet Case* (Cambridge, 1981).

Tara Magdalinski, 'Traditionspflege and the Construction of Identity in the German Democratic Republic, 1970–1979', *Occasional Papers in German Studies*, No.14 (December 1997).

Alan Nothnagle, 'From Buchenwald to Bismark: Historical Myth-building in the German Democratic Republic, 1945–1989', *Central European History*, 26, 1 (1993), 91–113.

Jim Riordan, *Sport, Politics and Communism* (Manchester, 1991).

Andrea Rögner-Francke, *Die SED und die deutsche Geschichte, Erbeaneignung und Traditionspflege in der DDR* (Melle, 1987).

Sport and the Scottish Office in the Twentieth Century: The Control of a Social Problem
Sport and the Scottish Office in the Twentieth Century: The Promotion of a Social and Gender Policy
Callum G. Brown

Callum G. Brown, 'Popular culture: the continuing struggle for rational recreation', in T.M. Devine and R. Finlay (eds.), *Scotland in the Twentieth Century* (Edinburgh, 1996).

May Brown, *Alive in the 1900s: With Reminiscences of the Scottish Council of Physical Recreation* (Edinburgh, 1979).

Jennifer Hargreaves, *Sporting Females: Critical Issues in the History and Sociology of Women's Sport* (London, 1994).

Grant Jarvie and Graham Walker (eds.), *Scottish Sport in the Making of the Nation: Ninety-minute Patriots?* (Leicester, 1994).

Bill Murray, *The Old Firm: Sectarianism, Sport and Society in Scotland* (Edinburgh, 1984).

Bill Murray, *The Old Firm in the New Age* (Edinburgh, 1998).

N.L. Tranter, 'The Cappielow riot and the composition and behaviour of soccer crowds in late Victorian Scotland', *International Journal of the History of Sport*, 12 (1995), 125–40.

Sport in the Slavic World before Communism: Cultural Traditions and National Functions
Wojciech Lipoński

Jerzy Gaj and Kajetan Hadzelek, *Dzieje kultury fizycznej w Polsce* (History of Physical Culture in Poland) (AWF Poznań, 1997).

Iwona Grys, 'Obce wplywy w dziewietnastowiecznym sporcie rosyjskim' (Foreign Influences in Nineteenth Century Russian Sport) in *Wychowanie Fizyczne i Sport*, 1 (1989).

Iwona Grys, 'Antecedencje rosyjskeigo sportu w osiemanstowiecznej tradycji plebejskiej i dworskiej' (Antecedents of Russian Sport in Eighteenth-century Plebeian and Court Traditions), in *Wwychowanie Fizyczne i Sport*, 3 (1986).

Alieksandar Janković *et al.*, 'Spomienitsa Srpski Sport 1918–1941' (Serbian Sport 1918–1941) (Belgrade, 1996).

Wojciech Lipoński, 'Still an Unknown Tradition: Polish Sport in the European Cultural Heritage', *International Journal of the History of Sport*, 13, 2 (August 1996).

Eugeniusz Piasecki, 'Wychowanie fizyczne wsrod narodow slowianskich' (Physical Education in the Slavonic Nations), *Kultura Slowianska* (Slavonic Culture), 1, 3 (1924).

František Potlacha, *Kniha o telesne vychove na vys, skolach v CSR* (Physical Education in High Schools in Czechoslovakian Republic) (Prague, 1925).

Angel Solakow (ed.), *Physical Culture and Sport in Bulgaria Through the Centuries* (Sofia, 1983).

'Sports and Games' in Michael Murray (ed.), *Poland's Progress* (London, 1939).

Index

Abell, H.F., 122, 124, 133–4
Access to Mountains Act 1939, 164, 193
Adams-Lehmann, H.B., 12
Aeneid, 212
Akademika YMKA, 236
Akademicki Zwiazek Sportowy, 237
Albermarle Committee report, 190
Alcock, C.W., 92, 112
Alliance Nationale, 45
Amateur Football Association, 120
amateurism, 4, 120–32, 183–4, 188, 191–2
Almond, H.H., 118–19, 122
Andrić, Ivo, 230
Angus, John, 172
Annual Drill Competition, 76
Anstey College of Physical Education, 185
anti-Semitism, 54–5
Arabadjiyata, Geno, 227
Arbeiderenes Idrettsforbund (AIF), 9
archery, 214–15
Arlott, J., 207
Arnold, Matthew, 66
Association for Supporting Agriculture,
   Cattle and Horse Breeding (Warsaw), 222
athleticism, 3, 118, 120, 134, 139–40; in
   elementary schools, 63–89
Athletic News, 131
athletics, 7–10, 27–8, 36, 38, 43, 76, 78,
   186–7, 194–7, 227, 234, 238–9, 242
Austria, 204, 227
Auto, L', 39
Aviemore, 193
Ayé, Louis, 227

Babák, Edward, 235
Baden-Powell, Robert, 123, 227
badminton, 9
Baer, Georg, 56, 58
bagatelle, 167
Bagot-Stack, Mary, 39
Bailey, Thomas Jerram, 77
Balfour, 6th Baron of Burleigh, 173
Balkan Games, 238–9
Balkan Peninsula, 204, 210, 217
Bandera, Stefan, 242
Barnard, H.C., 68
Barrio, Polo del, 5
basketball, 10, 38
battles, Tanneberg, 218; White Mountain, 218

Battling Malone, The, 41
Belgrade Civic Gymnastics Association, 219
Bellenden, The, 83
Bell, John, 35
Bell, P., 41, 43
Bell's Life in London, 96–7, 102
Belorussia, 204–5, 211–12, 232–3
Beneagh, J., 207
Bennett, Tony, 150
Beresford, Charles, 123
Berghofer, Ludwik, 224
Bergman-Osterburg, Madame, 31
Bernstein, Fritz, 58
betting, *see* gambling
Betting Houses Act, 168
Betting (Juvenile Messenger) (Scotland) Act
   1928, 169
Betting and Lotteries Act 1934, 170
billiards, 167–8, 170
Birmingham Athenic Institution, 100
Birrell, Augustine, 68
Blackwood's Magazine, 124
blood sports, 216
Board of Education, 67–8, 70, 74, 79
Bogacz, Ted, 34
Bohemia, 204, 218, 220, 225, 227, 232–3, 235
Bolton Evening News, 43
Bonafé, García, 17
Book of Routes and Kingdoms, 209
Borough Road College, 77
Borowski, Tadeusz, 244
Borrie, John, 243
Borzymowski, Marcin, 215
Botev, Hristo, 217
Bourke, Joanna, 34
Boverat, Fernand, 45
Boxer and Death, The, 244
Boxer a smrt, 244
boxing, 61, 167, 227, 243
Boys' Brigade, 189
Brand, Flora, 59
Brandt, Jósef, 215
Bridoux, Gaston, 32
Brno German Polytechnic, 235
British Football Association, 129
British Ladies' Football Club, 13, 28
British Workers' Sports Federation (BWSF),
   33
Broman, Allan, 69

Invitation

'Sport, Culture and Race'

The Editors of the journal *Culture, Sport, Society*, based at the International Research Centre for Sport, Socialisation and Society, Strathclyde University, Glasgow, Scotland, and published by Frank Cass, request the submission of articles for a special issue provisionally entitled 'Sport, Culture and Race'.

The issue will be edited by J.A. Mangan and Andrew Ritchie, and will be published as a volume in the Frank Cass series Sport in the Global Society. Provisional publication date is late 2000 or early 2001.

We invite submissions from writers/researchers exploring any aspect of the theme Sport, Culture and Race. Topics might examine questions of ethnicity, racial conflict or discrimination, interracial co-operation, distinct racial contribution, or examination of perceptions of race and ethnicity in the evolution of sport and its historiography. Articles may attempt a wide-ranging, survey-type approach exploring historical patterns and significance, or may narrow their focus to particular cases, personalities or incidents where race/ethnicity has been an issue in the history of sport. Articles may investigate any historical period, including recent attitudes and developments. Contributions from the European, Australasian, African and Asian, as well as American (North and South) contexts are encouraged.

Material should not have been published elsewhere, and finished articles should have a maximum length of 8,000 words, including endnotes. A short abstract should be submitted as soon as possible to:

Andrew Ritchie
1617 Oxford Street
Berkeley
California 94709
USA
Tel: (+001) 510-841-58809
Fax: (+001) 510-841-5809
E-mail: none